P9-BJV-596

VITA PATRUM
THE LIFE OF THE FATHERS
BY
ST. GREGORY OF TOURS

Translated from the Latin and French by
Fr. Seraphim Rose and Paul Bartlett

Edited, with introductory material
by Fr. Seraphim Rose

ST. HERMAN OF ALASKA BROTHERHOOD
PLATINA, CALIFORNIA

Copyright 1988 by the St. Herman of Alaska Brotherhood

St. Herman of Alaska Brotherhood
Platina, California 96076 U.S.A.

Front cover: St. Romanus in the Jura Mountains.
Back cover: St. Gregory of Tours with a map of Gaul and its major churches and
monasteries.

Illustrations by Fr. Damascene.

Library of Congress Cataloging in Publication Data

Gregory of Tours, St., 539-594.
    Vita patrum (the life of the fathers).
    Translated from the Latin and French. With introductory material by Fr.
Seraphim Rose.
    Bibliography.
    Index.
    1. Christian Saints—Patrology. 2. France (Gaul)—Church History. 3. Western
Fathers—6th-century.
    I. Title.

Library of Congress Catalogue Card Number 88-060562
ISBN 0-938635-23-9

A major work of Orthodox hagiography from the 6th century by a great Orthodox Saint of the West. Never before translated into Greek, Russian, or English, it is here presented and dedicated to the Blessed Memory of Archbishop John Maximovitch, himself the most recent of the great Orthodox Hierarchs of Gaul and new Apostle to the lands of the West.

†Hieromonk Seraphim Rose

CONTENTS

PREFACE

*The wilderness and the solitary
place shall be glad for them; and the
desert shall rejoice and blossom as the
rose. It shall blossom abundantly, and
rejoice even with joy and singing.*
Isaiah 35:1-2

The age of the Apostles was marked by great fervency of spirit among Christians. Since Christians in many places were threatened with martyrdom for their faith, they were vigilant, living in constant anticipation of the day when they would meet the Lord they served. When Christianity later became "legalized," it seemed not to require much of a Christian. It appeared that Christianity was no longer a matter of life and death. Many Christians, however, did not want to lose the fervency of the apostolic age. For them, Christianity was still "a matter of life and death," regardless of its cultural environment. To preserve the lamp of faith that was once enkindled within the dark catacombs hidden from anti-Christian authorities, these believers fled into the "desert" — that is, to uninhabited places where they could live a life of solitude and prayer. Denying themselves the comfort of worldly life that distracts the soul and body from the remembrance of God, they thus gave themselves up to a bloodless martyrdom, preventing the burning faith of the catacombs from being extinguished from the face of the earth. The desert came to preserve the savor of Christian pathos and hence rescued the whole of Christianity, which by adhering to its ascetic roots can keep its "first love" until the consummation of time.

The love of the desert was first instilled in the Christian communities of Palestine and Egypt. Later, the ideal of this way of life was brought to many other parts of the world, such as Greece, Italy, England, Ireland and France (Gaul). A pivotal figure in this westward movement was St. John Cassian, who in the 4th-century went to Egypt to learn the monastic rules and teachings and then brought this knowledge to his countrymen in Gaul. With the dissemination of St. John's writings, there occurred an exodus of monks and nuns into the wilderness of Gaul. This exodus produced saints whose lives were no less marked

9

by sanctity than those of their predecessors in the Middle East. So great was
their reputation among the faithful that the famous chronicler of that time, St.
Gregory of Tours, endeavored to record their lives in many books for the edification of future generations of Christians. One book, especially dedicated to his
native ascetic strugglers whom he even knew personally, he called *Vita Patrum*,
or *The Life of the Fathers*, as if these many men led *one* life before God—the
ultimate Christian virtue of *oneness of soul.*

    Vita Patrum has for the first time been presented in the English language,*
as a result of precisely the same passionate striving to acquire the same funda-
mental Christian pathos, the patristic oneness of soul, which the Fathers of the
ancient Egyptian desert and Gaul sought so earnestly. The compiler and transla-
tor of this book, the late Hieromonk Seraphim Rose, was himself an intense lover of the desert. During his many years as a monk in the forests of Northern California he strove to enter fully into the spirit of the Fathers of ancient Gaul.
From the introductory chapters by Fr. Seraphim, one can see that his research
into the monasticism of Gaul was no mere exercise of scholarship. Fr. Seraphim
was looking to the saints of Gaul for practical solutions to the malaise of modern
Christianity and the problems of contemporary monasticism. His intent was to,
while living in 20th-century America, act according to the same principles as the
early Christians, to *believe* as they did. Often when he was seen to be in a state
of deep contemplation, his monastic brothers would joke, saying, "Don't bother
him — he's in 6th-century Gaul."

    Fr. Seraphim did not try to escape into a bygone and irredeemable age;
rather, he hoped to meet the needs of his fellow Christians, strengthening his and
their faith so that they may not abandon the path of Christian struggle. To do
this, he tapped the well-springs of sanctity in ancient Gaul and uncovered this
true Christian treasure, inaccessible for over a thousand years. This book, published some years after his repose in 1982, is a fruit of his labor as a monk and
church writer. May the ideal of the desert, manifested in the lives of the saints
here presented and in Fr. Seraphim himself, inspire many to burn with love for
Jesus Christ. Such burning faith was once fostered in the catacombs and then in
the remote forests of Gaul.

    —And why not now, in the still fragrant wildernesses of the New Worlds:
in the Americas, Australia and New Zealand?

Abbot Herman and Fr. Damascene
Epiphany, 1985
Spruce Island, Alaska

---

* This first English translation of the entire *Vita Patrum* appeared in serial form in *The
Orthodox Word* several years before another translation was published by the Liverpool
University Press in 1985.

I

A Prologue of the Orthodox Saints of the West

by Fr. Seraphim Rose

St. Gregory the Dialogist   *St. Patrick of Ireland*

Great Monastic Leaders: Sts. Cassian, Martin, and Benedict

St. Ambrose of Milan

St. Irenæus of Lyons

St. Germanus of Auxerre

INTRODUCTION

Only if the sky can forego its stars, earth its grass, honeycombs their honey, streams their water, and breasts their milk will our tongues be able to renounce their praise of the saints, in whom God is the strength of life and the fame of death.
—St. Paulinus of Nola, *Poem 19* (405 A.D.)

Today we can clearly see that St. Herman of Alaska (1756-1836) came to America not merely to bring Holy Orthodoxy to the pagan Alaskan natives, but also to awaken the sense of the genuine Orthodox roots which lie deep underneath the fallen-away Christianity of the West, which is the spiritual background of America today. Even in our frightful times, when the foundations of any kind of decent life are collapsing, a chosen few are finding their way back to the Orthodoxy which, in the dim mists of history, was the patrimony of their own ancestors. Thus, this Prologue is devoted to the Orthodox patrimony of the sons of Western lands — to the Orthodox saints of the West, whose proper Orthodox veneration was so much desired by the great 20th-century apostle to the West, Archbishop John Maximovitch.

—Abbot Herman

13

A PROLOGUE of the
Orthodox Saints of the West

A TOUCHSTONE of true Orthodoxy is the love for Christ's saints. From the earliest Christian centuries the Church has celebrated her saints—first the Apostles and martyrs who died for Christ, then the desert-dwellers who crucified themselves for the love of Christ, and the hierarchs and shepherds who gave their lives for the salvation of their flocks.

From the beginning the Church has treasured the written Lives of these her saints and has celebrated their memory in her Divine services. These two sources — the Lives and services — are extremely important to us today for the preservation of the authentic Orthodox tradition of faith and piety. The false "enlightenment" of our modern age is so all-pervasive that it draws many Orthodox Christians into its puffed-up "wisdom," and without their even knowing it they are taken away from the true spirit of Orthodoxy and left only with the shell of Orthodox rites, formulas, and customs. Almost all Orthodox seminaries today (with the notable exception of Holy Trinity Seminary at Jordanville, New York) are centers for the propagation of modernism in the Church, and even when they cry "back to tradition" or "patristic revival," this is seldom more than another academic fashion, usually taking its inspiration from Roman Catholic scholarship, and leading not at all back to a truly Orthodox *spirit*, but only to yet more empty forms. To have a seminary education, even to have the "right views" about Orthodox history and theology — is not enough. A typical modern "Orthodox" education produces, more often than not, merely Orthodox rationalists capable of debating intellectual positions with Catholic and Protestant rationalists, but *lacking the true spirit and feeling of Orthodoxy*. This spirit and feeling are communicated most effectively in the Lives of saints and

14

in similar sources which speak less of the outward side of correct dogma and rite than of the essential inward side of proper Orthodox attitude, spirit, piety. Very many of these basic Orthodox sources, already translated into English, are lying unused by Orthodox Christians because a proper Orthodox approach or introduction to them has not been given. Let us attempt here to make this approach, particularly with regard to the Orthodox saints of the West who are as yet so little known to Orthodox Christians in America, even though a number of them have been revered for centuries in the East. May this our effort be a fitting "prologue" (we shall see in a moment what this word means in Orthodox literature) to a whole treasure-chest of Orthodox texts! May it help us all to put off our vain modern "wisdom" and enter more deeply into the spirit of Orthodox antiquity and its literature.

THE EARLIEST Lives of saints were the Acts of the Martyrs, followed in the 4th century, when the Egyptian desert began to blossom with monks, by the Lives of ascetics, the first of this form being the Life of St. Anthony the Great by St. Athanasius of Alexandria. Later, collections of such Lives were made, and they have been handed down to the present day in such works as the *Lives* of St. Demetrius of Rostov (†1709) in Slavonic and Russian, and the *Synaxaria* of St. Nicodemus of the Holy Mountain (†1809) in Greek. A person with a modern education must be taught how to approach these works, just as a person who has been trained in classical Western painting must be re-educated in order to understand the quite different art of the icon. Hagiography, like iconography, is a sacred art and has its own laws which are quite different from those of secular art. The Life of a saint is not a mere history of him, but rather a selection of the events in his life which reveal how God has been glorified in him; and its style is devout, and often exalted and reverential, in order to give a proper spiritual tone and feeling to the narration and arouse in the reader both faith and piety. This is why a mere retelling of a saint's life can never take the place of the original hagiographical account. A "Life" thus differs from a "biography" much as an icon differs from a naturalistic portrait.

Apart from actual Lives of saints, there is a second kind of hagiographical literature in the Orthodox Church. This is the material which has come down to us in the Orthodox *Prologues,* which include both brief Lives and edifying incidents from the lives of holy men as well as ordinary sinners. The name "Prologue" was given to collections of hagiographical literature as early as the 11th century in Byzantium; soon they appeared in Slavonic also and became greatly beloved by the Orthodox Russian people.

The *Prologue* is actually one of the *liturgical* books of the Orthodox Church. It is appointed to be read (not chanted, like the Psalms) after the Sixth Canticle of the Canon at Matins (in the Russian Church; in the Greek Church the *Synaxaria* are read here). The solemn and didactic prose of this book, giving first of all brief Lives of the saints of the day, does indeed serve as a "prologue" to the liturgical celebration of these saints in the Church's exalted poetry, much as the Acts of the Martyrs preceded the liturgical celebration of the martyrs in ancient times; this seems to account for the origin of its name. Yet it is of quite secondary importance whether the *Prologue* be read strictly "according to the Typicon" at its appointed place in the Divine services. The spirit of the Church is freedom, and various adaptations of ancient practice are possible, if only these serve for the edification and piety of the faithful. The *Prologue* (just like the Lives of saints) could be read at family morning or evening prayers, at mealtimes, on long winter evenings — a time now lamentably usurped even in most Orthodox homes by television, which inculcates its own crude, worldly tone and feeling. The book read need not be the *Prologue* (which does not exist in English, in any case),* but another book of similar inspiration may be used. Let us here only look briefly at the *Prologue* itself in order to discover something of its spirit — so important for us who live in the soul-less, spirit-less 20th century — before passing on to a discussion of books of similar inspiration in the West.

In the Slavonic *Prologue* printed at the St. Petersburg Synodal Press in 1896 (two large folio volumes of some 800 pages each — enough in itself to give us a glimpse of what our poor American Orthodoxy lacks!), under the date June 27 (chosen at random) we find the following:

First, "the commemoration of our holy Father Sampson the Hospitable," which gives a brief outline of the good deeds of this Saint (less than half a page). On most days there are several other similarly brief Lives, but on this day there is only the one Life, followed by a number of different edifying incidents. The first incident is a "Homily on Martin the Monk who was in Turov at the church of the holy Martyrs Boris and Gleb, living alone in God." This is an account of how Sts. Boris and Gleb appeared to one holy Russian monk in his illness and gave him to drink and healed him (half a page). This is followed by a little longer incident from the *Dialogues* of *St.* Gregory the Great, Pope of Rome, concerning the Presbyter Severus, who delayed in visit-

---

* Years after this article was written, The Prologue from Ochrid was published in English.

ing a dying man and found him dead on his arrival, but by his prayers brought him back to life for seven days in order that he might repent of his sins. Similar incidents are taken in other parts of the *Prologue* from such books as the *Lausiac History* of Palladius (5th century), the *Spiritual Meadow* of John Moschus (6th century), and the *Sayings of the Desert Fathers*. The final entry for June 27 is a brief Homily "That it is good to visit the sick," concluding with the Scriptural words of Christ: "For I was sick, and ye visited Me," and the standard conclusion of every day's readings: "To Him may there be glory, now and ever and unto the ages of ages."

It may readily be seen how foreign such readings are to the spirit and taste of our times. These are what might be called by some modern scholar "pious tales" or "miracle stories"; he would disdain them not only for their miracles, but just as much for their "moralizing." But it is just here that the searcher for the true spirit of Orthodoxy must question the "objective" scholar. Why is it that Orthodox Christians for nearly two millenia have found spiritual instruction and nourishment in such stories, and only quite recently, under the strong influence of modern Western "enlightenment," have our sophisticated Orthodox seminary graduates begun to disdain them? Is it because they are not true? — We shall see below that this is not the case at all. Is it because our Orthodox ancestors were really naive children who needed such tales, but we ourselves, being more sophisticated and mature, can do without them? — But then where do we derive our Orthodox nourishment outside of the few hours a week spent in church and church schools — from television?! Or could it be that our Orthodox ancestors had something which we lack, and which we desperately need in order to remain truly Orthodox and hand down the unchanging Orthodox faith and piety to our own offspring? Could it be that our ancestors understood something that many of us have lost through acquiring the habit of false, worldly knowledge? Perhaps, indeed, we may find in these miracles and morals that so insult the "modern mind" a missing dimension of the contemporary outlook, which in its elusive search for a two-dimensional "objectivity" has lost the key to much more of true wisdom than it thinks to have gained. "Scientific objectivity" has come today virtually to a dead-end, and every kind of truth has come into question. But this dead-end for worldly knowledge is perhaps the opening of a way to a higher knowledge, wherein truth and life are no longer divorced, where advance in true knowedge is impossible without a corresponding advance in moral and spiritual life. Involuntarily, the converts to Orthodoxy from Western lands — and the Westernized "native Orthodox" as well — have been transported back to that earlier time when the proud rationalism of pagan Rome was conquered by the true wisdom of Christianity. Let us therefore turn back to that earlier time in order to find something of the freshness and power of Orthodoxy as it conquered the Western mind. There we shall find also, to our great good fortune, materials for a Western "Prologue" (many of them already in English) not at all inferior to that of the East, as well as keys for understanding it and entering into its spirit.

Sts. Columbanus of Luxueil, Paulinus of Nola, and Clotilde the Queen

THE LANDS OF THE WEST, from Italy to Britain, knew both the preaching of the Apostles and the deeds of martyrs; here the Christian seed was planted so firmly that the West responded immediately and enthusiastically when it first heard of the great ascetics of Egypt and the East. St. Athanasius' *Life* of St. Anthony the Great was quickly translated into Latin, and the best sons and daughters of the West went to the East to learn from the great Fathers there. Many, including Blessed Jerome and the noble Roman ladies Paula and Melania, ended their days in the Holy Land; others, such as the Presbyter Rufinus, went on pilgrimage and brought back such valuable texts as the *History of the Monks of Egypt;* one — St. John Cassian the Roman — learned so thoroughly the spiritual doctrine of the Egyptian Fathers that his books (the *Institutes* and *Conferences*) became the chief foundation of the authentic monastic tradition of the West. The great seedbed of Orthodox monasticism in 5th-century Gaul — Lerins — grew up entirely under the influence of the Eastern monastic tradition.

    And then, even as the news of the phenomenon of Egyptian monasticism was still spreading through the West, the West produced its own ascetic miracle: St. Martin of Tours. Even before his death in 397, his manuscript *Life* was being circulated in Gaul, Spain, Italy, and elsewhere in the West, revealing him as a monastic Father and wonderworker in no way inferior to the desert Fathers in the East. From that time on the West had ascetic examples of its own to inspire its offspring, as well as able writers of their Lives, which to this day remain a chief primary source of the genuine Orthodoxy of the West. Among many others from the 5th to the 8th centuries, one may mention: in Gaul, the Eulogy of St. Honoratus, founder of Lerins, by St. Hilary, his successor as Bishop of Arles, and the Life of St. Germanus of Auxerre by Constantius of Lyons; in Italy, the Life of St. Benedict by St. Gregory the Great (Book II of the *Dialogues*), and the shorter Lives and incidents from the Lives of the Italian Fathers in the same work; in England, the Life of St. Cuthbert by Venerable Bede, and the Life of the great anchorite of the moors, St. Guthlac, by the Monk Felix; in Ireland, the Life of St. Columba by the Monk Adamnan.*

Here let us look more closely at three Western hagiographers of the 5th and 6th centuries. Their spirit is unquestionably and powerfully Orthodox.

1. SULPICIUS SEVERUS: THE *DIALOGUES* AND *LIFE OF ST. MARTIN*

Sulpicius Severus (363-420) is an excellent example of the proud Roman mind conquered by Christianity. Well educated, a successful lawyer, happily married, a writer of Latin prose (as even the critical historian Gibbon notes) in "a style not unworthy of the Augustan age" — he possessed all the characteristics needful for prosperity and success in the decadent Roman world at the turn of the 5th century. And yet, not only was he converted to the still-new religion of Christianity, he even abandoned the world and became the disciple of a wonderworking bishop and the writer of a Life of him that astonished the West by its miracles. Modern scholars, whether agnostic or "Christian," find him to be "one of the puzzles of history," because "no biographer of his period was better qualified to write a truthful life of a contemporary saint and no biographer of his period — we may almost say, of any period — has written a life more full of astounding prodigies." (F. R. Hoare, *The Western Fathers*, p. 4.)

§ Easily accessible collections of such original Lives in English include: *The Western Fathers* (chiefly of Gaul), ed. by F. R. Hoare, Harper Torchbooks, 1965; *Lives of the Saints* (of England), tr. by J. F. Webb, Penguin Books, 1970; *Anglo-Saxon Saints and Heroes*. tr. by Clinton Albertson, Fordham University Press, 1967; *The Anglo-Saxon Missionaries in Germany*, tr. by C. H. Talbot, Sheed & Ward, N.Y., 1954.

This "puzzle" remains unsolved for modern scholars; but how simple the answer to it is for someone unprejudiced by modern opinions of what is "possible" or "impossible." Sulpicius, both by his own experience and by the words of eyewitnesses he knew and trusted — discovered that *the miracles of St. Martin were true,* and he wrote of these "astounding prodigies" *only because they were true.* Sulpicius himself writes in the conclusion to his *Life*: "I am clear in my own conscience that my motives for writing were the certainty of the facts and the love of Christ, and that I have only related what is well known, only said what is true."

We who, even in these decadent latter times, have known Archbishop John Maximovitch (†1966), a wonderworker very similar in many respects to St. Martin, have no difficulty in believing the words of Sulpicius; they ring true to our own Orthodox Christian experience. It is only those who do not know the power of Orthodoxy in practice who find the *Life of St. Martin* a "puzzle." It is quite natural, in the Christian understanding, for the virtue of a man entirely dedicated to God and living already on earth an Angelic life, to result in manifestations which astound mere earthly logic, whether these be revelations of other-worldly humility and meekness, or outright miracles. The very word *virtus* in Latin signifies both "virtue" and "power," which in the Lives of saints is often "miraculous power," often translated simply "miracles."

The Orthodox tradition is by no means credulous in its acceptance of the miracles of saints. Great care is always taken to assure that the Lives of saints contain true accounts and not fables; for it is indeed true that, in the age of "romance" that began in the Western Middle Ages just after Rome's final separation from the Church of Christ (1054), such fables *were* introduced into many Lives of saints, rendering all later Latin sources especially suspect. Orthodox hagiographers, on the other hand, have always taken as their principle the maxim that St. Demetrius of Rostov placed on the first page of his *Lives*: MAY I TELL NO LIE ABOUT A SAINT. This is also why, in the Orthodox Church, great care is taken to transmit the *original sources* that tell of the saints: those Lives which are based on the author's immediate experience and the testimony of witnesses known to him personally. Thus the freshness and marvel of one who personally knew the saint is preserved, and there is transmitted to us directly, "between the lines" as it were, the authentic "tone" of a holy life.

Several years after the death of St. Martin, Sulpicius Severus composed two (sometimes divided into three) "Dialogues" on St. Martin.* This work, again, is greatly criticized by rationalist scholars, not merely for its miracles, but even more for its "anecdotal" character. One critic writes of it that by it "Sulpicius fixed for centuries a hagiographical tradition that rates the anecdotes of wonderworking above spiritual portraiture" (Hoare, *The Western Fathers*, p. 7). For Orthodox Christians precisely this "anecdotal" character is a source of immediate delight and makes the *Dialogues* of Sulpicius very close in spirit to the *Prologue*. Rationalist scholars are offended by these "anecdotes" because *they have lost the whole picture* into which these fragments fit. Orthodox Christians by no means see in such "anecdotes" the essence of a saint's life and character; but of course we take delight in the miracles of our saints and do not weary of them, knowing that in these *true stories* we can already see the breaking into this world of the entirely different laws of the spiritual, heavenly world, which at the end of time will entirely triumph over the laws of this fallen world. For us every "anecdote" that breathes the spirit of true Christianity in practice is a part of that one *Christian life,* the model for our own feeble struggle for salvation.

The *Dialogues* of Sulpicius are still somewhat "sophisticated" and therefore not as offensive to rationalist critics as later Orthodox works in the West. Sulpicius was trying to communicate to the educated Romans of his day the wonders of the new Christian life and frequently has in mind the weakness of his readers — whether their difficulty in believing some of his accounts, or their incapacity to fast like the ascetics of the East. Later, the materials for the Orthodox "Prologue" in the West become more "childlike" — not, primarily, because the level of education has decreased, but because Christianity has entered more deeply into the heart of the men of the West. Let us follow this development to see if we ourselves can learn from this childlikeness.

2. THE *DIALOGUES* OF ST. GREGORY THE GREAT (543-604)

The *Dialogues* of Sulpicius (400 A.D.) are an apologetic and missionary work, intended to convince men of the truth and power of Christianity, its saints, its miracles, its monastic life. The *Dialogues* of St. Gregory the Great,

---

§ English translation, together with the Life of St. Martin and Sulpicius' Letters about the Saint, in Hoare, *The Western Fathers.*

Pope of Rome, two centuries later (593) are a recalling to spiritual life in a
West already Christianized. St. Gregory's situation, then, is also that of us
today; for all but the freshest convert have experienced the waning of Christian
zeal and the awareness of the need to renourish one's spiritual faculties.

The holy hierarch begins his *Dialogues* in a melancholy frame of mind:
"My unhappy soul, weighed down by worldly affairs, calls now to mind in
what state it was when I lived in my monastery, and how then it was superior
to all earthly matters, far above everything transitory and corruptible, how it
did usually think upon nothing but heavenly things." He is further saddened—
but also inspired and roused to zeal — "by remembering the lives of certain
notable men, who with their whole soul did utterly forsake and abandon this
evil world... very many of whom, in a contemplative and retired kind of life,
greatly pleased God." He proceeds to "report only those things which I myself
have understood by the relation of virtuous and credible persons, or else learned
by myself, concerning the life and miracles of perfect and holy men." Thus,
the *Dialogues* too are one of those *original sources* so important for Orthodox Christians. There follow the four books of the *Dialogues,* which are so
much in the genuine Orthodox spirit that it is no wonder that they later became one of the chief sources for the incidents of the *Prologue* in the East,
being very early translated into Greek, and earned for St. Gregory the name by
which he is known to this day in the Orthodox Church: THE DIALOGIST.

Two of the books are devoted to the saints of Italy who lived before
St. Gregory — sometimes their Lives, but more often just incidents from their
lives which are capable of arousing piety and zeal. The Second Book, however,
is devoted entirely to one saint who inspired St. Gregory in Italy much as St.
Martin inspired Sulpicius in Gaul: St. Benedict (†543), a great Holy Father
of Western monasticism. This Book constitutes the earliest Life of this great
Orthodox saint, who has long had his place —just like St. Gregory himself
(March 12) — in the Orthodox Calendars of the East (March 14).

The first three books of the *Dialogues* of St. Gregory are, quite frankly,
"miracle stories," and the great hierarch makes no apology for handing them
down: these are the material of Christian hope and inspiration, and so deeply
had the West become Orthodox at this time that it received them eagerly.
But the Fourth Book of the *Dialogues* is the crowning insult to the modern
rationalist: these he would surely dismiss as "ghost stories." The Fourth Book
contains accounts — just as true and trustworthy as the "miracle stories" —
which demonstrate the truth of life after death. There are profitable tales of

the departure of men's souls, the state of souls in heaven and hell, the return of souls to their bodies after death, various apparitions of souls after death, and the like. Very similar tales may be found in a superb Orthodox book in England over a century later: the *Ecclesiastical History of the English People,* by Venerable Bede (Book V, chapters 12-14).

It must be said that the graduates of the modernist Orthodox seminaries, and "sophisticated" Orthodox today in general, find this part of ancient Christian literature the most difficult to accept. A few years ago a book of similar inspiration appeared in English: *Eternal Mysteries Beyond the Grave,* subtitled "Orthodox Teachings on the Existence of God, the Immortality of the soul, and Life Beyond the Grave" (Holy Trinity Monastery, Jordanville, N. Y., 1968). This work, the fruit of the missionary fervor of Archimandrite Panteleimon of Jordanville, consists of excerpts from the *Dialogues* of St. Gregory, the *Lives of Saints,* and similar standard Orthodox works, as well as Russian religious books and periodicals of the 19th century which give more recent incidents in the same spirit, together with excellent introductions to these excerpts, simple and straightforward and with just the right moral and pious tone so lacking in most Orthodox writings today. The book, while not an original source like St. Gregory's *Dialogues,* is of great value for Orthodox Christians. Anyone who has tried to interest children in Orthodox reading is well aware that this book, as perhaps no other book that now exists in English, is absolutely fascinating to children; a child of ten or twelve, if he first hears some of the profitable tales in it being read aloud at a family gathering, will later quite likely take the book himself and literally devour it, so interesting is it — not merely because the tales are "exciting" and quite capable of competing with the banal ghost stories of our day, but even more because he knows that *these stories are true and teach the truths of our Orthodox Faith.* How much energy "Orthodox educators" waste trying to arouse the interest of children in such inappropriate and soul-corrupting materials as cartoons and coloring books — while such a genuinely fascinating and authentic Orthodox book they overlook or disdain. Why is this? The answer to this question may clear away some of the difficulties that stand in the way of making maximum use of genuine Orthodox literature today.

In the 19th century Bishop Ignatius Brianchaninov, a great Orthodox Father of recent times, faced a similar problem when he tried to teach the Orthodox doctrine of heaven and hell, good and evil spirits, and life after death, to the Orthodox people of his time. Many "sophisticated" Christians objected, precisely because their own ideas of these realities were based

on Roman Catholic and Protestant, not Orthodox, ideas; and so Bishop Ignatius
devoted one entire volume of his collected works (v. 3) to this question, giving both the Orthodox and the Roman Catholic teaching. He found that the
Orthodox doctrine on all these questions — even though it does not, of course,
tell us everything about them — is quite precise in what it teaches, based on
Patristic writings such as the *Dialogues* of St. Gregory; while Roman Catholi-
cism, under the influence especially of modern philosophy from Descartes on-
wards, has come to teach a doctrine in which spiritual realities become increas-
ingly vague, corresponding to the ever greater preoccupation of modern men
with material things. Most Orthodox Christians today have picked up this
modernist-Papist teaching "in the air" of the contemporary world, and therefore if we do not consciously strive to discover the truth, we will be embarrassed when presented with the Orthodox teaching which is so definite, especially about the experiences of the soul after death. If we believe this teaching,
after all, we shall certainly be considered "naive" and "simple" even by other
believers, let alone by unbelievers. Some in their embarrassment may come to
think that these Orthodox teachings, which are so foreign to what "everybody
thinks" nowadays, are themselves somehow suspect, and they can point to Roman Catholics who claim that the Fourth Book of St. Gregory's *Dialogues*
teaches the Latin doctrine of Purgatory. Fortunately, however, this accusation
has already been raised and answered for us. Roman Catholic scholars proclaimed this very thing at the false council of Florence in 1439, and St. Mark
of Ephesus, the champion of Orthodoxy, gave the authoritative Orthodox answer: the teaching of St. Gregory in his *Dialogues* is Orthodox, and in fact he
clearly teaches *against* Purgatory.*

      The *Dialogues* of St. Gregory the Great, as well as *Eternal Mysteries
Beyond the Grave*, is excellent medicine for today's over-sophisticated Orthodox Christians. They can be a touchstone for us: if, reading them, we find them
"naive," "too realistic," or otherwise distasteful, we can know that we are still
too "sophisticated," not childlike and simple enough in our Orthodoxy. If we
are converts, we can know that we have not yet entered enough into the genuine spirit of Orthodoxy; if we are "native Orthodox," we can know that our
Orthodoxy has been corrupted by false modern Roman Catholic ideas. We will
have to struggle harder to approach such basic Orthodox literature like children,
without all our supposed "wisdom." Those who are accustomed to reading
the Orthodox literature of Christian antiquity have no difficulty with such books.

---

§ St. Mark of Ephesus, "First Homily on Purgatorial Fire (Refutation of the Latin
Chapters)," ch. 9; "Second Homily on Purgatorial Fire," ch. 23:9.

3. THE *BOOKS OF MIRACLES* OF ST. GREGORY OF TOURS

No writer in Latin in the Orthodox West was more devoted to the saints of Christ's Church nor more prolific in his praises of them than St. Gregory, Bishop of Tours (539-594). Although he is chiefly known today for his *History of the Franks*, he is more important to Orthodox Christians for his eight *Books of Miracles,* which are usually called his "minor works." In this 6th-century writer of Gaul there breathes the very spirit of the Orthodox East and the *Prologue.* Being especially under the influence of St. Martin, his own predecessor in the See of Tours, from whom he received miraculous healings, he devoted four of the eight books of this work to *The Miracles* (or rather, *Virtues*) *of Blessed Martin the Bishop.* But he also took all the saints as his concern, writing one book on *The Glory of the Blessed Martyrs,* another on *The Passion and Miracles of St. Julian the Martyr,* another on *The Life of the Fathers,* and a final one on *The Glory of the Confessors.* Taken together, these books — which deal mostly with the saints of Gaul — constitute the largest hagiographical material on the Orthodox saints of any land in antiquity. His aim in writing is moral and didactic, and he consciously turns his back on pagan learning. He himself writes: "We ought to pursue, to write, to speak that which edifies the Church of God and by sacred teaching enriches needy minds by the knowledge of perfect faith. For we ought not to recall the lying stories, or to follow the wisdom of the philosophers which is hostile to God, lest we fall under the judgment of eternal death by the decision of the Lord... I do not recall in my work the flight of Saturn, the wrath of Juno, the adulteries of Jupiter... Having glanced at all these events built on sand and soon to perish, we return rather to divine and evangelical miracles" (*The Glory of the Blessed Martyrs,* Preface).

"Miracles," indeed, are the subject matter as well as the title of these books. If rationalistic scholars are offended at the many miracles in the *History of the Franks,* they are absolutely scandalized by the *Books of Miracles,* which abound in them. But the reason why he writes of them, again, is because they are *true,* and he is careful to point out that he writes only what he knows from personal experience (having known many of the saints himself and witnessed many miracles) or from the testimony of reliable people. Thus, these books also are invaluable *original sources* of Christianity in practice.

Although St. Gregory is known in the East and mentioned in Orthodox Patrologies,* his writings were not translated into Greek or Slavonic. His con-

---

* For example, in the Patrology of Archbishop Philaret of Chernigov, St. Petersburg, 1882, vol. 3, section 191.

cern was too much with the West, and the East already had numerous collections on Eastern saints in exactly the same spirit.** More surprising, however, is it that the *Books of Miracles* (save for a few excerpts) has never been translated into English. This can only be a testimony to the rationalist superstition that has prevailed in the West in modern times, and also to the dying out of interest in the Orthodox saints of the West which has been continuing for many centuries now. Another reason why he has been disdained in the West is that his language falls short of the standards of classical Latin. He himself recognizes this and states that he undertook his *Books of Miracles* only at the command of the Lord in visions. In one dream, when protesting to his mother his lack of skill in writing, he received from her this answer: "Do you not know that on account of the ignorance of our people the way you can speak is considered more intelligible? So do not hesitate or delay doing this, because it will be a charge against you if you pass over these deeds in silence" (*The Miracles of Blessed Martin the Bishop,* Preface to the First Book). Even Blessed Augustine, as is well known, was reproached for his shortcomings in classical Latin, and he gave a sufficient reply, which will do for an answer to the detractors of St. Gregory's Latin also: "It is better that the grammarians reproach us than that the people not understand us."

Archbishop John Maximovitch of blessed memory gave as his testament to the Orthodox Christians of the West his love for the saints of Western lands. In fulfillment of this testament we now offer, as a separate book, the first English translation of the whole of the seventh of St. Gregory's *Books of Miracles* — THE LIFE OF THE FATHERS. No apology is necessary for presenting these twenty chapters on the monastic saints of Gaul in the 5th and 6th centuries. For the Orthodox Christian they are fascinating reading; the edifying homily that precedes each Life is most instructive for our spiritual struggle today; the spirit of the book is entirely Orthodox, and the Orthodox practices described in it have remained the inheritance of Orthodox Christians (but not of Roman Catholics) today, including the veneration of the "icons of saints" (the Latin text has *iconicas* instead of the more to be expected *imagines*) in chapter 12; and some of the incidents, just like the stories of the desert Fathers, have precise relevance for our problems today — for example, the story of the "charismatic" deacon who "healed in the name of Jesus" until St. Friardus exposed him as being in satanic deception (ch. 10).

---

§§ One of them, *The History of the Lovers of God* by Blessed Theodoret (5th century) — a collection of Lives of the Syrian Fathers — is an exact parallel to St. Gregory's *Life of the Fathers.*

It is our heartfelt wish that this book will take its place, together with the *Dialogues* of St. Gregory the Great, the *Lausiac History* of Palladius, and other BASIC ORTHODOX SOURCE-BOOKS, as part of the daily reading of those who are struggling for their salvation on the narrow Orthodox path. May it be read silently; may it be read aloud; may it become, like the other great books of Christian antiquity, a source of piety and the true spirit of Orthodoxy which is everywhere being overpowered today by the spirit of the world. May it help us in the all-important struggle to become and remain *conscious Orthodox Christians,* knowing what is the path of salvation, what is the savor of true Christianity, and how far we all fall short of these. May it be for us a beginning, a prologue, of true Christianity in practice!

II

The Life of
St. Gregory of Tours

539 - 594

by Abbot Odo

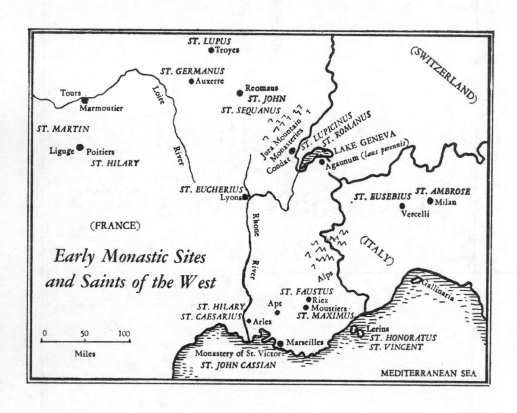

ST. LUPUS
● Troyes

ST. GERMANUS
● Auxerre

Tours
Marmoutier

Reomaus
ST. JOHN
ST. SEQUANUS

Loire

(SWITZERLAND)

ST. MARTIN

Liguge ● ● Poitiers
ST. HILARY

River

Jura Mountain
Monasteries
Condat

ST. LUPICINUS
ST. ROMANUS
● LAKE GENEVA
Aguanum (*laus perennis*)

ST. EUCHERIUS
Lyons●

ST. EUSEBIUS
● ST. AMBROSE
● Milan
Vercelli

(FRANCE)

*Early Monastic Sites
and Saints of the West*

Rhone

River

Alps

(ITALY)

ST. FAUSTUS
● Riez
● Moustiers
ST. MAXIMUS

Apt

Gallinaria

ST. HILARY
ST. CAESARIUS
● Arles

0   50   100

Miles

Marseilles

Lerins
ST. HONORATUS
ST. VINCENT

Monastery of St. Victor
ST. JOHN CASSIAN

MEDITERRANEAN SEA

INTRODUCTION

T HE LIFE OF THE FATHERS is one of the last of the many works of St. Gregory on the saints of Christ's Church. Completed only a year or so before his death (593), it contains accounts of monastic saints which are rather more detailed than his earlier works on martyrs and confessors, and much closer to what we would now call the *Lives* of saints. The book is of special value as an original source because many of the saints therein were known to him personally (the others having lived no more than about a century before his lifetime), and three of them were his own close relatives: his great-grandfather St. Gregory, Bishop of Langres (ch. 7), his granduncle St. Nicetius, Bishop of Lyons (ch. 8), and his uncle St. Gallus, Bishop of Clermont (ch. 6). The last part of this Introduction will place the Fathers whose Lives St. Gregory gives (most of the rest of them being abbots and hermits) in the whole context of the monasticism and Orthodoxy of 6th-century Gaul, which has its roots in the great Fathers of the 4th and 5th centuries: St. Martin of Tours, St. John Cassian of Marseilles, and the Fathers of the island monastery of Lerins.

The purpose of the Lives of saints is not to give abstract knowledge but, as St. Gregory himself often states in his works, to edify spiritually and to inspire to imitation. Thus it is that the surest proof of the value of St. Gregory's writings is his own life, which was wholly inspired by the saints he so loved.

31

The present-day Tours cathedral, built on the site of the cathedral in which St. Gregory was consecrated.

The Life of St. Gregory is in itself a remarkable document. Its author is identified in the manuscripts only as "Abbot Odo," evidently the Abbot Odo (879-942) who was a monk at St. Martin's monastery in Tours in the early years of the tenth century and wrote hymns in the Saint's praise, later becoming the second abbot of Cluny. The *Life* is remarkable in that it is almost entirely taken from the works of St. Gregory himself, who often spoke of his own experiences, and therefore has something of the value of an *autobiography* of a saint, wherein we can see clearly his temptations as well as the manifestations of God's grace in him. St. Gregory's descriptions of what he himself witnessed are so simple and straightforward that they are very moving for us today in our age of "sophistication" and lies. Abbot Odo usually paraphrases and condenses his excerpts from St. Gregory's works, but even so their original power shines through; and the Abbot's own comments show him to be a man of spiritual perception himself, handing down to us through the centuries the memory of one who — as the Orthodox reader will readily see — easily ranks with the great Fathers of Orthodox piety.

The complete *Life* is given here, presented for the first time in the English language. The titles of the sections and the footnotes have been added by the editors.

Fr. Seraphim
December, 1975
Optina Cell
St. Herman of Alaska Monastery

32

SANCTUS MARTINUS LUX ET APOSTOLUS GALLORUM

20th-century icon of St. Martin of Tours (†370),
who was a spiritual model of St. Gregory

SAINT GREGORY OF TOURS

The Life of St. Gregory of Tours

By ABBOT ODO†

PREFACE

IT IS RIGHT to venerate the memory of all the saints; but the faithful honor in the first place those who, whether by their doctrine or by their example have shone with greater splendor than the others. Now, that the blessed Gregory, archbishop of the metropolitan see of Tours, was one of these, and that he is resplendent with this double merit, is proved by documents which are by no means of negligible authority. It is therefore surely necessary to describe, even though incompletely, his actions, so that the renown of such a man may not be eclipsed one day by a cloud of uncertainty. Without doubt it suffices for his glory that he has, high in the heavens, the testimony of Christ, Whom he wished to please; but among us would it not, nonetheless, be something culpable to keep silent the praises of the man who exerted himself to publish those of so many saints? No matter how long this brief account might be, all these high deeds will not be related therein, because, neglecting several things which tradition recounts, we shall limit ourselves to a small number of those which are attested by his own books. If one demands miracles of him, measuring, in the manner of the Jews, the sanctity of each person by the number of his miracles — then what is one to think of the blessed Mother of God or St. John the Forerunner?* Let us judge more soundly and know that at the dreadful day of judgment many of those who have worked miracles will be rejected, and only those who have given themselves over to works of righteousness will be received at the right hand of the Sovereign Judge. Therefore, it is not for having worked miracles that we recommend our Metropolitan — even though his life is by no means utterly devoid of them — but we hope to demonstrate that he, meek and humble of heart, walked in the steps of Christ.

1. THE SAINT'S PARENTAGE

GREGORY WAS A NATIVE of the Celtic region of the Gauls; he was born in the land of Auvergne. His father was Florentius, his mother Armentaria; and, as if nobility in this world approached in some respect the Divine generosity, his parents were rich in goods and illustrious by their origin. How-

---

† Latin text in Henri Bordier, *Les Livres des Miracles* (de Saint. Gregoire), Paris, 1864. vol. 4, pp, 212—233; French translation (apparently the only one hitherto into a modern language) in the Introduction of the same author's French translation of *The History of the Franks*. Paris, 1859,
* I.e., who did not work miracles during their lifetime, as recorded in the Gospels.

ever, something more important, they showed themselves so attached by a remarkable devotion to the duties of service toward God, that every member of
this family who might have been irreligious had the merit of being regarded
as degenerate. We shall demonstrate this by saying something of those who
were closest to him.

George, who in his lifetime was a senator, took for wife Leucadia; she
was a descendent of the race of Vectius Epagatus who, according to the account of Eusebius in the fifth book of his History, suffered martyrdom and died
at Lyons with other Christians of the same time, perhaps even more gloriously
than they [A.D. 177]. This Leucadia brought into the world St. Gallus, Bishop
of the see of Auvergne, and Florentius, who had the child of whom we are
now speaking. Of this Florentius his father, of Armentaria his mother, of
Peter his brother, of his sister the wife of Justin, and of his two nieces
Heustenia and Justina the disciple of St. Radegunde, Gregory relates in his
Books of Miracles things which reveal that their faith and their merits were not
of negligible glory. Thus, of old Leucadia bore her head so high in this Auvergne, native land of the child, that she dominated among the senators like
the statue of Rome.

It was from such persons that the lineage of St. Gregory came:** it furnished senators, judges, and everything that I could cite as being in the first
rank of the most distinguished citizens. Let us say with assurance of his parents
that, as the Lord is manifest in giving one the descent of which he is worthy,
it is a fact which should serve for the praise of Gregory that he seemed to have

** This lineage included many other illustrious names as well, including thirteen of
the eighteen Bishops of Tours who preceded him. The genealogical chart below shows
only his closest relatives:

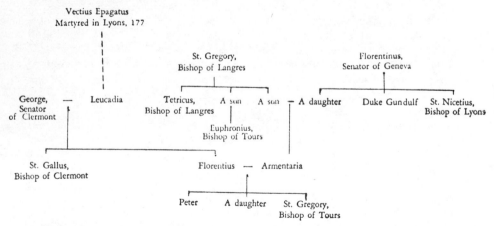

THE GENEALOGY OF ST. GREGORY

SAINT MARTIN OF TOURS,
*spiritual model of St.
Gregory, as a young
soldier divides his cloak
with a beggar, and at night
sees in a dream that
he has given it to Christ.*
(11th c. Tours manuscript)

been naturally borne by his ancestry to the renown of sanctity. Fortunatus,* in speaking of the race and native land of Gregory, has said:

"Honor of thy house, sublime head of the city of Tours, thou appearest among the Alps of the Auvergne as a mountain higher than they themselves."

And in addressing his mother:

"Twice fortunate for her merits, both for herself and for the world, was that Maccabee who gave to heaven seven children worthy of the palms of martyrdom [II Macc., ch. 7]; and thou also, Armentaria, thou art truly a fortunate mother, thou who, brilliant in thy child, adorned with the works of thy son, receivest as a crown the steadfast sanctity of Gregory."

Thus, of a noble race an offspring yet more noble, like a rose that charms all the more when removed from its stem, he returns upon his parents the honor increased by a generous nature. And although it is not necessary to seek in names the majesty of the mysterious, still he, by a fortunate omen — as the event has demonstrated — received the name of Gregory.** It is thus that, in Greek, one calls the *vigilant* man; for he knew how to keep, not only the third

---

* Venantius Honorius Clementianus Fortunatus, the celebrated Christian poet of Gaul, c. 540-600. A close friend of St. Radegunde of Poitiers, he wrote her Life (in prose) as well as several other Lives (St. Hilary of Poitiers, St. Germanus of Paris). St. Gregory encouraged his literary labors, and he wrote poems (quoted here) on the occasion of St. Gregory's accession as Bishop of Tours (573) and on his completion of the new basilica of St. Martin (590). He ended his days as Bishop of Poitiers.

** Actually, at baptism he was called Georgius Florentius; later, in honor of his great-grandfather, the Bishop of Langres (see The Life of the Fathers, ch. 7), he took the name of Gregorius at his tonsure.

37

vigil, but also the second, which is more difficult, and even the first, something one sees very rarely; and because he bore the yoke of the Saviour from his infancy, he sits solitary, following the expression of Jeremiah [Lamentations 1:1], or at least in the company of St. Martin. When he came to the age of a boy, he was consecrated to the study of letters, a labor where his tender intellect received its earliest development under Bishop Gallus, his uncle.

2. His Introduction to Miraculous Signs

He WAS ALREADY being made to learn the letters of writing, when the Divine will introduced him to miraculous signs and ennobled his holy childhood by showing him wondrous things. His father, overtaken by a violent malady, had taken to his bed. Fever had begun to devour the marrow of his bones, the venom of gout to swell his body, a fiery hue to inflame his visage — when a man, appearing in sleep to the child, said to him: "Have you read the book of Joshua?" The child replied: "I know nothing but the letters of the alphabet, and I am grieved at studying them, to which I have been assigned against my will. I know nothing at all of the existence of this book." The man replied: "Go and take a small rod of fashioned wood to someone who can place this name there, and when it shall be written with ink, place it upon the bed of your father, by the side of his head. If you do this, he will be comforted."

When morning came, he informed his mother of what he had seen. The young child of pious spirit understood, in fact, that it was not he but his mother who should judge whether this thing should be done. His mother commanded that it should be done as in the vision. This is what he did, and immediately recovered his health.* And what, in truth, is more reasonable than the fitness of the name of Jesus [Joshua] and of the wood on which it was written, in order to restore health?

3. His Granduncle, St. Nicetius of Lyons

His PARENTS, in their capacity as nobles, were possessors of a vast estate in Burgundy. As they were neighbors of St. Nicetius, a man of all sanctity who governed [as bishop] the city of Lyons, the latter had the young Gregory come to be near him. When he was brought into the bishop's presence, the holy man regarded him for some time, and having observed in this child I know

---

* The Glory of the Confessors, ch. 40. The "fashioned wood" in all likelihood was the form of the holy Cross, or a type of it.

not what of the Divine, he asked that the child be lifted up to him — for he was lying down in his bed — and, like a dweller of paradise foreboding a future companion, he began to warm him by pressing him in his arms, but (a detail one should not pass over in silence) only while covering himself entirely with his tunic for fear of touching the child's naked skin, even if it might be with the tip of his fingers. This same child, when he became a man, would often relate to his listeners this trait of chastity and would counsel them to judge, by this precaution of a man who was perfect, how much we, as frail as we are, should avoid the contact of the flesh. Nicetius, therefore, blessed the child, and after having prayed for his happiness, he restored him to his own people.**

4. HIS FATHER IS HEALED A SECOND TIME

ABOUT TWO YEARS after the miracle which we have related, Florentius was again overcome by a malady; a fever was kindled, the feet became swollen and were contorted with extreme pain. He was under the weight of his approaching end and lay already almost enclosed in the tomb. However, the child saw again in his sleep the same person who asked of him whether he knew the book of Tobit. "Not at all," he replied. The person continued: "Know that Tobit was blind, and that his son, accompanied by an angel, healed him with the liver of a fish. Do, therefore, the same, and your father will be saved." He reported these words to his mother, who immediately sent servants to the river. A fish was caught, and the part of the viscera which had been commanded was placed on burning coals. The fortunate conclusion of the miracle was not long in coming, for as soon as the first emanation of the odor had penetrated the nostrils of the father, the whole tumor and all the pain disappeared immediately.* If it is an admirable thing that the mouth of Zachariah was opened by the merit of John, it is no less a thing that Florentius was, not once but twice, healed by his son. This Florentius and his wife understood by this that their son would be a capable and blessedly inspired man; they could not but be aware, in fact, that the Divine wisdom had formed him for yet more delicate tasks. However, they did not have him tonsured immediately, desiring, I think, that he should consent himself to accept the clerical state; but he was assigned with yet greater care to literary studies.

** *The Life of the Fathers*, ch. 8, §2, where St. Gregory states that he was eight years old at this time.

* *The Glory of the Confessors*, ch. 40. See Tobit 6:1-8, where the angel explains that the smoke from the heart and liver of the fish is a remedy against evil spirits.

The Puy-de-Dome
near Clermont,
birthplace of St. Gregory

5. HE IS HEALED, AND ENTERS THE CLERICAL STATE

HE WAS STILL but a layman and had increased in spirit and body when, being suddenly seized by a chest cold and a violent fever, he fell gravely ill; and then his weakness increased from day to day, being in no way improved by medical skill. His uncle Gallus visited him often, and his mother surrounded him, as mothers do, with continual groans. But at the moment when all hope in human help had already been given up, heaven inspired the young lad to have recourse to Divine assistance. He asked, therefore, that he be transported to the tomb of Saint Illidius (for it was nearby), but this did him little good, for he yet delayed to accomplish that to which this malady was meant to lead him. Having returned home, he began after a short time to be so tormented that he was regarded as hastening to his end. The suffering finally made him understand the matter; he consoled those weeping over him and told them: "Carry me once more to the tomb of St. Illidius; I have faith that he will promptly grant healing for me, and joy for you." Having thus been transported there, he prayed as mightily as he was able, promising, if he would be delivered from this ill, that he would take the clerical habit without any delay. As soon as he had said this, he felt his fever dissipate itself immediately; he emitted through the nostrils a quantity of blood, and his malady disappeared entirely, as a messenger hastens to depart after having obtained that for which he had come. The hair of his head, therefore, was cut, and he gave himself over entirely to religious duties.*

* *The Life of the Fathers,* ch. 2, §2.

40

Mountains of the Auvergne
—native land of St. Gregory
(near Le Sancy)

6. His Literary Studies

WHEN ST. GALLUS had been called to receive the just reward of a pious life, Avitus,† the man of God, received the lad. After having tested his character and his moral habits, he confided him to the care of masters, with whose help he made him climb the steps of wisdom as rapidly as their activity and the industry of their disciple permitted. You will find this in the Life of Illidius which has already been mentioned.* However, he exercised himself in the study of letters with such discernment that he kept himself from a double excess: he was not altogether horrified at the foolishness of the poets, and yet he was not devoted to them either, as many become in an unbefitting manner, and his soul was not a slave of their seductions. Doing what was required, he sharpened as upon flint the point of his spirit, and by this way, acting as if he had borrowed golden vessels from Egypt in order to go and eat manna in the desert, he penetrated to the examination of the power which the Divine

† Then (551) Archdeacon in Clermont, later Bishop of Clermont; 517-594.

* *The Life of the Fathers*, ch. 2, Preface, where St. Gregory says that it was from Bishop Avitus that he acquired his basic knowledge of Christian doctrine and learned how to honor the saints of God.

Scriptures conceal. This is what he demonstrates when he says, speaking of himself: "I do not speak of the flight of Saturn, the wrath of Juno, the adulteries
of Jupiter"; and, continuing his discourse, he cites other fabulous persons, until
he says: "Despising all that was destined soon to perish, I return rather to Divine things and to the Gospel, for I have no wish to be caught and enveloped
in my own nets." He demonstrates in this passage** that he knew many
things, but that his enlightened judgment rejected them.

7. HE GROWS IN SANCTITY BY THE EXAMPLES OF THE SAINTS

AT THE ESTABLISHED TIME† he was ordained deacon. There was
then a man from the land of Auvergne who had carried away some wood
from the all-holy sepulchre of the blessed Martin; but when this man carelessly
failed to pay the respect due to this wood, his whole family fell gravely ill.
Soon the illness grew worse; and being in ignorance as to what might be the
cause of this, he did not correct himself until he saw in a dream a terrible figure
who asked him why he was acting thus in this regard. The man said that he did
not know what was being spoken of. "This wood which you have taken from the
couch of lord Martin," was the reply, "you are keeping without care; this is
why you have incurred these evils. But go now and bring it to the Deacon
Gregory."†† The latter, I am persuaded, was already a worthy priest, since the
lord Martin entrusted to him the most precious thing that his flock possessed.

There were in Auvergne at this time many persons who shone forth in
the ecclesiastical calling and whom this young man visited, whether when he
was with the blessed Avitus or when alone,* so that now he would take from
them examples of piety, and now, by a return of mutual love, he would offer
them that which they might lack themselves. He revered Christ in them, and,
since Christ cannot be beheld in His Own Person, he saw Him in them as one
sees a ray of the sun shining brightly on the mountain peaks. Directing his efforts towards this aim, therefore, he sought to accomplish, whether by their example or by the example of those who had already preceded them to heaven,
all that could serve for the glory of Christ.

** *The Glory of the Martyrs*, Preface.
† At the canonical age of 25, that is, in about the year 563.
†† *The Miracles of Blessed Martin*, Book I, ch. 35.
* For example, the recluse Caluppan, whom he visited with Bishop Avitus. See *The Life of the Fathers*, 11, §3.

8. HE IS HEALED BY ST. MARTIN

AMONG THESE EXEMPLARS in whose midst, as we have just said, Christ shines forth as on mountain peaks, he had noticed the glorious lord Martin, who surpasses the others like an Olympus, and being closer to the fires of the upper air, reflects the stars themselves with greater brilliance: Martin, for whose veneration the whole world rightly conspires, and towards whom Gregory aspired with an ardent desire. Constantly bearing him both in his heart and on his lips, he spread his praises everywhere. But while he applied himself mightily with all the resources of his spirit to the practice of the virtues, his flesh lost its strength, as usually happens. It is the same cause which made Daniel, on arising after having beheld his angel in a vision, find his body deprived of strength (Daniel 10:8, 16, 17), and become sick for many days. As for the virtues, Gregory profited, but as for the health of the body, he was weak; and once he found himself fallen prey to a fever and to an eruption of the skin which ended by overwhelming him to such an extent that, being no longer able either to eat or to drink, he lost all hope of preserving his life. One thing only remained to him: the trust which he had placed in Martin had never been shaken. On the contrary, burning with a yet more fervent love, he conceived such a desire for this Martin that, even though his head had scarcely come through the blows of death, he did not hesitate to set out to visit the Saint's tomb; his own people could not dissuade him from this, and he persisted obstinately, for the fever of his body was less strong than the fever of his love. After two or three stopping-places, his weakness increased with the progress of the journey. But even then nothing could restrain his impatience to have recourse to Martin with the same faith, and in the name of the Divine majesty he supplicated those who wished to divert him from this, to present him, whether alive, or in any case dead, before the tomb of the Saint.

What more shall I say? He arrived, as much well as ill, and his faith, justified, obtained the healing which he expected. And not only he, but also one of his clerics named Armentarius, who had been almost at the point of death, owed his own health to the merit of this faith. Gregory, therefore, offering thanks as much for the latter as for himself, returned to his own land satisfied, or rather, consumed more than ever by the love of Martin.*

---

* *The Miracles of Blessed Martin*, Book I, ch. 32.

9. He Works a Miracle, and His Pride is Humbled

ONCE WHEN HE WAS GOING from Burgundy to Auvergne, a violent storm arose above him. The dense air gathered in storm-clouds; the sky began to sparkle with repeated flashes, to resound with vast rumblings of thunder; and everyone felt himself grow pale and dreaded the danger that threatened. But Gregory, with tranquil soul, drew from his breast — for he always carried them around his neck — some relics of saints, which he raised in the direction of the clouds, to which he opposed them with perseverance; and the clouds instantly separated, some to the right and the others to the left, offering to the travellers an undisturbed route. But pride, which is so frequently nourished by virtues, stole into the soul of this young man; he rejoiced within himself and attributed to his own merits that which had just been accorded to his relics.** But what is nearer to presumption than a fall? And in fact, the horse on which he was mounted fell at this very place and threw him down to the ground so severely that, bruised in every part of his body, he could scarcely get up again. Understanding the cause of his misfortune, he took care in future never to let himself be vanquished by the stings of a vain glory, but every time that the Divine virtue acted through him, to ascribe the honor of it not to his own merits, but to the power of the relics which, as we have said, he carried. And if you weigh well this incident, you will see that it is more admirable to have corrected one's pride than to have separated the clouds.

10. The Vision of Light in the Temple of the Mother of God

GREGORY WAS ASSIDUOUS at prayer, especially during the hours of the night consecrated to repose. The feast of the Blessed Virgin Mary arrived. There were relics of Her† in Auvergne, in the village of Marsat. Gregory, who was there at this time, undertook out of duty, following his custom, to go to perform his prayers secretly while everyone else was immersed in sleep, and looking at it from a distance, he saw the oratory shining with a great light. He imagined, therefore, that some fervent ones had preceded him in the celebration of the vigil; nonetheless, astonished to see this great light, he directed himself toward the place from whence it proceeded: all was shrouded in silence.

** St. Gregory himself expresses this even more humbly: "I boasted before my travelling companions that God had wished to show that my innocence merited this grace" (*The Glory of the Martyrs*, ch. 84).

† Most likely a piece of Her sash or robe; such relics are preserved in Orthodox churches to this day.

He sent to search out the watchman of the building; but during this time the door opened by itself, and, realizing that this place was the object of a Divine visitation, he entered with reverence into the midst of an angelic vigil. The light which he had seen from outside ceased immediately, and he no longer saw anything but the virtue of the glorious Virgin.*

11. He is Elected Bishop of Tours

In the year 172 after the death of St. Martin, the twelfth of the reign of King Sigibert,** the blessed Euphronius, who, grown old in the midst of virtues, had been enriched by a grace so great that he seemed to have in him the spirit of prophecy, was laid beside his fathers.† The time had come when Gregory, inflamed with the love of blessed Martin and become capable of exercising the pastoral office, should take up in his place the government of his episcopal see. The blessed Euphronius thus being dead, the people of the diocese of Tours assembled to make a choice of his successor, and as a result of an affable discussion all were persuaded that Gregory was the preferable choice. They were acquainted with him by his very frequent presence in this land and knew of him a great number of actions worthy of a man of decorum.

All, therefore, joined together with a single voice, and by the favor of God his cause prevailed. In fact, the multitude of clerics and noble persons, as well as the people of the country and the towns, cried out all with the same opinion that the decision should be for this Gregory, equally illustrious by his brilliant merits and by his nobility, eminent in wisdom, surpassing all others in generosity, known by the princes, revered for his uprightness and capable of all the duties of the office. Messengers were directed to the king at a moment when, by the Lord's dispensation, Gregory himself was present [with the king]. Informed of what was happening, with what humility he strove to decline! By how many means he endeavored to escape! But where the will of God is, there everything else must yield. The king charged him to obey his authority; Queen Brunhilde pressed him to submit. And because true humility does not refuse obedience, he finally gave his consent.

---

* *The Glory of the Martyrs*, ch. 9,
** King of Austrasia and Auvergne, 561-576.
† A.D. 573, actually the year 176 after the death of St. Martin. Bishop Euphronius, who was a cousin of St. Gregory's mother, ruled the Diocese of Tours 556-573,

Immediately —for fear, I think, that any delay would give him a pre-text to flee — Egidius, Archbishop of Reims,†† consecrated him, as the poet Fortunatus has written in these verses:

"Saint Julian* sendeth to Saint Martin his dear disciple; the one who was so pleasing to him, he giveth to his brother: it is he whom the venerable and paternal hand of Egidius hath consecrated to the Lord so that he might direct the people, he whom Radegunde loveth; joyful Sigibert encourageth him, and Brunhilde giveth him honor" (Bk. V:2).

Thus the episcopal see of Tours, eighteen days after having lost Eu-phronius, received Gregory. When the inhabitants of Tours solemnly came out before their new pastor, the same poet composed again in his honor the verses that follow:

"Applaud, O fortunate people, whose desire hath now been accom-plished. Your hierarch arriveth; it is the hope of the flock that cometh. May lively childhood, may the old and bent with age celebrate this event; may each proclaim it, for it is the good fortune of all."

And the poet continues in showing Gregory celebrated by the people of Tours and enthroned, according to the forms, in his see.

12. He Restores the Basilica of Saint Martin

To SAY BRIEFLY what he was and how great he was when he was in-vested with the episcopacy: it may be seen in the several churches which he newly constructed or whose roofs he restored, and it is demonstrated at once by the books which he composed in praise of the saints or for the explanation of the Divine Scriptures. The mother church which the lord Martin had con-structed, and which was in ruins as a result of age, was restored by him in arch-form, and he adorned the walls of it with histories having for subject the ex-ploits of the same Martin.** Our poet is not silent about this, saying, among other things (Book X:2):

"By the aid of Martin, Gregory raiseth the ediface; we find again in the new man that which was the celebrated man of old."

And again:

"In restoring these ancient foundations, the excellent bishop giveth them the splendor with which they shone before."

---

†† Who later became involved in a political plot, was convicted of treason against King Childebert and deposed from the priesthood, and died in exile. See *The History of the Franks,* especially Book X, 19.

* The Martyr of Clermont, buried in Brioude. His tomb was the chief holy place of Auvergne, as St. Martin's was of Touraine. St. Gregory wrote a book on his miracles.

** See the Introduction following this Life for more sources on iconography in Gaul in the 6th century.

He also restored, as we have said, and as one may find in his own chronicles, several churches, such as the church of the Holy Cross in the village of
Marsat.†

13. INSTRUCTOR OF MONKS

THE FERVOR with which he gave himself over, whether to the construction of religious edifaces or to the care of his flock, is what one principally
notices when one considers that he could not receive even from the most holy
men the model of his perfection. In fact, to say nothing of those whose sins
are manifest, as the Apostle says (all that we could say of them would be su-
perfluous), let us take only two among those whose marks of sanctity are such
that no one but Gregory could answer them well; and let us show how delicate
he manifested himself in a worthy matter.

Not long after Gregory's ordination, the holy abbot Senoch left his cell
and went to greet him. The holy man received him with great respect, and
after gradually becoming acquainted with him in the exchanges of conversation,
he was not slow in seeing him to be infected with the disease of pride. But he
healed him completely of this pride by means of the heavenly grace which
aided him in penetrating to the evaluation of spiritual things.*

He had no less power and no less concern with regard to St. Leopardus,
whom the evil spirit was disturbing with sinister thoughts to the point where
he had decided, following a verbal injury which had been made him, to leave
the cell where he had long been enclosed. But he was unable to incur this fall,
since he merited to have Gregory for support. The latter, in fact, going in the
usual way to Marmoutier** in order to kiss there the sacred marks left by the
memory of Martin, turned aside toward the hut of Leopardus in order to be
informed, as a concerned pastor, how a sheep chained in the love of Christ was
governing himself. Leopardus soon opened to him the secrets of his heart which
the devil had represented to him as reasonable. Gregory, his spirit filled with
keenness, immediately discovered the designs of the devil, and, sighing with
extreme anguish, he began to admonish this man and to unveil for him, by his
conversation filled with good sense, the diabolic trick; then, having returned to
his house, with a pious concern he sent to him some books which were in harmony with the monastic calling. Leopardus, after having read them thoroughly

---

† At the end of the 17th century Dom Ruinart mentions this church as still existing.
* *The Life of the Fathers*, ch. 15, §2. where a much fuller account is given.
** *Major Monasterium*: St. Martin's monastery outside the city of Tours. The
original monastery (or rather, hermitage) is described by Sulpicius Severus in Chapter 10 of his *Life of Saint Martin*.

was not only healed of the temptation which he had suffered, but was subsequently endowed with a much more penetrating spirit.† Seek nothing more ex-. cellent, expect nothing more remarkable that one might say in praise of Gregory. If the soul is worth more than the body, it is a sufficiently great miracle to resurrect it in someone; the liar himself [the devil] would not dare to deny it. As for how commanding his voice was, and how authoritatively the example of his life imposed itself upon his subordinates, the careful reader will ascertain this in his own books.

14. A TEMPTATION

PHYSICAL WEAKNESS often troubled him, for he took no care at all for what concerns the flesh; but each time illness too severely tormented his body, fatigued by the rigorous practice of austerities, he had recourse to his dear Martin and immediately he was healed: this happened very often. When this happened, and in what circumstances, is related, in a manner to delight the reader, in his history of the miracles of Saint Martin. As a man humble and prudent, he would begin by applying to himself material medicines; but the more he sought after these with modesty, judging himself unworthy to receive the assistance of a miracle, the more the Divine generosity held its power in reserve for him as the sole medicine. Once it happened to him that, healed of a pain in the temples by the customary virtue of blessed Martin, he conceived a little later, at the instigation of the tempter, the thought that this agitation of the veins could be calmed by a blood-letting. While he was reflecting on this within himself, he felt the veins in both temples begin to beat violently, and the pain came upon him again with great force; immediately he hastened, troubled, to the basilica, first implored pardon for the thought which he had had, then touched his head to the veil of the sacred sepulchre, and departed from there healed.*

15. HIS RELIQUARY MIRACULOUSLY OPENS

HE HAD ALREADY COMPOSED several writings in praise of diverse persons; and although he burned with love for Martin more than for any other,

---

† *The Life of the Fathers*, ch. 20, §3, where the fuller account specifies that the books which St. Gregory gave him were the "Lives of the Fathers" (that is, of Egypt) and the "Institutes of the Monks" of St. John Cassian.

* *The Miracles of Blessed Martin*, Book II, ch. 60.

A typical peasant hut of ancient Auvergne (see §16)

he did not judge himself worthy in any way to recount what there was to write about his miracles — when, being warned two and three times during his sleep, he saw himself threatened with incurring a severe accusation by his silence.

He had had the oratory of St. Stephen, located in the outskirts of Tours, enlarged, and the entire altar transported a little farther back than it had been; but not finding any relic in this place, he sent one of the abbots to the bishop's house to take the relics of the holy Martyr Stephen. But he forgot to give him the key, so that the abbot, finding the relic-casket locked, was uncertain what to decide upon. If he returned to the bishop to obtain the key, it would mean a delay; if he brought the entire casket, he knew that it would be displeasing to the bishop, because it contained relics of a great number of saints. While he was hesitating within himself, he saw the bars withdraw and the casket open as if to attest that Divine grace was associated with the labors of Gregory. The abbot, giving thanks to God, carried the relics to Gregory amidst the general astonishment; and the latter, on his return, found the casket locked, just as he had left it.**

** *The Glory of the Martyrs*, ch. 34.

16. He Stops a Fire with his Relics

GREGORY did for the healing of the sick many things which it would be too long to relate here; however, he gave the honor for this to the saints whose relics he carried, and he endeavored to divest himself of the merit for himself. The more it was true that they were done by him, the more humbly he would attribute it to others. Here is an example:

He was proceeding once on the highway carrying around his neck a cross of gold in which there were relics of the Blessed Mary Ever-Virgin, or of blessed Martin. He perceived not far from the road a poor man's hut which was burning; it was covered, according to the custom of poor people, with leaves and small branches, that is, with flammable materials. The unfortunate one was running hither and thither, with his wife and children; he was crying out, throwing water, but all in vain. Already the flames were prevailing and one could no longer stop them. But then Gregory hastened there, raised the cross against the sheets of flame, and soon the whole fire was so paralyzed at the sight of the holy relics that it could burn no more, not even a little, the parts which it had already seized.†

17. His Closeness Heals a Deaf Man

THERE WAS a matter for which he had to go to the town of Reims. After having been graciously received by Bishop Egidius, he spent the night there and the next day, which was a Sunday. When day had come, he went to the church in order to converse with the bishop. As he was awaiting his arrival in the sacristy (for he did not wish to speak in the church), Siggo, formerly the referendary* of King Sigibert, approached him, and Gregory, after having embraced him, made him sit at his side. They spoke for some time together, and Siggo, who was listening attentively to Gregory, felt one of his ears, which had been deaf for some time, suddenly open with an unusual noise. He began to make known these acts of grace, relating what had just been done in him by the closeness of Gregory. But the man of God did not forget his habitual humility and, endeavoring to remove from this man the judgment which he had made, he said: "It is not to me that you should render thanks, my dear son, but to the blessed Martin, by whose relics — which I, unworthy one, am carrying — your hearing has been restored and your deafness dissipated."

---

† *The Glory of the Martyrs*, ch. 11.
* Legal secretary, in charge of the royal signet-ring by which documents were signed. On Siggo see *The History of the Franks*, V, 3.

The Merovingian King Sigibert I
(from a medieval design on his grave).

A 6th-century reliquary of Gaul.

18. HE INVITES HIS ATTACKERS TO EAT WITH HIM

L OVE WAS TO SUCH an extent the dominating virtue in him that he had feelings of tenderness even for his enemies, as the following example will demonstrate. He happened one time to be going to Burgundy to see his venerable mother.** In a remote forest on the other side of the river Barberon he encountered some robbers, who rushed after him with such force that they seemed to wish not merely to rob him, but to kill him as well. But their appearance could not frighten Gregory, who walked surrounded by the protection of Martin: he invoked his succour, and he experienced its presence so promptly that the robbers took flight more swiftly than they had appeared. Gregory, making use of his habitual love, and without being disturbed in the midst of the disorder, called back the fugitives and invited these enemies to take something to eat and drink. But one might have believed them pursued by the blows of a staff and their horses carried away in spite of themselves with a speed beyond their own power, so that they could not hear the voice that called them back.† Thus Gregory was shown to be both favorably heard on high, and devoted to works of love.

** Who had moved to the family's Burgundian estates after the death of St. Gregory's father. The river Barberon is a tributary of the Dolon, which flows into the Rhone near Vienne.
† *The Miracles of St. Martin*, Book I, ch. 36.

19. The Healing of A Paralytic at St. Martin's Basilica.

Thanks to Gregory, the faith of the people and their devotion grew abundantly. And so it happened that the malicious adversary, tormented by a lively anguish and being unable to control the efforts of his wickedness, endeavored with all his might to overthrow the trust both of the pastor and the flock. The very day of the Lord's Nativity, as Gregory came to celebrate the feast pontifically, according to custom, in the chief basilica of the city, one of the more violent of the possessed began to run wild beyond measure, and going before the groups that surrounded Gregory in front and behind, he cried out: "It is in vain that you approach Martin's threshhold; it is for nothing that you come near his temple; for, because of your crimes without number, he has abandoned you, he has fled from you in abhorrence, and it is at Rome that he performs miracles." As the devil was panting these and similar words at the crowded throng, his voice not only troubled the hearts of the country people, but struck with fear also the clerics and Gregory himself. They entered the basilica shedding abundant tears, and all prostrated themselves on the pavement while praying in order to be worthy of the presence of the holy man. A man who, for over three years, had had both hands and a foot paralyzed, was prostrate like the others before the holy altar, imploring the aid of the blessed Martin, when, being suddenly overcome by fever, he began to suffer as if he had been under torture. Nonetheless, the sacred solemnities were celebrated; and at the moment when the holy hierarch, his tears flowing more copiously, was awaiting the coming of the blessed Martin — when, according to custom, he was covering with a veil the instruments of the Divine Mystery — the sick one was fully restored to health.

Immediately Gregory, full of joy, gave thanks to God Almighty and, his eyes filled with a rain of tears, he burst out with these words which he addressed to the people: "May fear depart from your hearts, my brothers, for the blessed confessor dwells with us, and you should by no means believe the devil who is a liar from the beginning of the world and has never known the truth." After he had given the people these words of consolation, and others also, the universal grief was turned to joy, and all, thanks to Martin and to Gregory, returned home happier than when they had come.*

---

* *The Miracles of St. Martin*, Book II, ch. 25.

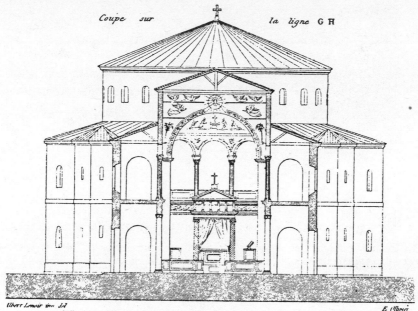

The Basilica of St. Martin in Tours in the 6th century
(as reconstructed from the writings of St. Gregory)

20. His Fervor is Spurred by an Angel.

SINCE WE HAVE just spoken of the Lord's Nativity, we shall mention what happened to our bishop one Nativity day. During the most sacred night of this solemnity, fatigued by the ceremonies of the vigil, he had lain down for a moment on his bed, when a man advanced quickly towards him and said to him: "Arise and return to church." He awoke, made the sign of the cross, and went back to sleep. The man did not desist, but gave him a second warning; but feeling himself still heavy on awakening, he fell asleep again. Then this man, coming for the third time, gave him a slap on the cheek and said to him: "It is you who should admonish the others to make them go to the vigil, and here it is you who let yourself be so long overcome by sleep." Struck by these words, Gregory returned to church with a rapid step.** He was so pleasing in the eyes of the Most High that he was not permitted, even under the excuse of human weakness, to neglect his salvation for a moment.

** *The Glory of the Martyrs*, ch. 87.

53

St. Radegund's wooden
reading desk, preserved
at her convent, Poitiers

21. An Angel Reproves Him.

WE BELIEVE we must add to this account how God wished to reprove him so that he might not sin even as a result of the levity of others. As the blessed Martin had healed him of a hopeless malady, so that he could go the next day to church, still, in order not to weary himself during the ceremonies of the liturgy, he had ordered one of his priests to perform the celebration. But this priest pronounced the sacred words with I know not what crudity, and several of the assistants began to ridicule him, saying that he would have done better to be silent than to speak so crudely. That night, Gregory saw in sleep a man who told him that one should make no observation at all on the Mysteries of God. From this it resulted for him that he should not permit foolish or light-minded men to disparage the blessed solemnities in his presence.

22. St. Radegund and the Relic of the Holy Cross.

OFTEN THE MAN OF GOD, as a true guardian of himself and of his flock, would travel far, whether for the benefit of his people, or for his own salvation. Once, while going to pray at the tomb of St. Hilary,* he turned aside in order to visit the holy queen Radegund.** The two of them, like unto dwellers of paradise, were conversing of heavenly things, when the oil which ordinarily flowed drop by drop before the relics of the holy Cross became so

---

* St. Hilary, Bishop of Poitiers, a theologian and spiritual father of St. Martin of Tours; † 368, January 13.
** St. Radegund († 587, August 13), daughter of the king of Thuringia, was taken prisoner by the Frankish King Clotaire I and was forced to marry him. Later she took refuge with St. Medardus, Bishop of Soissons, became a nun and founded a convent in Poitiers under the rule of St. Cæsarius of Arles.

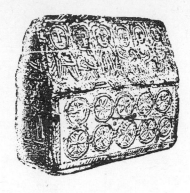

Left: St. Radegund's reliquary of the True Cross, before which St. Gregory prayed, as it survives today (see sketch of whole reliquary, next page).

Right: 6th-century reliquary used in Gaul.

abundant at the arrival of the bishop that in the space of less than an hour more than a pint of it flowed.†

"The Cross of the Lord, which had been discovered by the Empress Helen at Jerusalem, is venerated on Wednesday and Friday of each week. The queen Radegund, whom one might, both in merit and faith, compare to Helen, asked for a portion of this Cross and placed it with devotion in the monastery of Poitiers which had been established by her efforts. Then she sent again servants to Jerusalem and into all the East and they, going about the tombs, brought back the relics of holy martyrs and confessors, which she placed, together with this holy cross, in a casket of silver; and they produced a great number of miracles of which she was vouchsafed to be a witness....

"I had often heard that the lamps which burned before these holy relics would begin to boil by a divine power, and that they caused the oil to overflow to such an extent that a vessel placed underneath was filled most of the time. However, in the foolishness of a hardened spirit I could not decide to believe this, until this same power, which had already been manifested to others, acted in my presence and ended by triumphing over my brute indifference. I shall tell, therefore, what I saw with my own eyes.

† The account of St. Gregory himself (*The Glory of the Martyrs*, ch. 5), being much more detailed, is here added to the text of Odo (within quotation marks).

The original reliquary of St. Radegund (6th century), with icons of the saints whose relics are contained in it (from an 18th-century drawing).

Before St. Radegund's reliquary of the precious Cross, I saw that there was a lamp which was lit. Having noticed that frequent drops of oil were issuing from it, I believed — God is my witness — that the vessel was cracked, all the more because underneath it there had been placed a dish in which the flowing oil was received. Turning then to the abbess, I said to her: 'Are you so careless that you cannot prepare a lamp that is intact, in which the oil burns, in place of this one which is cracked and from which the oil is leaking?' She replied: 'My lord, it is not that, but the power of the holy cross which you see.' Then, turning within myself and remembering what I had heard before, I looked at the lamp and saw it boiling in great waves and overflowing its edges, like a pot over a hot flame — a phenomenon which, as I think, in order the better to convince my unbelief, increased yet more and more, so that in the space of an hour the vessel, which held no more than a quart, had poured out a pint. I marvelled in silence, and from that moment I proclaimed the virtue of the precious Cross."

When this blessed queen was on the point of being called before the King of Heaven, Gregory, the man of God, received the news that she was at her end; but she had already departed when he hastened to her, and he gave burial to her holy body. At the same time he solemnly blessed the altar erected over the grave, reserving, however, to the bishop of the place, who happened then to be absent, the care of closing the coffin.

The Baptistery of St. John in Poitiers (4th century)
much as it looked in St. Gregory's time.

St. Radegund is tonsured by St. Medardus of Soissons
(10th century manuscript)

SAINT GREGORY THE DIALOGIST (10th-century illumination, Regensburg)

23. HE IS SAVED FROM PERIL BY ST. ROMANUS.

THERE WAS a matter that obliged him to cross the river Garonne near the castle of Blaye; but this river had become so swollen that it inspired not a little fear, just to behold it. Not far from there reposed St. Romanus, the priest whom Martin had buried, as is related in his Life.* As the gusts of wind on the one hand, and the mountains of waves on the other, placed the voyager in great peril, he raised his eyes to heaven, then beheld the church of this Saint Romanus, and the entire sea soon levelled itself out so completely that every ominous sound disappeared and he was transported to the other bank without incurring any danger **

24. HE GOES TO ROME.

HE HAD ALREADY completed sixteen years of his episcopate when his namesake, the great Gregory, was placed in the apostolic see.† It is believed that they were for some time attached one to the other by a close friendship; and this feeling would only be natural, for Fortunatus compares this Pope to Gregory of Nazianzus*** and says that the latter was as a gift made to the East, Gregory of Rome a gift made to the South, and our Gregory a gift to the West. This latter having gone to the church of the Holy Apostles [in Rome], the holy Pope received him with great reverence; and having conducted him to the place where St. Peter had confessed Christ, he stopped at his side, waiting until he should arise. And while he waited, he considered with astonishment— for he was a profound genius — the secret dispensations of God with regard to the man whom he had before his eyes and who, small in stature, had received from heaven such an abundance of grace. The latter perceived this instantly by a Divine perception, and, arising after his prayer, he turned towards the Pope with the calm air which he always preserved and said to him: "It is the Lord Who hath made us, and not we ourselves; He is the same in small things as in great." The holy Pope understood that these words were an answer to his thought and, all rejoicing at this observation, he began to profess a profound veneration for this grace which until then he had only admired in Gregory, and he honored the episcopal see of Tours with the gift of a chair of

---

* St. Romanus of Bordeaux, † 382, November 24.
** *The Glory of the Confessors*, ch. 46, where St. Gregory states that those in danger of shipwreck on the Garonne are saved by crying out: "Have mercy on us, St. Romanus, confessor of God."
† St. Gregory the Dialogist. Pope of Rome from 590 to his death in 604 (March 12).
*** St. Gregory the Theologian, Archbishop of Constantinople, † 390, January 25.

gold which was always to be preserved there.*

25. The Apparition of Mystical Fire.

ALREADY SAINT MARTIN, glorifying everywhere his disciple Gregory, had manifested in many ways how much he favored him; but, desiring even to cooperate in his works, he deigned sometimes to be present with all the splendor which accompanied him, all the while remaining invisible.

Having the intention to consecrate an oratory in a hall which had served as an office for his predecessor, Gregory transported there some relics of Saint Saturninus,** which he had taken with great respect from the basilica of the lord Martin. There was a considerable choir of priests and deacons in white robes, a noble assembly of citizens decorated according to their office, a numerous throng of people of the second rank; the tapers shed a majestic radiance, crosses were raised high in the air.

When the door was reached, an awesome flash suddenly filling the room struck all eyes in a great outburst, and, being prolonged, sped here and there like lightning. All, seized by a mighty fear, prostrated themselves upon the ground. But Gregory, as if he had been admitted to the secret of this so great miracle, exhorted all with firmness and said to them: "Fear nothing. Remember in what manner a globe of fire was seen to come from the head of the blessed Martin and to ascend toward heaven,† and believe that he is come himself with his holy relics in order to visit us." Then all glorified God, and this venerable man repeated with the clerics: "Blessed is he that cometh in the name of the Lord; God is the Lord and hath appeared unto us" (Ps. 117:26).††

---

* These lines of Abbot Odo seem to be the only historical mention of the journey of St. Gregory to Rome, and for this reason modern historians tend to doubt that it occurred. We do know, however, that St. Gregory greatly respected his namesake the Pope, and that his Deacon Agiulf had been in Rome in 590 when the latter was elected Pope, giving St. Gregory an eyewitness account of events in Rome, including the only remaining text of the address of the Dialogist to the people of Rome on this occasion. See *The History of the Franks,* Book X, ch. 1,

** First bishop of Toulouse, martyred in the 3rd century, November 29.

† While the Saint was celebrating the Divine Liturgy; see Sulpicius Severus, *Dialogues,* II, 2.

†† *The Glory of the Confessors,* ch. 20, where in St. Gregory's much longer account he makes clear that he was bringing also some relics of St. Martin to the oratory. He also told the people: "It is the virtue (power) of the saints which you see," and concludes the chapter with a theological explanation: "I think that this was a mystical fire, because it illumined without burning."

26. THE REPOSE OF SAINT GREGORY.

LET THESE FEW WORDS on our bishop suffice. We do not recommend him by means of a quantity of miracles, such as one usually attributes even to the reprobate, although this sort of glory was not lacking to him either. But it is sufficient, to make his honor shine, that he followed, humble of heart, the example of Christ, and that he did not place his hope at all in treasures of gold. To have been able, as we have shown above (in part at least), to keep himself from the bonds of sin — is certainly to have done miraculous things. To be free from sins is a glory superior to any other.

In the twenty-first year of his episcopate, that is to say, at the moment when he had completed the number of three times seven years in faith in the Holy Trinity (594), he was placed beside his fathers, less full of days — for he had been ordained at the age of about thirty years — than full of perfection. However, one is not entirely sealed in the tomb if his word itself is living in the world; and similarly, we believe that Gregory is united to blessed Martin in Heaven, just as his holy body is near his in the grave. The inhabitants of Tours, therefore, if they do not wish to pass for ingrates, having regard for the Divine gifts which they have received, should always remember how much God has protected them. The patron whom He has given them is not an ordinary saint; it is Martin, of whom one does not know where to begin one's praises, nor what particular praise to make of him, since his least actions are manifestly greater, as has been written, than the greatest actions of others. All the nations of the world, so to speak, testify what honor we should bear him when they cherish him with an affection so intimate that even in our times, when love has become so cold, we see flocking to his most holy grave a throng of people of unknown country and language, so that one can say with justice of this Martin: "All the earth is eager to see him." Their zeal forcefully and rightly condemns the inertia of us who are near him; but it is clear that it is not without a Divine dispensation that his love has penetrated all hearts to the extent of making his memory everywhere fragrant, as that of a second Josiah, and that it is so widespread through all the countries of the earth that wherever the name of Christ reigns, there Martin is honored.*

---

* In fact, the name of St. Martin is to be found in Greek and Russian Calendars,

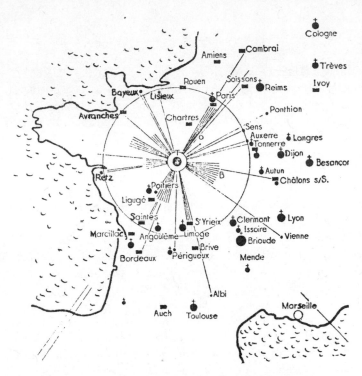

PLACES OF PILGRIMAGE IN 6TH-CENTURY GAUL

(Tours occupies the central place; the small rectangles indicate
other relics of St. Martin, the circles with crosses, other tombs of saints.)

What is more, the inhabitants of Touraine have been given Gregory, a man remarkable not only for sanctity, but also for knowledge, to the end that the city of Tours should not be a city without splendor and destitute of the practice of letters, but that it should be illustrious through him after being such through Martin, just as the city of Romulus (Rome), after the Apostles, was adorned by another Gregory.

Let us be assured that we have Gregory for advocate and for guardian, whether with God or with the blessed Martin, and that we can entrust to him our needs so that he might satisfy them. Gregory, in fact, will not at all lose the memory of the goodness which animated him just as it did Martin, whose compassionate heart he has made known to us with such concern. In order to show us this compassion, he collected the miracles of the Saint, so that all those in the future who should know what an enormous number of them he worked, and of what importance they were and what hopeless maladies he healed, might never doubt his power. And if it should happen, in consequence of the difference of times, that the material miracles should cease, let us nonetheless always believe that he works in our souls miracles which sustain them by his virtue.

Let Gregory, then, who experienced the compassion of Martin, ever remind him of his flock, ever ask of him the maintenance of the holy place where Martin reposes, and implore of him the prosperity of the entire kingdom. Let us not forget, either, how he preserved even in his own burial his habits of humility. He had himself buried in a spot placed in such a manner that he would always be trampled under foot by everyone, and one would necessarily be prevented by the disposition of the place from ever rendering him any respect.* But the flock of the blessed Martin, being unable to support such things, removed from this place the friend of their Lord, and placed him with the proper respect in a splendid mausoleum erected at the left of the holy sepulchre (of Martin). He died on November 17, in the very week consecrated to Martin;** so that, after having commenced, already ill, to celebrate the feast of Martin, he could complete it together with him in Heaven, by the grace of the Lord Jesus Christ, the living God, Who reigns with the Father and the Holy Spirit unto the ages of ages. Amen.

A NOTE ON THE RELICS AND SEPULCHRE
OF STS. MARTIN AND GREGORY OF TOURS

OWING TO HIS extraordinary life and many miracles, the importance of St. Martin as an intercessor for the Orthodox people before God only increased after his death in 397, and his sepulchre soon became a place of pilgrimage. His successor as Bishop of Tours, St. Brice, erected a church over the tomb, where there was also a basin with healing waters wherein the faithful would immerse themselves. Later Bishop Perpetuus replaced this first church with a spacious basilica, which was consecrated on July 4, 470, and was perhaps the most striking monument of Christian Gaul, being, outside of Rome, the chief center of Christian pilgrimage in the West. This is the basilica described by St. Gregory. In the 5th century also the tomb was covered by a slab of white

---

* Compare the testaments of Sts. Nilus of Sora and Alexander of Svir in Russia.
** Who died on November 11.

GITUR CHRODICILDIS REGINA
I plena dierum bonis que operibus pre
orta Apud urbem Turonicam obiit
tempore Iniuriosi episcopi, Quae a pa
risius cum magno psallentio deport
tata in sacrario basilicae scipe triad
latus chlodovechi regis sepulta est
a filiis suis childeberto atque chlo
thario regibus Nam basilicam illam
ipsa construxerat in quac igenue
nia beatissima est sacpulta

Denique chlotharius rex in dixe
rat ut omnes aecclesiae regni sui
tertiam partem fructuum fisco dissol
verent, quodlicet inuri cum omnes e
piscopi consensissent atque subscrip
sissent. Uiriliter hoc beatus iniurio
sus respuens subscribe dedignatus
est dicens. Si uolueris res dī tollere dns
regnum tuum uelociter aufert, quia
niquum est ut pauperes quos tuo debes
alere horreo ab eorum stipe tua reple
antur. Et iratus contra regem nec illa
ledicens abscessit Tunc conmotus rex
timens etiam uirtutem beati martini

A 7th-century manuscript of St. Gregory's *History of the Franks*

18th-century view of the Cathedral built in 1008 over the relics of
St. Martin of Tours (with later additions); destroyed in 1793.

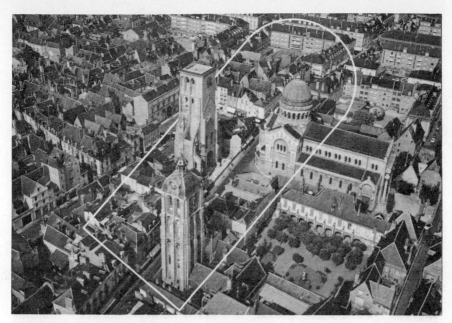

Above: the site (represented by the white line) of the cathedral with the relics of Sts. Martin and Gregory, which was destroyed in 1793 during the French Revolution.

At left: the cathedral built in 1860 over the site of St. Martin's sepulchre. This cathedral (which also appears in the above photograph) still stands today.

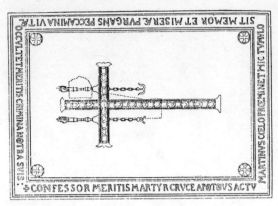

The marble slab sent by
St Euphronius of Autun
to cover the relics of
St. Martin (reconstructed
from pieces found in 1860)

marble sent by St. Euphronius of Autun. The tomb of St. Gregory was placed near that of St. Martin, and at the end of the 7th century it was rebuilt into an impressive monument itself by St. Ouen. The basilica suffered various injuries over the centuries, especially from the Norman invasions, and finally in 997, shortly after Abbot Odo was there, it was totally destroyed by fire. The relics of Sts. Martin and Gregory, however, were preserved and placed in the new cathedral which was dedicated on July 4, 1008. Partially rebuilt in the 11th to 13th centuries, this church survived to the French Revolution, but historians note that the veneration of St. Martin never regained the power it had during France's Orthodox era (before 1054).

In 1562, on May 25, the relics of Sts. Martin and Gregory were profaned and given over to flames by Protestant Huguenots. The next year a bone of St. Martin and some pieces of the skulls of Sts. Brice and Gregory were recovered together with some ashes of their relics, which were placed again in the cathedral. In 1793, in the midst of the most ferocious anti-Christian revolution before our own century, the cathedral was leveled to the ground, and the very site was covered with houses and paved streets in a deliberate attempt to blot out the memory of the saints. Only in 1860, in a commendable spirit of repentance for the revolutionary sacrilege (something worthy of imitation in the future Russia!), did some devout Roman Catholics seek out the sepulchre of the holy Hierarchs of Tours and find the very place of their burial, together with parts of the marble slab which had covered St. Martin's grave since the 5th century (illustrated here). Subsequently a new cathedral of St. Martin was built on this spot, where some fragments of his relics are still venerated; but of the relics of St. Gregory nothing remains.

III

Introduction to Orthodox Gaul

by Fr. Seraphim Rose

The 10-century monastery of St. Martin at Canigou in the south of
France (Rousillon): a fruit of the last period of Orthodox Gaul's monastic
fervor, whose flourishing period of the 5th and 6th centuries is described by
St. Gregory of Tours in *Vita Patrum*.

1

Orthodox Christianity in 6th-Century Gaul

THE 20TH-CENTURY Orthodox Christian will find little that is strange in the Christianity of 6th-century Gaul; in fact, if he himself has entered deeply into the piety and spirit of Orthodoxy as it has come down even to our days, he will find himself very much at home in the Christian world of St. Gregory of Tours. The externals of Christian worship — church structures and decoration, iconography, vestments, services — after centuries of development, had attained essentially the form they retain today in the Orthodox Church. In the West, especially after the final Schism of the Church of Rome in 1054, all these things changed. The more tradition-minded East, by the very fact that it has changed so little over the centuries even in outward forms, is naturally much closer to the early Christian West than is the Catholic-Protestant West of recent centuries, which had departed far from its Orthodox roots even before the present-day "post-Christian" era arrived.

Some historians of this period, such as O.M. Dalton in the Introduction to his translation of St. Gregory's *History of the Franks* (Oxford, 1927, two volumes), find much in Christian Gaul that is "Eastern" in form. This observation is true as far as it goes, but it is made from a modern Western perspective that is not quite precise. A more precise formulation of this observation would be the following:

In the 6th century there was one common Christianity, identical in dogma and spirit in East and West, with some differences in form which, at this early period, were no more than minor and incidental. The whole Church met together in councils, both before and after this century, to decide disputed dogmatic questions and confess the one true Faith. There were numerous pil-

69

grims and travellers, especially "Westerners" going to the East, but also "Easterners" going to the West, and they did not find each other strangers, or the Christian faith or piety or customs of the distant land alien to what they knew at home. The local differences amounted to no more than exist today between the Orthodox Christians of Russia and Greece.

The estrangement between East and West belongs to future centuries. It becomes painfully manifest (although there were signs of it before this) only with the age of the Crusades (1096 and later), and the reason for it is to be found in a striking spiritual, psychological and cultural change which occurred in the West precisely at the time of the Schism. Concerning this a noted Roman Catholic scholar, Yves Congar, has perceptively remarked: "A Christian of the fourth or fifth century would have felt less bewildered by the forms of piety current in the 11th century than would his counterpart of the 11th century in the forms of the 12th. The great break occurred in the transition period from the one to the other century. This change took place only in the West where, sometime between the end of the 11th and the end of the 12th century, everything was somehow transformed. This profound alteration of view did not take place in the East, where, in some respects, Christian matters are still today what they were then — and what they were in the West before the end of the 11th century." (Yves Congar, O.P., *After Nine Hundred Years,* Fordham University Press, 1959, p. 39, where he is actually paraphrasing Dom A. Wilmart.)

One might cite numerous manifestations of this remarkable change in the West: the beginnings of Scholasticism or the academic-analytical approach to knowledge as opposed to the traditional-synthetic approach of Orthodoxy; the beginning of the age of romance," when fables and legends were introduced into Christian texts; the new naturalism in art (Giotto) which destroyed iconography; the new "personal" concept of sanctity (Francis of Assisi), unacceptable to Orthodoxy, which gave rise to later Western "mysticism" and eventually to the innumerable sects and pseudo-religious movements of modern times; and so forth. The cause of this change is something that cannot be evident to a Roman Catholic scholar: it is the loss of grace which follows on separation from the Church of Christ and which puts one at the mercy of the "spirit of the times" and of purely logical and human ways of life and thought. When the Crusaders sacked and desecrated Constantinople in 1204 (an act unthinkable in earlier centuries for the Christian West), they only revealed that they had become total strangers to Orthodoxy, and therefore to the Eastern Christians, and that they had irretrievably lost what their own ancestors in 6th-century Gaul had preserved as the apple of their eye: the unbroken tradition of true Christianity.

We shall mention here only some of the most obvious Orthodox forms of 6th-century Gaul, as a helpful background to the reading of St. Gregory's *Life of the Fathers*.

THE CHRISTIAN TEMPLE: THE BASILICA

W HEN CHRISTIANS finally emerged from the catacombs in the reign of St. Constantine the Great, it was natural that they should begin to build churches in great numbers. For nearly three centuries, under conditions of persecution and the threat of persecution, the basic forms of Christian faith and piety had been nurtured literally underground and in private home churches; now, with Orthodox Christianity first given freedom, and then recognized as the religion of the State, Christian houses of worship were erected in conspicuous places in all cities and major towns of the Roman Empire, in East and West alike. The type of building found most suitable to the needs of Christian worship was not the pagan temple, where idols were worshipped in dark and confining interiors, but the Roman basilica or "royal hall," a secular building used and adapted for various public functions, in many of which the emperor himself would be present (whence the name). Such buildings are known from the second century B.C., but the first Christian basilica dates only from shortly before the time of St. Constantine, and the 4th century is the first great age of its construction. For many centuries this was the standard Christian temple both in East and West; in style there is but little variation from Syria to Spain and Britain, from Africa to Germany. It is from the basilica that the Christian temples of later centuries, whether East or West, are derived.

The standard basilica plan includes a long nave (where the believers would stand), usually flanked by aisles on both sides, ending in a semi-circular apse where the sanctuary or altar-area was located; often there was a narthex in the rear and an atrium or courtyard outside with a fountain where the faithful would wash their hands before entering the church. The nave was supported by columns which separated it from the aisles, and the columns were topped by a band of wide windows which gave abundant opaque light (being made of mica or similar material, there being no glass then) which rendered especially bright the iconographic mosaics or (more commonly in Gaul) frescoes which adorned the apse and the upper walls of the basilica. The interior was also ornamented with numerous gold decorations, chandeliers, etc. The basic structure would be of stone or brick, surmounted by a flat ceiling, with open timbers usually visible. Already by the 6th century, the flat roof was often replaced by a dome.

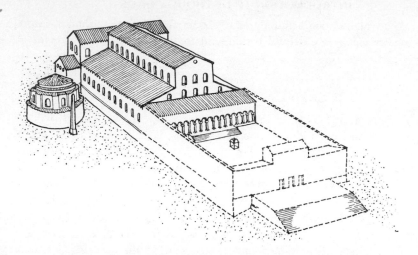

The original Basilica of St. Peter in Rome (5th century)
with atrium and adjoining baptistery
(according to the reconstruction by Krautheimer)

There are a number of excellently preserved basilicas especially from the 5th and 6th centuries in Rome and Ravenna, and many others are well known from foundation remains, excavations, and contemporary descriptions. The first impression created by such buildings is one of majesty and beauty. This is the aspect emphasized in the first detailed descriptions we have of a Christian basilica, that of the Basilica of Tyre in the East (consecrated in 317), in the *Church History* of Eusebius (Book X, 4): "The basilica itself he (the builder) has furnished with beautiful and splendid materials, using unstinted liberality in his disbursements. Its splendor and its majesty surpass description, and the brilliant appearance of the work, its lofty pinnacles reaching to the heavens, and the costly cedars of Lebanon above them. . . the skillful architectural arrangement and the surpassing beauty of each part."

The purpose of such splendor is to inspire and elevate one, to open up a new heavenly world to those born of earth. But the entrance to this world is gained only by those who go on the narrow path of ascetic Christianity. To remind the faithful of this, St. Paulinus had his own verses inscribed over the doors to his basilica in Nola in Italy (early 5th century). Over one door he wrote: "Peace be upon you who enter the sanctuary of Christ with pure minds and peaceful hearts"; over another, together with a representation of the cross: "Behold the wreathed cross of Christ the Lord, set above the entrance hall. It promises high rewards for grinding toil. If you wish to obtain the crown, take up the cross"; and inside one door, visible to the people as they leave: "Each of you that departs from the house of the Lord, after completing your prayers in due order, remove your bodies but remain here in heart." (St Paulinus of Nola, Letter 32.)

Unfortunately, none of the basilicas of Gaul in this period have survived, but from the numerous literary descriptions of them that we do have it is obvious that they were identical in style to those of Rome and the East. From descriptions in the writings of St. Gregory of Tours it has been possible to reconstruct the approximate appearance of the Basilica of St. Martin in his time. He has an interesting description also of the basilica of his native Clermont, built by St. Namatius in the 5th century: "It is 150 feet long, 60 feet wide inside the nave, and 50 feet high as far as the vaulting. It has a rounded apse at the end, and two wings of elegant design (one variation of the basilica-style) on either side. The whole building is constructed in the shape of a cross. It has 42 windows, 70 columns, and eight doorways. In it one is conscious of the fear of God and of a great brightness, and those at prayer are often aware of a most sweet and aromatic odor which is being wafted towards them. Round the sanctuary it has walls which are decorated with mosaic work made of many varieties of marble." *(History of the Franks,* II, 16.)

Between the nave and the altar area there was often, even in the earliest Christian basilicas, a kind of screen. A description and explanation of this is given by Eusebius when, in describing the Basilica of Tyre, he ends with "the holy of holies, the altar, and, that it might be inaccessible to the multitude, he enclosed it with wooden lattice-work, accurately wrought with artistic carving, presenting a wonderful sight to the beholders." Evidently, from the very moment the Church left the catacombs, it was felt necessary to screen the holy of holies from the people so that the Mysteries might not be profaned by the ever-present temptation, in times of peace and ease, to take them for granted. This screen, the "chancel," is the beginning of the later iconostasis in the East and the rood-screen in the medieval West. Many traces of the chancel may be seen in the oldest Roman basilicas today, and in all likelihood they were present in the basilicas of Gaul as well.

The altar-tables in the early Christian basilicas were virtually identical with those still used in the Orthodox East, rather than with the later elaborate Latin altars of the West. Made at first usually of wood, and later of stone, they were generally square in shape, as is the oldest surviving altar-table of Gaul, found at Auriol near Marseilles (5th century). The altar-tables visible in the 6th-century mosaics of Ravenna square and entirely hidden by cloth

The earliest altar-table of Gaul still extant
(found at Auriol near Marseilles)

coverings, are in no way different from the altar-tables that may be seen in any Orthodox church today.

The saint to whom a basilica would be dedicated would be most often buried under the altar, sometimes in a special crypt; thus it was in the Basilica of St. Martin in Tours.

Baptisms were conducted in a separate building (baptistery) near the basilica. Several baptisteries from this period have been well preserved in Italy, and the baptistery in Poitiers is the only substantially intact church building of the whole Merovingian (pre-Charlemagne) period in Gaul.

The church furnishings of the basilica would be familiar to today's Orthodox Christian. There would be many oil-burning lamps, some in chandeliers hanging from the roof, others before the tombs of saints or before icons or relics. The poet Fortunatus and his fellow student Felix were healed of an eye affliction by rubbing the affected spot with oil from the lamp burning before the icon of St. Martin in his church in Ravenna. A remarkable miracle in the Life of St. Gregory of Tours (ch. 22) occurred with the oil lamp which hung before the relic of the Holy Cross in St. Radegund's convent in Poitiers. Beeswax candles were used, both as offerings and carried in processions.

The vestments of the clergy were also very similar to those still in use today in the Orthodox Church. The characteristic vestment of deacons (who at this time were still a separate order of the clergy, as in the East today, and not simply a stage on the way to the priesthood, as they became in the Latin church), was the alb, a long white tunic of silk or wool, identical with the Eastern sticharion; later in the West this was much modified. Deacons also wore a stole or orarium over the left shoulder — the orarion of Orthodox deacons today. Priests wore the chasuble, which in distinction from the Eastern phelonion had a hood (cucullus), as mentioned in the *Life of the Fathers* (VIII, 5), and also wore cuffs, as in the East today. The distinctive mark of the bishop was the pallium (given only to some bishops in the beginning), which in later centuries became much simplified in the Latin church, but in this period, according to Prof. Dalton, "in form corresponded almost exactly with the omophorion of the Greek Church" (vol. 1, p. 334). These vestments were chiefly adapted for use from the ceremonial dress of the Roman imperial court; as in the case of

6th-century Basilica of Sant' Apollinare in Classe, Ravenna

Interior of the Basilica of St. Demetrius in Thessalonica (5th century)

Apse of the Basilica of Sant' Apollinare in Classe, Ravenna

Mosaic from the Church of San Vitale, Ravenna
(showing Altar-table in use in the 6th century)

Right wall of the nave, showing procession of the martyrs, in
Saint Martin's Basilica in Ravenna (Sant' Apollinare Nuovo)

St. Apollinaris, first Bishop of Ravenna
with the priestly vestments in use in the 6th century:
alb (sticharion), chasuble (phelonion), cuffs, and the bishop's
pallium (omophorion)
(Mosaic from the apse, Sant' Apollinare in Classe, Ravenna)

the Christian basilica, the Church used for its external forms what it found when it emerged from the catacombs and hallowed it for use by succeeding generations.

The daily cycle of services followed the same pattern which has been preserved up to now in the Orthodox Church: Vespers and Matins, the Hours (First, Third, Sixth and Ninth), Compline and Nocturn. The specific content of the services (for example, which psalms were read in which services) was different from that of the East, but the general nature of the material used (psalms, antiphons taken from the psalms, readings from the Old and New Testaments, newly-composed hymns) was the same. Nocturn and Matins were combined to form the Vigil (vigilia) before the great feasts. The services in monasteries were generally longer than those in parish churches and cathedrals.

The Gallican Rite, which differed from the Roman Rite in a number of details, was used in Gaul and Spain. Attempts have been made in modern times to reconstruct this rite, which was supplanted in Gaul by the Roman Rite in the 8th and 9th centuries, and later died out completely in the West; but the texts from this period that have come down to us give only the general outline of some of the services, and not their full texts. The Gallican Mass (missa, as the Liturgy was universally called in the West) has some interesting points of agreement with the Easern Liturgy as opposed to the Roman Mass, most notably the presence of a "Great Entrance" with the unconsecrated bread and wine after the dismissal of the catechumens. However, even the Latin Mass at this time was less different from the Eastern Liturgy than it became in later centuries, and no problems were encountered on the frequent occasions when Christian clergy from the West would concelebrate the Liturgy in Constantinople, or Eastern clergy would do so in Rome.

The liturgical year was basically the same as that known today in East and West alike. Great feasts such as Christmas and Epiphany, Pascha, the Ascension and Pentecost were celebrated with special solemnity, as were saints' days such as those of St. John the Baptist and Sts. Peter and Paul. The Calendar of saints in the Roman Church included many thousands of names, and the memory of local saints was kept with great reverence; in Tours, as St. Gregory informs us, special vigils were kept for the feasts of Sts. Martin, Litorius and Bricius of Tours, St. Symphorian of Autun, and St. Hilary of Poitiers (HF X, 31). Whereever there were relics of saints, they were venerated with special solemnity; the relics of St. Martin in Tours, in particular, were the object of pilgrimages from all over Gaul. The fast of Great Lent was kept strictly, and Wednesdays and Fridays of most weeks were fast days, in addition to extra fast days before Christmas and at other times.

The days of rogation mentioned by St. Gregory were special days of fasting and prayer before the feast of the Ascension; these were instituted by St. Mamertus of Vienne in the 5th century and later spread to the whole of Gaul and the West (*HF* II, 347).

ICONOGRAPHY

From THE BEGINNING, the Christian basilicas were adorned with mosaics or frescoes, at first in the apse, and very soon on the walls as well. Those in Gaul were lost together with the churches that housed them, and so we can only judge of them by contemporary descriptions and by surviving examples, especially in Italy, which was in close contact with Gaul at this time.

The iconography of the 4th century is rather close in style to the realism of later Roman painting, although by the end of the century, even in Rome, it is already changing towards the Byzantine style; in content it combines themes from the symbolic paintings of the catacombs (Christ as the Lamb, the Good Shepherd, etc.) with scenes from the Old and (more and more with time) from the New Testament. The Basilica of St. Ambrose in Milan, dedicated in 386, contained frescoes (as we know from the inscriptions of the Saint himself) from the Old Testament, and the following ones from the New Testament: the Annunciation, the conversion of Zacchaeus, the woman with an issue of blood, the Transfiguration, and St. John leaning on the breast of the Saviour. Judging from the contemporary mosaics at St. Pudentiana in Rome, the style of these icons was already very close to the later Byzantine style. In the Basilica of St. Paulinus in Nola (404), the two sides of the nave contained scenes from the Old and New Testaments, and in the space between the windows above were apostles and saints, with Christ the King in the apse. There was as yet no fixed rule for the depiction of various feasts or scriptural events, and there was no formal canonization of the saints who might be portrayed in icons; apostles, martyrs, and even recent bishops and ascetics were depicted according to their local veneration. There is even a case where, in the baptistery of the monastery of Sulpicius Severus at Primuliacum in southern Gaul, the recently-reposed St. Martin is depicted on one wall, and the still-living Bishop Paulinus of Nola on the opposite wall — something which aroused the good-natured protest of St. Paulinus, who wrote Severus: "By depicting me alone on the opposite wall, you have contrasted my lowly figure, shrouded in mental darkness, with Martin's holy person" (St. Paulinus, Letter 32).

The distinctive Byzantine style is already evident in the 5th century, and the 6th century is the age of an already developed and perfected art. The

great basilicas of Ravenna are monumental triumphs of Byzantine iconography
— an art which in style and subject-matter has not changed essentially through
the ages, and is still very much alive today. The Byzantine style was universal
in the Roman Empire, as may be seen in the icons even of the remote border
area of Mt. Sinai, where the mosaic of the Transfiguration in the apse is identical with later icons of the feast down to our day. This is the Christian art that
was known to the great Western hierarchs of the 6th century, St. Gregory, Pope
of Rome, and St. Gregory of Tours.

In Gaul, mosaic icons are known (*HF* II, 16; X, 45), but more commonly we hear of frescoes. The original basilica of St. Martin had frescoes
which were restored by St. Gregory, as he himself relates (*HF* X, 31): "I found
the walls of St. Martin's basilica damaged by fire. I ordered my workmen to use
all their skill to paint and decorate them, until they were as bright as they had
previously been." These frescoes must have been impressive, for when treat-
ing of the stay of a certain Eberulf in the basilica (under the law of sanctuary
which then prevailed), St. Gregory writes: "When the priest had gone off,
Eberulf's young women and his men-servants used to come in and stand gaping
at the frescoes on the walls" (*HF* VII, 22). St. Gregory has preserved for us
also a brief account of how the frescoes were painted (5th century): "The wife
of Namatius built the church of St. Stephen in the suburb outside the walls of
Clermont-Ferrand. She wanted it to be decorated with colored frescoes. She
used to hold in her lap a book from which she would read stories of events
which happened long ago, and tell the workmen what she wanted painted on the
walls" (*HF* II, 17). This "book" might have been the Scriptures, the Life of
a saint, or even, as Prof. Dalton suggests, "some sort of painter's manual like
those used in the East" (vol. 1, p. 327).

When restoring the main basilica of Tours (distinct from the basilica
where St. Martin's relics reposed), as Abbot Odo informs us precisely in his
life of St. Gregory (ch. 12), the latter "decorated the walls with histories
having for subject the exploits of Martin." It so happens that we have a list of
these iconographic scenes in a poem of Fortunatus describing the basilica (*Car-
mine* X, 6). They are: (1) St. Martin curing a leper by a kiss; (2) dividing his
cloak and giving half to a beggar; (3) giving away his tunic; (4) raising three
men from the dead; (5) preventing the pine tree from falling on him by the
sign of the Cross; (6) idols being crushed by a great column launched from
heaven; (7) St. Martin exposing a pretended martyr. We can only regret the
disappearance of such a notable monument of Orthodox Christian art, just one
of many in 6th-century Gaul, the likes of which were not to be seen in later

centuries in the West (where the Roman-Byzantine style was gradually lost); but we may gain a general idea of its appearance in the contemporary basilicas of Ravenna with their mosaic icons. One of these basilicas, indeed, was dedicated originally to St. Martin of Tours, the dedication later being changed to Sant' Apollinare Nuovo.

Separate panel icons also existed at this time. In the history of Bede it is stated that St. Augustine of Canterbury and those with him, after landing in Britain in the year 597, came to King Ethelbert of Kent "bearing a silver cross for their banner, and the image of our Lord and Saviour painted on a board" (*Ecclesiastical History of England,* Book I, ch. 25). In the *Life of the Fathers* (XII, 2) we read of "the icons (Latin *iconicas*) of the apostles and other saints" in the oratory where St. Bracchio prayed. It should be noted that the oratories and small village churches of Gaul would not, of course, be in basilica style or usually made of stone; they were generally of wood, and the icons in them were painted on boards and hung on the walls. The most detailed reference to these 6th-century panel icons is in St. Gregory's *Glory of the Martyrs* (ch. 22), where we read, in the account "of the Jew who stole an icon (Latin *iconica,* or in one manuscript, *icona*) and pierced it," the following, which is also an impressive testimony of the truly Orthodox attitude of the Church of Gaul at this time, as contrasted with the iconoclast sentiment which seized part of Gaul (as it did also of the Christian East) in the century of Charlemagne. Here are St. Gregory's words: "The faith which has remained pure among us up to this day causes us to love Christ with such a love that the faithful who keep His law engraved in their hearts wish to have also His painted image, in memory of His virtue, on visible boards which they hang in their churches and in their homes. . . A Jew, who often saw in a church an image of this sort painted on a board (Latin *imaginem in tabula pictam*) attached to the wall, said to himself, 'Behold the seducer who has humiliated us'. . . Having come then in the night, he pierced the image, took it down from the wall, and carried it under his clothes to his house in order to throw it into the fire." He was discovered when it was found that the image shed copious blood in the place where it had been pierced (a miracle which occurred also later in Byzantium with the Icon of the Iviron Mother of God, and in Soviet times in Kaplunovka in Russia with a crucifix).

A number of such panel icons on wood have come down to us from 6th-century Mount Sinai; they are identical in appearance to the icons which pious Orthodox Christians cause to have painted for their churches and homes even today.

THE MOST HOLY THEOTOKOS
6th-century Mosaic
in St. Martin's basilica
(Sant' Apollinare Nuovo, Ravenna)

SAINT MARTIN OF TOURS
Probably the earliest
surviving icon of the Saint
(Sant' Apollinare Nuovo, Ravenna)

Mosaic of Christ from the Basilica
of St. Pudentiana, Rome, about 385

6th-century Mosaic of Christ, from Sant' Apollinare Nuovo, Ravenna

The Transfiguration of Christ (6th-century mosaic at Mt. Sinai)

Saint Martin before the Saviour
(Sant' Apollinare Nuovo, Ravenna)

CHURCH ORGANIZATION

THE CHURCH GOVERNMENT of Gaul in the 6th century was, in the words of Prof. Dalton, according to the "Eastern system" (vol. 1, p. 272) — that is, according to Orthodox and not Papal principles.

At this time there were about 130 bishops in Gaul, of whom eleven were Metropolitans, or bishops of the chief cities of the land, with certain rights of precedence over the other bishops of the metropolitan district. The Metropolitans of Arles (in the south) usually held a seniority over the other Metropolitans, and especially during the episcopate of St. Caesarius of Arles (first half of the 6th century), it was he who convoked and presided over councils of bishops. There were no vicar bishops; each bishop governed his own see, and questions affecting many bishops were decided in councils, where all the bishops had an equal voice.

The Pope of Rome, while of course respected as Patriarch of the West, was still "first among equals" and exercised authority about equal to that exercised in later centuries (before the fall of Byzantium) by the Patriarch of Constantinople over the Church of Russia. Pope Gregory the Great at this time specifically protested against the assumption by the Patriarch of Constantinople (or any Patriarch, including himself) of the title "Ecumenical Patriarch": "What will you say to Christ, Who is the Head of the universal Church, in the scrutiny of the last judgment, having attempted to put all His members under yourself by the appellation of Universal,. . . Certainly Peter, the first of the Apostles, himself a member of the universal Church, Paul, Andrew, John, — what were they but heads of particular communities. . . And of all the saints, not one has asked himself to be called universal. . . The prelates of this Apostolic See, which by the Providence of God I serve, had the honor offered them of being called universal. . . But yet not one of them has ever wished to be called by such a title, or seized upon this ill-advised name, lest if, in virtue of the rank of the pontificate he should take to himself the glory of singularity, he might seem to have denied it to all his brethren." (*Letters of St. Gregory the Great*, Book V, 18.)

The very title of "apostolic see," although applied with special reverence to the See of St. Peter, was in this period given not only to Rome but to all episcopal sees, at least in Gaul, as may be seen in the letter of St. Radegund preserved in the *History of the Franks* (IX, 42): "To the holy fathers in Christ and to the lord Bishops, worthy occupants of their apostolic sees. . ." The "apostolic see" of Bordeaux is mentioned specifically by St. Gregory in the *History of the Franks*.

87

Even the famous case of St. Hilary of Arles, which is sometimes viewed as an example of "Papal intervention" in the affairs of the Church of Gaul, in the eyes of Pope St. Leo himself had entirely another meaning. The Pope — who, indeed, was recognized as having jurisdiction when appealed to by other bishops in the West — overturned St. Hilary's deposition in 444 of a certain bishop in Gaul, whom St. Leo found innocent of the charge against him, not in the name of any "Papal rights" but rather with the intention of restoring the ancient rights of the local bishops of Gaul. He accused St. Hilary of "claiming for himself the ordinations of all the churches throughout the provinces of Gaul, and transferring to himself the dignity which is due to Metropolitans," thus "claiming for himself the ordinations of a province for which he was not responsible." St. Leo concludes his letter to the bishops of the Gallic province of Vienne: "We are not keeping in our own hands the ordinations of your provinces, but we are claiming for you that no further innovations should be allowed, and that for the future no opportunity should be given for the usurper to infringe your privileges." (*Letters of St. Leo the Great,* Letter X.)

It was only in later centuries that Papal "universality" began to be asserted by the Popes, and only after the Schism that the present-day concept of "Papalism" was developed. In the 5th and 6th centuries the government of the Church of Gaul was very much in the "Eastern" way. The Metropolitans had no direct jurisdiction even over the bishops of their own province. When Felix, Bishop of Nantes, made false accusations against St. Gregory of Tours, his own Metropolitan, out of spite for being unable to take away some church property from the latter's diocese, St. Gregory could do nothing but express his exasperation at such un-Christian conduct in a reply not lacking in St. Gregory's dry humor: "What a pity that it was not Marseilles that elected you its bishop! Instead of bringing you cargoes of oil and other wares, its ships could have carried only papyrus, which would have given you more opportunity for writing libellous letters to honest folk like me" (*HF* V, 5).

CONCLUSION: THE MEANING OF SIXTH-CENTURY GAUL FOR TODAY

TO SUM UP this brief description of 6th-century Christian Gaul, we may say that here we find already the historical Orthodox world which is familiar even today to any Orthodox Christian who is at home in true (not modernized or renovated) Orthodoxy. The scholar of Late Latin could find ample opportunities for further research in this field, whether in the works of St. Gregory of Tours or in numerous other texts of this time (which have been surprisingly little studied or translated up to now); the material given above is no more than an introduction. In modern times, 6th-century Gaul may most accurately be likened to 19th-century Russia. Both societies were entirely permeated with Orthodox Christianity; in them the Orthodox *standard* was always the governing principle of life (however short of it the practice might fall), and the central fact in the life of the people was reverence for Christ, the holy things of the Church, and sanctity. In the 6th century (as opposed to the 4th, which is still a time of development), the outward things of the Church had already received their more-or-less final forms, which subsequently changed very little in the Orthodox East; thus, we are able to feel very much at home with them. At the same time, there is a freshness and newness about the Church's forms and its life which is very inspiring to us today, when it is very easy either to take the age-old forms of Orthodoxy for granted, or to feel that they have no "relevance" to modern life.

So much for the outward side of Orthodoxy; but what of its inward side? Does the Christian world of St. Gregory of Tours have any spiritual significance for us today, or is it of no more than antiquarian interest for us, the "out-of-date" Orthodox Christians of the 20th century?

Much has been written in modern times of the "fossilized" Orthodox Church and its followers who, when they are true to themselves and their priceless heritage, simply do not "fit in" with anyone else in the contemporary world, whether heterodox Christians, pagans, or unbelievers. If only we could undersand it, there is a message in this for us, concerning our position among others in the world and our preservation of the Orthodox Faith.

Perhaps no one has better expressed the modern world's bewilderment over genuine Orthodox Christianity than a renowned scholar precisely of St. Gregory of Tours and the Gaul of his times. In his book, *Roman Society in Gaul in the Merovingian Age* (London, 1926), Sir Samuel Dill has written: "The dim religious life of the early Middle Ages is severed from the modern mind by so wide a gulf, by such a revolution of beliefs that the most cultivated sympathy can only hope to revive it in faint imagination. Its hard, firm, realistic faith in the wonders and terrors of an unseen world seems to evade the utmost effort to make it real to us" (p. 324). "Gregory's legends reveal a world of imagination and fervent belief which no modern man can ever fully enter into, even with the most insinuating power of imaginative sympathy. It is intensely interesting, even fascinating. But the interest is that of the remote observer, studying with cold scrutiny a puzzling phase in the development of the human spirit. Between us and the early Middle Ages there is a gulf which the most supple and agile imagination can hardly hope to pass. He who has pondered most deeply over the popular faith of that time will feel most deeply how impossible it is to pierce its secret" (p. 397).

And yet, for us who strive to be conscious Orthodox Christians in the 20th century it is precisely the *spiritual* world of St. Gregory of Tours that is of profound relevance and significance. The material side is familiar to us, but that is only an expression of something much deeper. It is surely providential for us that the material side of the Orthodox culture of Gaul has been almost entirely destroyed, and we cannot view it directly even in a museum of dead antiquities; for that leaves the spiritual message of his epoch even freer to speak to us. The Orthodox Christian of today is overwhelmed to open St. Gregory's "Books of Miracles" and find there just what his soul is craving in this soulless, mechanistic modern world; he finds that very Christian path of salvation which he knows in the Orthodox services, the Lives of the Saints, the Patristic writings, but which is so absent today, even among the best of modern "Christians," that one begins to wonder whether one is not really insane, or some literal fossil of history, for continuing to believe and feel as the Church has always believed and felt. It is one thing to recognize the intellectual truth of Orthodox Christianity; but how is one to live it when it is so out of harmony with the times? And then one reads St. Gregory and finds that all of this Orthodox truth is also profoundly *normal*, that whole societies were once based on it, that it is unbelief and "renovated" Christianity which are profoundly abnormal and not Orthodox Christianity, that this is the heritage and birthright *of the West itself* which it deserted so long ago when it separated from the one and only Church of Christ, thereby losing the key to the "secret" which so baffles the modern scholar — the "secret" of true Christianity, which must be approached with a fervent, believing heart, and not with the cold aloofness of modern unbelief which is not natural to man but is an anomaly of history.

But let us just briefly state why the Orthodox Christian feels so much at home in the spiritual world of St. Gregory of Tours.

St. Gregory is an historian; but this does not mean a mere chronicler of bare facts, or the mythical "objective observer" of so much modern scholarship who looks at things with the "cold scrutiny" of the "remote observer." He had a point of view; he was always seeking a pattern in history; he had constantly before him what the modern scientist would call a "model" into which he fitted the historical facts which he collected. In actual fact, all scientists and scholars act in this way, and any one who denies it only deceives himself and admits in effect that his "model" of reality, his basis for interpreting facts, is unconscious, and therefore is much more capable of distorting reality than is the "model" of a scholar who knows what his own basic beliefs and presuppositions are. The "objective observer," most often in our times, is someone whose basic view of reality is modern unbelief and scepticism, who is willing to ascribe the lowest possible motives to historical personages, who is inclined to dismiss all "supernatural" events as belonging to the convenient categories of "superstition" or "self-deception" or as to be understood within the concepts of modern psychology.

The "model" by which St. Gregory interprets reality is Orthodox Christianity, and he not only subscribes to it with his mind, but is fervently committed to it with his whole heart. Thus, he begins his great historical work, *The History of the Franks,* with nothing less than his own confession of faith: "Proposing as I do to describe the wars waged by kings against hostile peoples, by martyrs against the heathen and by the Churches against the heretics, I wish first of all to explain my own faith, so that whoever reads me may not doubt that I am a Catholic." ("Catholic," of course, in 6th-century texts, means the same thing that we now mean by the word "Orthodox.") There follows the Nicene Creed, paraphrased and with certain Orthodox interpretations added.

Thus in St. Gregory we may see the *wholeness* of view which has been lost by almost all of modern scholarship — another one of those basic differences between East and West that began only with the Schism of Rome. In this, St. Gregory is fully in the Orthodox spirit. In this approach there is a great advantage solely from the point of view of historical fact — for we have before us not only the "bare facts" he chronicles, but we understand as well the context in which he interprets them. But more important than this — particularly when it comes to chronicling supernatural events or the virtues of saints — we have the inestimable advantage of *a trained observer on the spot,* so to speak — someone who interprets spiritual events (almost all of which he knew either from personal experience or from the testimony of witnesses he regarded as reliable) on the basis of the Church's tradition and his own rich Christian experience. We do not need to guess as to the meaning of some spiritually-significant event when we have such a reliable contemporary interpreter of it, and especially when his interpretations are so much in accord with what we find in the basic source books of the Orthodox East. We may place all the more trust in St. Gregory's interpretations when we know that he himself was granted spiritual visions (as described in his life) and was frank in admitting when he did not see the spiritual visions of others (*HF* V, 50).

Sir Samuel Dill notes that access is denied him, as a modern man, to the world of St. Gregory's "legends." What are we, 20th-century Orthodox Christians to think of these "legends"? Prof. Dalton notes, regarding the very book of St. Gregory which we are presenting here, that "his *Lives of the Fathers* have something of the childlike simplicity characterizing the *Dialogues* of St. *Gregory the Great*" (vol. 1, p. 21). We have already discussed, in the "Prologue" to this book, the value of this "childlikeness" for Orthodox Christians today, as well as the high standards of truthfulness of such Orthodox writers as St. Gregory the Great (as contrasted with the frequent fables of the medieval West). The extraordinary spiritual manifestations described by St. Gregory of Tours are familiar to any Orthodox Christian who is well grounded in the ABC's of spiritual experience and in the basic Orthodox source-books; they sound like "legends" only to those whose grounding is in the materialism and unbelief of modern times. Somewhat ironically, these "legends" have now become a little more accessible to a new generation that has become interested in psychic and occult phenomena as well as actual sorcery and witchcraft; but for them also the whole tone of St. Gregory's writings will remain foreign unless they obtain the key to its "secrets": true Orthodox Christianity. St. Gregory's "wonders and terrors of an unseen world" open up for us another reality entirely from that of modern unbelief and occultism alike: the reality of spiritual life, which is indeed more unseen than seen, which does indeed account for many extraordinary phenomena usually misunderstood by modern scholarship, and which begins now and continues into eternity.

There is, finally, another aspect of St. Gregory's writings which modern historians find generally not so much baffling as disdainfully amusing, but to which, again, we Orthodox Christians have the key which they lack. This aspect is that of the "coincidences," omens, and the like, which St. Gregory finds significant but which modern historians find totally irrelevant to the chronicling of historical events. Some of these phenomena are manifestations of spiritual vision, such as the naked sword which St. Salvius (and no one else) saw hanging over the house of King Chilperic, portending the death of the king's sons (*HF* V, 50). But other of the manifestations are simply dreams or natural phenomena of an extraordinary kind, which either fill St. Gregory with foreboding (*HF* VIII, 17) or of which he says in all simplicity, "I have no idea what all this meant" (*HF* V, 23). The modern historian is only amused at the idea of finding a "meaning" behind earthquakes or strange signs in the sky; but St. Gregory, as a Christian historian, is aware that God's Providence is at work everywhere in the universe and can be understood even in small or seemingly random details by those who are spiritually sensitive; he sees also that the deepest causes of historical events are by no means always the obvious ones. Concerning this theological point we may cite the words of a contemporary of St. Gregory in the East, St. Abba Dorotheus, to whom the writings of St. Gregory would have been not in the least strange. "It is good, brethren, to place your hope for every deed upon God and to say: Nothing happens without the will of God; but of course God knew that this was good and useful and profitable, and therefore he did this, even though this matter also had some outward cause. For example, I could say that inasmuch as I ate food with the pilgrims and forced myself a litle in order to be host to them, therefore my stomach was weighed down and there was a numbness caused in my feet and from this I became ill. I could also cite various other causes (for one who seeks them, there is no lack of them); but the most sure and profitable thing is to say: In truth God knew that this would be more profitable for my soul, and therefore it happened in this way." (St. Abba Dorotheus, *Spiritual Instructions,* Instruction 12.)

St. Gregory, like St. Abba Dorotheus, was always seeking first of all the *primary* or inward causes of events, which concern the will of God and man's salvation. That is why his history of the Franks, as well as of individual saints, are of much greater value than the "objective" (that is, purely *outward*) researches of modern scholars into the same subjects. This is not to say that some of his historical facts might not be subject to correction, but only that his *spiritual* interpretation of events is basically the correct, the Christian one.

It remains now, before proceeding to the texts of St. Gregory himself, to examine only one more major aspect of the historical context of *The Life of the Fathers:* the monasticism of 6th-century Gaul. Here again we shall find St. Gregory's Gaul very "Eastern," and perhaps here more than in any other aspect of that early Orthodox age will we find cause for spiritual inspiration, and perhaps even some hints that will help our own poor and feeble Orthodox monasticism in the 20th century.

2

Orthodox Monasticism
in 5th and 6th-Century Gaul

THE HEART of the Christian life of early Orthodox Gaul was monasticism. Orthodox monasticism sprang up on the soil of Gaul almost as soon as news of the great Egyptian Fathers reached the West; and once Christian Gaul had been given the example of its first great native monastic saint, St. Martin of Tours, its monastics already numbered in the thousands, some 2,000 of whom attended the funeral of St. Martin in 397. With the founding of the monastery of Lerins in the Egyptian tradition, at the dawn of the new century, and the writings of St. John Cassian on the spiritual teaching of the Egyptian Fathers early in the 5th century, the golden age of monasticism in Gaul may be said to have begun. We know of the founding of some 200 monasteries in Gaul in the next two centuries, and probably there were many more; and the wonderworking saints from among these communities were already past counting.

But the history of Orthodox monasticism in Gaul in this period is not at all one of institutions. The monastic "orders" of the medieval West, with their centralized government and uniform rule, were of course unheard of in this early period of fresh monastic fervor; and even the dominance of the Rule of St. Benedict (+529) over the monastic institutions of the West (a dominance which, for all its good points, also indicated a waning of the early monastic fervor of the West) was still several centuries away. The spiritual tone of monastic Gaul in these centuries was set by the Orthodox East.

The most general picture of the monasticism of these centuries in the West is to be found in the writings of St. Gregory of Tours, particularly in the *Life of the Fathers*, but also scattered throughout the pages of the *History of the Franks* and his other works. But we will look at his writings in vain for an account of monastic *institutions;* we will find there the names of few monasteries, and there is almost nothing on monastic rules or government. He is interested first of all not even in monks or nuns (i.e., formally tonsured monastics), but in *ascetic strugglers and their spiritual deeds.* For the most part he recounts the exploits of ascetics renowned for their sanctity and miracles; but he also recounts tales of those who went astray, holding these up as a warning to those who would undertake the path of spiritual struggle. The center of his attention, and that of monastic Gaul, is *spiritual struggle* itself. The forested "desert" of Orthodox Gaul at this time breathes the same freshness and fervor and freedom as the Egyptian and Palestinian deserts, as chronicled in the *Lausiac History* and other such classic accounts of early Eastern monasticism. Let us see if we can recapture something of the spirit of the "flight to the desert" in 5th and 6th century Gaul by examining some of the texts of the great Western monastic Fathers of this time.

THE TEACHING OF ST. JOHN CASSIAN

W E KNOW LITTLE of the written sources by which the Orthodox monastic teaching was given to St. Martin's disciples and other early monastic strugglers in Gaul; probably there was not much more than St. Athanasius' *Life of St. Anthony* and one other of the early Latin versions of the Lives and Sayings of the Egyptian Fathers. In the presence of a living model of the monastic ideal such as St. Martin was, these sources were sufficient; but when the monks of Gaul became numbered in the thousands and numerous new monasteries were being opened, the need for a rather "systematic" written account of the monastic teaching became acutely felt. As with one voice, the monastic fathers of Gaul turned for this account to St. John Cassian, abbot of a newly-founded monastery in Marseilles, who had just returned from a long sojourn in the monastic deserts of Egypt and Palestine. Having thoroughly absorbed the teaching of the Eastern Fathers, and being a man of spiritual discernment himself, he answered their plea with two books: the *Institutes,* setting forth the outward order of monasticism (dress, services, discipline, etc.) and the spiritual teaching on an elementary level, and the *Conferences,* giving the profounder monastic teaching of the great Egyptian Fathers. These works, addressed and dedicated to various abbots and monastic founders in Gaul, were by far the most influential monastic source-books in 5th and 6th century Gaul and. (albeit, to a lesser extent) in other Western countries as well. To understand the monastic movement which St. Gregory describes, we can begin in no better way than by a brief account of the teaching of St. Cassian, and in particular of the "ABC's" of monasticism contained in the *Institutes,* the single book that is most often mentioned in the monastic accounts of this period. (All citations translated here, with book and chapter number, are from the Russian translation of Bishop Peter of Ufa, Moscow, 1892.)

The book is dedicated to Castor, Bishop of Apt (a short distance north of Marseilles) who had just established a coenobitic monastery in his diocese. In his Introduction St. Cassian explains what is demanded of him, and what he intends to give: "Desiring that the coenobitic monasteries in your region should be ordered according to the rules of the Eastern, and in particular the Egyptian monasteries . . . you demand of me, poor in word and knowledge, that I set forth those monastic rules which I saw in Egypt and Palestine, and of which I heard from the Fathers, so that the brethren of your monastery might know the way of life which the saints lead there." Following in the footsteps of monastic teachers "outstanding in life, understanding, and eloquence, such as Basil the Great, Jerome, and others," he promises to speak of the monastic rules, the origin of the eight chief vices, and of how they may be uprooted, on the basis of what he learned in the East, for "there can be no new brotherhood in the West, in the land of Gaul, better than those monasteries."

Although St. Cassian notes, in this same Introduction, that not all the monastic rules of the Egyptian desert may be applicable in Gaul, "owing to the severity of the climate and the difficulty and difference of manners," and in general he is condescending to "Western" weakness — still, he is rather merciless in castigating any aspect of Gallic monasticism in practice that smacks of self-pampering or idleness. Then, even as today, a large part of the interest in monasticism was a product of idle dreaming which would rather not face the daily struggles and humiliations necessary for the forging of true spiritual life according to the Gospel. Thus St. Cassian places much emphasis on the necessity of just plain *work.* "The cause of the fact that in these (Western) regions we do not see monasteries with such a multitude of brethren (i.e., thousands and tens of thousands) is that they are not supported by what their own labors can acquire; but if the generosity of another might furnish them sufficient food, then a love of idleness and distraction of heart do not allow them any longer to remain in that place. Therefore, there is a saying among the ancient Fathers of Egypt: a laboring monk is tempted by one demon, while a lazy one is attacked by a numberless multitude of demons" *(Institutes* X, 23). The Eastern Fathers "think that the more fervent they will be in handiwork and labors, the more will be born in them the desire for the higher purity of spiritual contemplation" (II, 12). There is a definite correlation between willingness to work and a genuine striving for spiritual attainments: "Equally exercising the powers of body and soul, they equalize the gain of the outward man and profit to the inward man, opposing to the passionate movements of the heart and the inconstant wave of thoughts the heaviness of handiwork, as some kind of firm, unwavering anchor, by which one can restrain the distraction and wandering of the heart within the cell as in a safe harbor" (II, 14). Zeal for work, in fact, is a measuring stick of spiritual advancement: "The Egyptian Fathers in no way allow monks to be idle, especially the young, measuring the condition of their heart and their advancement in patience and humility by their zeal for work" (IX, 22). Awareness of this basic principle of spiritual life is what produces the "down-to-earth", even "rough" quality of a genuine Orthodox monastery even today. A novice being formed in such a spiritual atmosphere often finds himself in hectic circumstances that test his natural love of idleness and repose. Thus Abba Dorotheus, author of a 6th century "ABC" of monasticism, describes his own monastic training: "When I was living in coenobitism, the Abbot, at the advice of the Elders, made me the receiver of visitors, while not long before this I had had a severe illness. And thus it happened that visitors would come in the evening and I would spend the evening with them; then camel-drivers would come, and I would serve them; and often after I had gone to sleep, another need would arise, and they would wake me up, and meanwhile the hour of the Vigil would also be approaching. Hardly would I have fallen asleep when the canonarch would wake me up; but from labor or from illness I would be exhausted, and sleep would again take such possession of me that, weakened by fever, I would not remember myself and would answer through sleep: 'Very well, my Lord, may God remember your love and reward you; you have commanded, I will come, O Lord.' Then when he went out, I would again fall asleep and be very sad that I was late in going to church. And since the canonarch could not wait for me, I begged two brethren, one to wake me up, and the other not to let me doze at the Vigil; and believe me, brethren, I revered them as if through them my salvation was accomplished, and maintained toward them great piety" (Abba Dorotheus, *Spiritual Instructions*). A similar hectic novitiate, in modern times, was spent by the Optina elder Joseph, who for a private cell was given the busy waiting room of Elder Ambrose! The idle dreamers among monastic aspirants do not survive under such conditions; they often leave because the monastery is "not spiritual enough" — not realizing that thus they are depriving themselves of the spiritual "anchor" without which they will wander in vain dissatisfaction at not finding their "ideal monastery."

Laziness is not the worst sin of monastic aspirants; but without love of labor they will never even enter into the struggle of monastic life nor understand the most elementary principles of spiritual combat.

If the novice has zeal for work, there is hope that he can acquire understanding of the other ABC's of monastic life. The first of these is *cutting off the will*. "The elder strives first of all to instruct the novice to conquer his will, desiring that through this he might gradually ascend to the highest perfection; and for this he deliberately orders him to do what he does not like. By much experience it has been shown that a monk (especially a young one) cannot bridle his desires if he has not learned through obedience to mortify his will. Therefore they say that he who has not first learned to conquer his will can in no way suppress anger, despondency, fleshly lust; he cannot have true humility, constant unity and harmony with the brethren, and long remain in the community" (IV, 8). The novice who is unwilling to cut off his will by monastic obedience often finds that he is "not understood" by the monastic authorities, or that he is forced to do things "unsuited" to him, or that his "zeal" in performing ascetic labors (according to his own understanding, of course) is not appreciated; but the true lover of obedience, like the lover of labor, rejoices in the midst of the hard work of going against his own will, even when it may seem to his earthly logic that he is "right" and his spiritual father is "wrong".

Another important part of the monastic basic training is learning *not to trust one's own judgment*, which is closely bound up with *revelation of thoughts*. "If we wish to follow the commandments of the Gospel and be imitators of the Apostles and the whole of the early Church, or of the Fathers who in our times have followed their virtues and perfection, we should not trust our own opinions, promising ourselves evangelical perfection from this cold and pitiful condition; but following their steps, we should strive not to deceive ourselves, and thus we shall fulfill the good order and the commands of the monastery, so that we might renounce this world in truth" (VII, 18).

"Giving novices the beginning instruction, they strive to raise them to greater perfection, at the same time finding out whether their humility is true or pretended. And the more easily to attain this, they teach them not to hide any of the thoughts of their hearts out of false shame, but to reveal them to their elder immediately after they arise, and in the judging of them not to trust their own opinion, but to consider bad or good only what the elder shall recognize as such. Because of this the cunning enemy cannot catch the inexperienced young monk in anything; he can in no way deceive one who trusts not his own but his elder's judgment" (IV, 9).

Despite the ascetic prodigies for which the Eastern Fathers are noted, the emphasis of their spiritual teaching is not at all on outward asceticism. "The infirmity of the flesh does not hinder purity of heart, if wc use only the food that is needful for strengthening our infirmity, and not that which desire demands . . . Fasting and continence consist in moderation . . . Each must fast as much as necessary for the taming of fleshly warfare" (V, 7, 8, 9).

The purpose of the monastic discipline is to *uproot the passions and acquire the virtues*. In Egypt, the elders see that novices "discover both the causes of the passions by which they are tempted, and the means against them. . . These true physicians of souls, averting by spiritual instruction as by some heavenly medicine the afflictions of heart that might arise in the future, do not allow the passions to grow in the souls of youths, revealing to them both the cause of the passion that threatens, and the means for healing" (XI, 16). It may well be imagined what pain this process of self-knowledge causes in the soul of the novice, who usually comes to a monastery full of illusions about himself.

All of the virtues must be sought together, and all of the passions fought at the same time, for "he who does not possess several of the virtues has not mastered any of them to perfection. For how can one quench the blazing heat of lust, which is kindled not merely from the desire of the body, but also from the fault of the soul, if he cannot tame the anger which bursts forth from the incontinence of the heart alone? Or how can he handle the sensuous arousal of the flesh and soul if he cannot conquer the simple vice of pride?" (V. 11).

The spiritual battle to acquire virtues and uproot passions is above all an *inward* battle: the chief enemy is not outside of us, but in our own passionate nature; our advancement in virtue is judged not chiefly by our outward actions, but by our inward state; the means of battle is not primarily outward acts (such as avoiding people, in order to avoid occasions of temptation), but working on one's inner man. "It is clear that disturbance occurs in us not always because of others, but more often from our own faults, because we have in us the hidden causes of offense and the seeds of vices, which, as soon as the rain of temptation pours on our soul, immediately produce sprouts and fruits" (IX, 5). "Perfection of heart is acquired not so much by going away from people as by the virtue of patience. If patience will be made strong and sure, it can keep us peaceful even with those who hate peace; but if it will not be acquired, we shall be constantly in discord even with those who are more perfect and better than we" (IX, 7). "If we wish to receive that higher divine reward of which it is said: Blessed are the pure in heart, for they shall see God (Matt. 5:8), then it is not only in our actions that we must suppress anger, but it must be torn up by the roots from the hidden part of the soul as well" (VIII, 19). "For those who seek perfection, it is insufficient merely not to become angry at another. For we remember that when we were in the desert we became angry at a writing reed when its thickness or thinness did not please us, as also at a knife when it did not cut quickly with a dull blade, and at a flint if a spark did not quickly fly from it when we were hastening to the reading; the flash of dissatisfaction went so far that we could put down and pacify the disturbance of soul in no other way than by pronouncing a curse on the unfeeling objects, or at least on the devil" (VIII, 18). "We have nothing to fear from the foe without; the enemy is concealed within ourselves. In us there proceeds a daily inward warfare; after gaining a victory in it, everything is reconciled to the warrior of Christ and submits to him. We shall not have a foe whom we have to fear outside of us, if what is within us will be conquered and subjugated to the spirit . . . The forcing of the flesh, joined with contrition of spirit; comprises a sacrifice most pleasing to God and a worthy dwelling of sanctity in the hidden parts of a pure, well-adorned spirit" (V, 21).

Most important is it for the monastic struggler in this inner warfare to *judge himself and not others.* "A monk is subjected to the same guilt and vices for which he has thought to judge others. Therefore, each should judge only himself, should cautiously, carefully look after himself in everything, and not examine the life and conduct of others" (V, 30).

One key to the acquirement of other virtues is *chastity,* which must be of soul as well as body. "We should most fervently struggle not only in continence of body, but also in contrition of heart, with frequent sighs of prayer, so that the furnace of our flesh, which the Babylonian king constantly ignites by the arousal of fleshly lust, may be put out by the dew of the Holy Spirit which descends into our heart" (VI, 17). "It is possible to acquire purity without the gift of knowledge; but it is impossible to acquire spiritual knowledge without the purity of chastity" (VI, 18).

Eight of the twelve books of the *Institutes* are devoted to a description of the eight primary vices and the struggle the monk must make against them. These eight are: gluttony, fornication, love of money, anger, sorrow, despondency, vainglory, and pride. These chapters are very practical and contain numerous instructive examples taken from the experience of the desert Fathers. One memorable example among these, illustrating the sin of vainglory, may be taken as an apt warning against the tendency, so present in 20th century monastic aspirants also, of spiritual fakery and "posing", based on an elementary self-love and idleness.

"When I lived in the desert of Scetis, I remember an elder who, going to the cell of a certain brother for a visit, when he drew near to the door and heard him saying something inside, stopped a little, desiring to find out whether he was reading from the Sacred Scripture or, as was the custom, was reciting something from memory while working. When this pious tester, putting his ear close, heard more clearly, he discovered that the brother had been so deceived by the spirit of vainglory that he pretended to be delivering a sermon of admonishment to the people in church. When the elder, continuing to stand, heard that he had finished the sermon and, changing his role, was giving the deacon's dismissal to the catechumens — he knocked on the door. The brother met the elder with his usual respect and, leading him in, being wounded in conscience for his dreams, asked whether he had been there for a long time, or whether, standing for a long time at the door, he had endured some unpleasantness? The elder, joking, tenderly replied: I came when you were giving the dismissal to the catechumens" (XI, 15). The fantasies of 20th century monastic aspirants are not far from this classic example!

As for the chief of the vices or passions, pride, St. Cassian is, as always, down-to-earth and practical, and spends most of this chapter describing the lower or "fleshly" type of pride that is one of the commonest pitfalls for monastic aspirants, ancient as well as modern. "This fleshly pride, when it settles in the soul of a monk who has placed a cold or bad beginning to his renunciation of the world, not allowing him because of his former worldly arrogance to come to the humility of Christ, at first makes him insubmissive and stubborn, then does not allow him to be meek and affable, as likewise to be equal with the brethren and sociable, nor to leave all possessions and remain in poverty according to the commandment of our God and Saviour . . . He does not wish to bear the burden of the monastery's life, does not accept the instruction of any elder. For whoever is possessed by the passion of pride not only considers it unworthy of him to observe any kind of rule of submission or obedience, but does not even allow into his ears the very teaching concerning perfection; in his heart there grows such a repulsion for spiritual words that when such a conversation takes place his gaze cannot stay in one place, but his wandering look is directed this way and that, the eyes turned the other way, obliquely . . . As long as the spiritual conversation continues, he imagines that he is sitting on crawling worms or sharp sticks, and no matter what the simple conversation might utter for the edification of the hearers, the proud one thinks that this is said to put him to shame. And the whole time the talk on spiritual life is taking place, he, being occupied with his own suspicions, catches and intercepts not what he should accept for his own advancement, but with preoccupied mind seeks out the reason why this or the other is being said, or with secret disturbance of the heart he invents what he might reply to them; so that from a soul-saving inquiry he can receive nothing at all, or correct himself in any way" (XII, 25, 27). As an example of this lower kind of pride: "I have heard that in this very country (something strange and shameful to relate) one of the younger ones, when his Abba began to rebuke him, asking why he had begun to abandon the humility which he had preserved for such a short time after renouncing the world, and had become arrogant with diabolical pride, replied with extreme haughtiness: 'Did I really humble myself for a time so as to be *always* in submission? At this brazen, criminal reply the elder was so astonished that all talk was cut off, as if he had received these words uttered from Lucifer himself" (XII, 28).

The aim of all this monastic warfare and struggle, which St. Cassian describes so concretely, is to raise one's mind to the eternal and unchanging and prepare one for the blessedness of the Kingdom of Heaven. "The work of the monk's calling is nothing else than the contemplation of divine purity, which surpasses everything" (IX, 3). "We can in no way despise the satisfaction of the food before us unless the mind, giving itself over to Divine contemplation shall take greater enjoyment of the love of virtue and the beauty of heavenly objects. And thus, everyone shall despise everything here below as quickly passing away, when he will uninterruptedly direct the gaze of his mind towards the unwavering and eternal, and when, still being in the body, he will contemplate the blessedness of the future life" (V, 14).

The monastic aspirant who allows earthly things or his own passions to draw him away from heavenly things is invariably entangled in the things here below and perishes; St. Cassian's warning regarding this is equally applicable to our own day. "The mind of a lover of idleness has nothing else to think about than only food and the belly, until, having contracted friendship with some man or woman, who has been weakened by an identical coldness, he binds himself with their doings and needs, and thus little by little becomes entangled in harmful occupations, as it were is constrained by serpentine meanderings, and finally is in no condition to untie himself in order to acquire the perfection of his earlier (monastic) vow" (IX, 6).

Therefore, St. Cassian gives an inspiring word of encouragement to those who wish to follow the monastic life to its goal. "Know that you are in the number of the few who are chosen, and beholding the example and the coldness of the many, do not grow cool, but live as the few live, so that with these few you might be vouchsafed the Kingdom of Heaven. For many are called, but few are chosen, and small is the flock to whom the Father has been pleased to give the Kingdom" (IV, 38).

The foundation of this whole monastic struggle is *humility* and *fear of God,* without which all ascetic labors are vain and empty: "If we wish to bring our (spiritual) building to completion, so that it might be perfect and pleasing to God, let us hasten to place its foundation not according to the will of our passion, but according to the precise teaching of the Gospel; this foundation can be nothing else than the fear of God and humility, which latter proceeds from meekness and simplicity of heart. Humility cannot be acquired without (spiritual) nakedness. Without the latter one can in no way acquire either readiness for submission, nor the strength for patience, nor the calmness of meekness, nor the perfection of love, without which things our heart can not at all be the dwelling of the Holy Spirit" (XII, 31). "It is precisely necessary that in the beginning, with a sincere disposition of heart, we should manifest true humility to our brethren, taking care not to offend or grieve in any way, something we can in no way fulfill if there will not be established in us, out of love for Christ, true self-renunciation, which consists in the abandoning of all possessions and non-acquisitiveness; and then, if we will not take up the yoke of obedience and submission with a simple heart, without any pretense, so that no will of our own should live in us at all, apart from the Abba's orders. This can be done only by one who considers himself not only dead for this world, but also foolish and stupid, and will fulfill all that the elder commands him without any investigation, considering this as sacred and as announced by God" (XII, 32).

Finally, the struggler must be fully aware that the attainment of his goal — victory over the passions and the salvation of the soul — comes not from his own efforts, as essential as they are, but from the grace of God. "It is impossible for anyone to be perfectly cleansed of fleshly vices unless he is aware that all his labors and striving cannot be sufficient to attain such perfection, and unless he becomes convinced that he attains it not otherwise than by the mercy and with the help of God" (XII, 13). "The attainment of perfection is the work not of the one who desires or struggles, but of the merciful God (Rom. 9:16), who makes us victors over vices not at all as a reward for the merit of our labors or struggle . . . The action of every good thing proceeds from the grace of God, Who has given us with great bounty such an eternity of blessedness and limitless glory for our weak fervor and our short, small struggle" (XII, 11). The whole book of the *Institutes* ends with the following words: "We must acknowledge that we in ourselves, without the help of God's grace, can do nothing at all with regard to the doing of virtues, and we must be assured in truth that even that which we have been vouchsafed to understand is the gift of God" (XII, 33).

It may be seen from this brief exposition of the teaching of the *Institutes* that the monastic life in 5th and 6th century Gaul had a solid foundation under it. The teaching of St. Cassian is not for idle dreamers or those fleeing from the responsibilities of life in the world. With its sober, down-to-earth tone, and its insistence on work, ascetic struggle, and coming to know and overcome one's own passions, it is rather a manual for serious, energetic, determined Christian fighters who are looking for *greater,* not lesser, struggles than the Christian finds in normal worldly life.

It is above all the *Institutes* that set the tone for the monasticism of this period. St. Gregory of Tours himself, when he had occasion to give spiritual instruction to a recluse of his diocese, "sent him books with the Lives of the Fathers and the Institutes of the Monks, so that he might learn what recluses ought to be and with what prudence monks ought to behave. When he had read and re-read them, not only did he drive out of his mind the bad thoughts which he had had, but even more it so developed his knowledge that he astonished us with his facility in speaking of these matters" (*Life of the Fathers,* XX, 3). These same two books (as we shall see below) are the ones that St. Romanus took with him when he set out for his hermit's life in the Jura mountains. But even apart from its direct influence on monastic aspirants, the *Institutes* may be seen also clearly reflected in the teaching of the monastic Fathers of Gaul who came after him.

SAINT FAUSTUS OF LERINS

CHIEF OF THE monastic Fathers of Gaul in the 5th century, after St. Cassian himself, was St. Faustus (+490), who was abbot of Lerins during the

St. Cassian's Monastery of St. Victor,
overlooking the Port of Marseilles (1655)

Atrium of the ancient basilica
of St. Cassian's Monastery

The first hermitage of St. Honoratus:
Grotto at Sainte Baume near Cannes.

last years of St. Cassian's lifetime, and was later Bishop of Rhegium (Riez), less than a hundred miles north of Marseilles.

Noted for his defense of the "Eastern" teachings on such questions as the relative corporeality of the soul (God alone being perfectly incorporeal) and grace and free will (and probably for this reason much neglected in the later West), he was first and foremost a teacher of monastic life, and had more direct influence on the great monastic Father of the 6th century, St. Caesarius of Arles, than did St. Cassian. (Citations here are from Abbe Alliez, *Histoire du Monastere de Lerins*, Vol. 1 (Paris, 1861); and A. Malnory, *Saint Cesaire, Eveque d'Arles*, Paris, 1894.)

In his instructions to his monks he has the same emphasis as St. Cassian on unremitting struggle and the avoidance of idleness and repose: "It is not at all for peace and quiet, not for security, that you have come to this island, but rather to struggle and combat vigorously . . . We have come to these remote shores, into the ranks of this spiritual army, in order to struggle every day against our passions . . . Our profession obliges us to reject all that the present life can offer of consolation or of glory. The sweetest things of the earth should be foreign to us; our thoughts should be intent solely on the eternal rewards which are promised us. To rejoice at living in dependence and wretchedness, to seek fervently poverty, to uproot from our hearts not only the attachment to created things, but the will itself — these are our means to perfection" (Homily *Ad monachos* I). "A ship, after having braved the billows of the open sea, can be in danger even in the middle of what seems the safest port, and is in peril of sinking there. Likewise, in the refuge of religion to which the Saviour has led you, do not be without fear; force yourselves, with the help of Christ, to avoid the least negligence, the slightest faults; they act on the soul like drops of water entering a ship's keel by imperceptible fissures" (*Ad monachos* II).

With St. Cassian, St. Faustus teaches the *inward* nature of the monastic struggle. "Of what benefit is it to live in this silent place, if one suffers within oneself the torment of the passions? Will there be tranquility without, and a storm within? Is it worth the trouble of abandoning the world which is down there far away, in order to keep the passions shut up in oneself? (Homily *Sicut a nobis*).

Above all St. Faustus, like St. Cassian, emphasizes the virtue of obedience and the ruinousness of disobedience and pride. "The strength which the work of salvation requires, God refuses to him who does not know how to obey . . . Obedience is a necessity for youth, and at the same time old age finds therein its glory . . . The habit of disobedience obscures the intelligence and falsifies the judgment. The heart of the guilty one becomes so hard that, if he does not by an extreme effort suddenly humble himself in order to correct his fault, he will dare to battle against his superior, will go on to insult him and to say: How strongly I resisted! How well I did to disobey! With what haughtiness I replied! He believed that I would *always* humble myself before him!" (Homily VII).

St. Faustus, seeing the rapidly growing monastic movement of Gaul, saw also the tragedy of "runaway" monks — those who had tasted the monastic life but did not have the patience to persevere in it. His forceful words on remaining in the monastery where one has made one's renunciation of the world anticipate the emphasis on monastic *stability* in the 6th-century Fathers, St. Caesarius of Arles and St. Benedict of Nursia. Referring to the sea around Lerins, he told his monks: "This sea is the world; the monastery is the harbor. What should the true monk propose for himself? — to fix his anchor forever in the harbor. Would he return to the world? These rocks, against which the sea is breaking down there, are the image of the reefs against which the monk inconstant in his path is sure of breaking himself" (Homily, *Sicut a nobis*). "What in truth is more cruel than to uproot yourself so suddenly, like a migrating bird, from the place where your God has called you, where He illumined you with the first rays of His light, and which He opened up to you like a harbor against the raging of the storm? Do you so quickly forget your brothers and companions who applied themselves to console you? Is it thus that you abandon the place where you put off the clothes of this world and changed the name you bore when you were there? . . . But you are so wanting in good sense as to prefer to the favors of God your own will and whim, and to place yourself at the mercy of your own ideas! Do you not feel to what shipwreck you are rushing?"

The true monastic path, according to St. Faustus, is one of humility, patience, and obedience, which can change those around one and make the monastic community indeed a paradise on earth. "Oh, how blessed by God is he whose humility has diminished the pride of his brother, whose patience has extinguished the wrath of his neighbor, who by his obedience and fervor corrects in others lukewarmness and sloth, whose consoling examples or words restore light in the heart which anger has rendered blind" (*Ad monachos* I).

POET OF THE WESTERN DESERT
SAINT EUCHERIUS OF LYONS:

IN GENERAL, the "desert" in 5th and 6th century Gaul refers to the deserted places, outside of cities, suitable for the habitation of monks, those who have abandoned worldly ways. There is, however, another more specific meaning of the word "desert" which St. Cassian uses: the place for those who wish to lead the solitary, anchoretic life away even from the coenobitic or semi-coenobitic communities wherein most monks dwelt. St. Cassian sets forth in the *Institutes* the conditions for entering upon this higher way of life. "We set out to look at a special, higher kind of monks, who are called anchorites. At first they live for a long time in a community, until they learn patience, discernment, humility, non-acquisition, and totally uproot in themselves all vices; then, intending to enter into the fiercest battle with demons, they go away to the remote places of the desert" (V, 36). "The desert should be sought by those who are perfect, cleansed of every vice, and one should go into it after being perfectly cleansed from vices in the community of the brethren, not out of faintheartedness but for Divine contemplation, with the desire of higher vision, which can be acquired only in solitude and only by the perfect" (VIII, 17).

This higher kind of desert life had a definite attraction for the monastic aspirants of St. Gregory's Gaul, not actually as a separate form of monastic life, but as a higher ideal of the one common monastic life. We shall see several of such advanced desert-dwellers in the *Life of the Fathers*. Here above all, however, we must be aware of the context of hard ascetic struggle, usually in a monastery, that invariably precedes such desert-dwelling, as well as the down-to-earth monastic teaching which underlies it. St. Cassian's *Institutes* are the ABC of this kind of monasticism also, while his *Conferences* contain a more advanced teaching for desert-dwellers (as well as coenobites).

The very idea that the "desert" could be found in Gaul itself was not one that was immediately evident. Even after the example of St. Martin and his disciples, St. Honoratus set out to find his desert in the East; it was only owing to the death of his companion that he returned after traveling only as far as Greece and retired first to a cave on the mainland, and then to the island of Lerins off the coast of southern Gaul, where with his followers he founded a monastery as much as possible in the tradition of the East. We do not have a detailed description of his original monastery at Lerins, but the few brief references to it show it to be a close imitation of the semi-hermitic lavras of the

The island of Lerins, with the fortress where the relics
of St. Honoratus were treasured for several centuries.

East. St. Eucherius, disciple of St. Honoratus, describes it as a place of "holy
elders living in separate cells." We have a more detailed description of the same
kind of monastery in Sulpicius Severus' *Life of St. Martin:*

"The place was so secluded and remote that it had all the solitude of
the desert. On one side it was walled in by the rock-face of a high mountain, and
the level ground that remained was enclosed by a gentle bend of the River Loire.
There was only one approach to it, and that a very narrow one. His own cell was
built of wood, as were those of many of the brethren; but most of them had
hollowed out shelters for themselves in the rock of the overhanging mountain.
There were about eighty disciples there, being trained in the pattern of their
most blessed master. No one possessed anything of his own; everything was
put into the common stock . . . It was seldom that anyone left his cell except
when they assembled at the place of worship." (*Life of St. Martin,* ch. X, F. R.
Hoare translation).

As such monastic settlements grew in 5th-century Gaul, the need to go
to Egypt to see the Christian "desert" became less and less urgent. It was above
all St. Cassian who put to rest the idea of "going to the East" for monastic training when he provided in his books the spiritual teaching of the great
elders of Egypt. When he heard that St. Eucherius, even after being in Lerins,
was thinking of going to Egypt, he dedicated to him (and to his great Abba, St.
Honoratus) seven books of his *Conferences,* with this preface: "O holy brethren,
Honoratus and Eucherius, you have become so inflamed by the praise of those
exalted men from whom we have received the first instructions of the anchoretic
life, that one of you, being head of a great coenobium of brethren, desires that
his community, which is edified by the daily sight of your holy life, should be
instructed furher by the commandments of those fathers, while the other has
desired to set out for Egypt so as to be edified also by seeing them in the body,
so that, leaving this region, numbed by the severity of the Gallic frost, he would
fly like a pure turtledove to the lands which, being more closely illuminated by
the Sun of Righteousness, also abound with mature fruits of virtue. This has involuntarily aroused a love in me, so that, being consoled by the desire of the
one and the labor of the other, I have not shunned the peril of writing in brief,
if only to increase the authority of the former among his monks themselves, and
to divert the latter from the necessity of a dangerous voyage" (Preface to Con-
ference XI).

St. Eucherius, clearly, took the words of St. Cassian to heart. Not only
did he not go to Egypt, but he also became the great church poet of the des-

ert of Gaul. Perhaps it is a matter of his (and our) "Western" temperament and experience, or perhaps it is only the "Northern" setting of his writings, made familiar to us in recent centuries by the great monastic strugglers of the "Northern Thebaid" of Russia, down to St. Seraphim of Sarov and other holy monks and nuns right up to our own century — that makes us feel something very kin to us in the writings of St. Eucherius, and in particular his *Praise of the Desert (De laude eremi)*. Let us quote here from this work, which, albeit in a different way, helps set the tone for the monastic strugglers of 5th and 6th century Gaul almost as well as St. Cassian's *Institutes*. This little book is not one of monastic *teaching* as such, but gives us a good view of the impulse of soul which inspired young men (and women) to go to the desert in the Gaul of his time. (Citations from an unpublished manuscript translation by James Graves.)

"Let him who burns with divine fire abandon his abode in order to choose the desert; let him prefer it to his close ones, his children . . . For the Christian who abandons his native soil, let the desert become a temporary fatherland, from which let nothing call him back, neither fear, nor desires, nor joy, nor sorrows. Yes, one can well pay for the happiness of solitude by the sacrifice of all that one loves."

"How sweet, for those who thirst after God, are these remote solitudes with their forests! How pleasant, for those who thirst after Christ, are those retreats, extending far and wide, where only nature wakes! All things are hushed. Then, as if under the goad of silence, the mind is aroused joyfully towards its God, and quickens with unutterable transports. No shrill distraction is met there, no word, except perchance with God. That sweet din alone breaks in amid the hush of the remote abode. An uproar sweeter than silence interrupts that state of placid silence, a holy tumult of modest converse . . . Then the deceitful enemy roars vainly like a wolf within the folds where the sheep have been penned. Back and forth along Jacob's wondrous ladder, a choir of rejoicing angels makes watchful call upon the desert expanse and illumines the solitude with the thronging of unseen visitation (Gen. 28:12). Moreover, lest those who guard the city stand their watch in vain, Christ guards and hedges His property within. He wards off its foes from the circuit of the desert in such a way that, though God's adopted people lie exposed to the expanse of the desert, yet they are hedged from their foes. Within, moreover, the Bridegroom reclines in that noontide, and the desert dwellers, wounded by His loving kindness, contemplate Him, saying, *We have found Whom our soul loveth. We shall hold Him, nor shall we let Him go"* (*Cant. 3:4*) (*chs. 37, 38*).

"The soil of the desert is not unfruitful, though it is commonly thought to be so . . . In the desert the husbandman reaps harvests bearing a rich yield . . . In that place is found the bread of life which descends from heaven. Amid those crags burst forth refreshing fountains, even the living waters, with power to quench not only thirst for water, but thirst for salvation as well. Here is the meadow and the pleasure of the inward man . . . The same desert of the body is the paradise of the soul" (ch. 39).

"Rightly then, O land deserving reverence, you have come forth as a dwelling lately fit for habitation by the saints who dwell in your confines . . . Whoever has sought out your brotherhood of saints, has found God. Each who has cultivated you has found Christ in you. He who dwells in you rejoices in the Lord Who dwells there also. The same man is at once your possessor and a divine possession. He who does not flee your dwelling becomes himself a temple of God" (ch. 41).

"Indeed, to all deserts illumined by the retreats of the pious I owe meet honor. Yet before all others I embrace my Lerins, which receives in its most pious arms those who come there scattered by the shipwrecks of the stormy world. Those tossed by the billows of the world it leads gently within its shades, so that there within that inward shade of the Lord they may catch their panting breath. Bubbling with streams, green with grass, bright with vineyards, joyful in its sights and scents, it reveals itself as a paradise for those who possess it . . . It now has those wondrous holy elders who, living in separate cells, have brought the Egyptian Fathers to our Gaul" (ch. 42).

"What gatherings and assemblies of saints, O good Jesus, have I myself seen there, fragrant with the precious scent of sweet ointments in boxes of alabaster! The fragrance of life breathes everywhere. They prefer the appearance of the inward man to the garb of the outer one. Strengthened in loving-kindness, downcast in lowliness, most gentle in piety, most strong in faith, modest in gait, swift in obedience, silent upon encounter, majestically serene in feature: in a word, they display ranks of angelic peace in unremitting contemplation. They long for nothing, they desire nothing, save only when they long for Him Whom alone they desire. While they seek a blessed life, they live it; and even while they strive after it presently, already they achieve it.

"Do they wish, then, to be set apart from sinners? They have already been set apart. Do they choose to possess a life that is pure? They possess it. Do they strive to keep all their time for the praises of God? They keep it. Do they yearn to rejoice in the gatherings of saints? They rejoice in them. Do they desire to enjoy Christ? They enjoy Him. Are they eager to gain the life of the desert? In their heart they gain it. Thus, through the most bountiful grace of Christ, here and now they earn many of those blessings which they long for in the time to come. While following the hope, though at a distance, they seize its substance now. Even their toil itself brings great reward, for their future recompense lies, as it were, within their present work" (ch. 43).

Lest it be thought that this lavish "praise of the desert" is some kind of "Western romanticism", let us put beside it the words of the great monastic Father of the East in the preceding century, St. Basil the Great (as quoted in the Life of the great Father of Russia's "Northern Thebaid," Elder Nazarius of Valaam). Inspired by the outwardly very different deserts of Egypt and Cappadocia, St. Basil sees, just like the Western poet, the same *paradise of the heart* of him who has abandoned everything for God:

"O life of solitude, house of heavenly learning and divine knowledge, school wherein God is everything that we learn! O desert of sweetness, where fragrant flowers of love now blaze with fiery color, now shine with snow-like purity. With them is peace and quiet; and those who live beneath them remain unmoved by the wind. There, is the incense of complete mortification, not only of flesh, but, what is more praiseworhy, of the will itself, and the censer of perpetual prayer burns ceaselessly with the fire of divine love. There, are diverse flowers of virtue, resplendent with diverse adornments, blossoming with the grace of unfading beauty. O desert, delight of holy souls, paradise of inexhaustible sweetness! Thou art a furnace, the power of whose blazing flame the Three Youths make cool by prayer, and by means of burning faith they extinguish around themselves the fierce flame in which both arrows and chains burn away, but those in chains do not burn, only the bonds of sin are loosed, and the soul is led up to the singing of divine praise, exulting: *Thou has burst my bonds asunder; I will offer Thee the sacrifice of praise*" (Ps. 115:7-8).

Love for the desert, as a refuge from the storms and occupations of the world and a place of intense spiritual combat for the sake of the heavenly kingdom; and reverence before the holy monks who dwelt there and were already making the lands of the West fragrant with their deeds of asceticism and piety — these were the impulses which inspired the young, newly-converted Christians of the West to seek out the deserts of Gaul and learn there at first hand, from experienced elders and in their own practice, the spiritual teaching of the Eastern Fathers. There were many casualties and spiritual disasters, as the very ferocity of the battle would promise; but those who persevered against all obstacles and truly planted the seeds of Eastern monasticism in Western soil have left a fragrant memory and example which is not dead even today, for those who wish to seek it out and be inspired by it.

Of the lives of the early desert-dwellers of Gaul, none is so fascinating and inspiring as the one with which St. Gregory begins the *Life of the Fathers:* the Life of Sts. Romanus and Lupicinus. As it happens, there exists a much longer Life of these Fathers than St. Gregory's, written in their monastery within a few decades of their death. This Life gives the most detailed account we have of the early monastic fervor of Gaul, and a summary of it will give the most fitting completion for this introduction to the Orthodox Gaul of St. Gregory.

Saints Romanus and Lupicinus

The Desert-Dwellers of the Jura

FOURTH-CENTURY GAUL had St. Martin with his ascetic prodigies and his communities of anchorites; the turn of the new century saw the foundation of the island monastery of Lerins, which brought the tradition of the Egyptian Fathers to Gaul and produced a number of bishops and monastic founders; the first decades of the 5th century saw the establishment of numerous monastic communities in the south of Gaul, usually near cities and often founded by bishops, and the spread of the Eastern monastic rule and teaching through the writings of St. Cassian. By the end of St. Cassian's life (434), Orthodox monasticism was thus already well-established in Gaul.

Then occurred a phenomenon which is familiar to us from the later history of the "Northern Thebaid" of Russia from the 14th to the 17th centuries: the flight of monks and monastic aspirants not only from cities and other inhabited centers, but even from established monasteries, into the absolute isolation of the forested wilderness of Gaul. Doubtless such books at St. Eucherius' *Praise of the Desert* had an influence on this movement; but the main impulse was the same one that had produced the original flight to the Egyptian desert a century earlier: the elementary Christian impulse to give up everything for God, to abandon all things and influences of this world in order the better to prepare oneself for the Kingdom of Heaven.

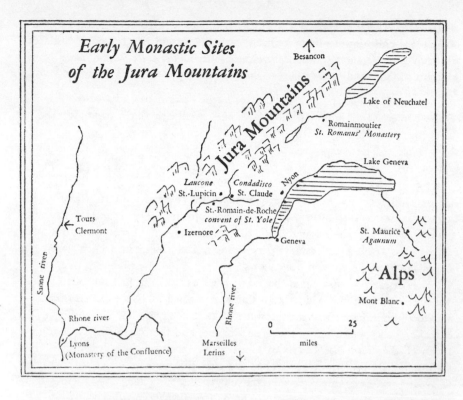

Early Monastic Sites of the Jura Mountains

Besancon

Jura Mountains

Lake of Neuchatel

Romainmoutier
St. Romanus' Monastery

Lake Geneva

Nyon

Laucone
St.-Lupicin • Condadisco
• St. Claude •

St.-Romain-de-Roche
convent of St. Yole

Tours
Clermont

• Izernore

Geneva

St. Maurice
Agaunum

Alps

Mont Blanc •

Saone river

Rhone river

Rhone river

0   25

miles

Lyons
(Monastery of the Confluence)

Marseilles
Lerins

Among the first of such desert-dwellers who literally turned the "deserts" of Gaul into cities populated with armies of mŏnks, were Sts. Romanus and Lupicinus. It is not by accident that St. Gregory begins his *Life of the Fathers* with them; for already before his time their exploits had become legendary in Gaul, and they were taken as the purest examples of the monastic desert life. Their Lives, together with the Life of their disciple St. Eugendus, were written by an anonymous disciple of the latter about the year 520. This document, the *Life of the Jura Fathers (Vita Patrum Jurensium)*, gives not only a much more detailed account of the Lives of Sts. Romanus and Lupicinus than does St. Gregory, but also furnishes invaluable information on the monastic teaching of these Fathers, on the monastic life in general in 5th-century Gaul, and on the everyday life and the growth of the Jura monasteries during the first 75 years or so of their exist- ence. The following pages are a summary of the parts of this document which best illustrate these points, with citations from it according to chapter, as a sup- plement to chapter one of the *Life of the Fathers. (Francois Martine, Vie des*

115

Peres du Jura, Paris, 1968, Latin and French text with copious notes; other information, and almost all illustrations, are taken from the thorough historical work of Paul Benoit: *Histoire de l'Abbaye et de la Terre de Saint-Claude,* Montreuil-sur-Mer, 1890, 2 vols.)

THE JURA is a mountain range in the eastern part of France, near the Swiss border, some hundred miles long and twenty or thirty wide. While not as spectacular as the Alps, which are visible in spots to the east, these mountains have a rugged beauty of their own. They proceed from west to east in three "steps," each about 1000 feet higher than the one below, from the plains to the "high Jura," which is a mountainous plateau of peaks and gorges, with elevations up to 5500 feet. Even today the mountains are covered with fir forests, with numerous waterfalls, lakes and treacherous streams. The towns which now occupy the sites of the original monastic settlements are tourist centers for such activities as fishing and camping in summer, and skiing in winter, when the mountains are covered with deep snows.

In early Roman times the lower parts of the Jura had inhabited towns, but the "high Jura" — which Julius Caesar described as *Jura mons altissimus* — was totally uninhabited. With the wane of Roman power and the incursions of barbarians, the population of this area declined, and the forests quickly overgrew much of the land that had been taken from them by the advancing Roman civilization. By the 5th century, when the wild Burgundians and Franks roamed this part of Gaul, only a few of the old towns were left; they were largely Christian, and the old pagan temples here were already in ruins.

Ruins of the pagan temple at Izernore, birthplace of the Jura saints

It was near one of these towns that all three of the Jura Fathers were born. St. Eugendus, as the *Life* states (ch. 119) was born not far from Izernore, site of an important pagan temple dedicated to the god Mercury, which had been partially destroyed (its ruins may still be seen today); and he was a "fellow-

The forested Alps of Eastern France, adjoining the Jura Mountains —
the habitat of Sts. Romanus and Lupicinus

The forest of the Jura

citizen" of St. Romanus and Lupicinus, who were thus born either here or in a nearby village.

St. Romanus was the elder brother of St. Lupicinus and was the first to go into the wilderness (St. Gregory's account is much more general and omits details like this). He was born probably in the last decade of the 4th century, the decade of the death of St. Martin. "Before him in this province no kind of monk had devoted himself either to the solitary life or the life in common" (ch. 5). Concerning his monastic preparation the *Life* devotes only one sentence: "Before embracing the religious life, he had known the venerable Sabinus, Abba of the (Monastery of the) Confluence of Lyons, as well as his strenuous rule and the life of his monks; then, like a bee in search of booty, after having gathered from each of them the flowers of their perfections, he returned to where he came from" (ch. 11). Nothing more is known of this Abba Sabinus, nor is it known of which of the several island monasteries of Lyons (which is situated at the "confluence" of the Saone and Rhone rivers) he was Abba. It is known, however, that Lyons, some 200 miles inland from Marseilles, was already a monastic center early in the 5th century; a disciple of St. Martin of Tours, St. Maximus (whose brief Life is given by St. Gregory in his *Glory of the Confessors*, ch. 22), was for a time in one of the island monasteries; and St. Eucherius, author of the *Praise of the Desert*, became bishop of Lyons in about 434 and was known to spend the time of Lent in one of these monasteries in prayer, fasting, and the writing of books. Judging from the information given in the Life, St. Romanus could have been in Lyons during the episcopacy of St. Eucherius, although it is more likely that he was there a few years before it; in any case, he could have read the *Praise of the Desert*, which was written in about 428, before leaving himself for the wilderness. His reason for going to Lyons was probably a simple one: most likely it had the nearest monastery to his home, being no more than a hundred miles from the Jura mountains and being connected with them by the river Rhone and its tributaries.

It is not stated that St. Romanus became a monk in this monastery, only that he received his knowledge of monasticism there. And then, " from this monastery, without manifesting anything of his most holy aspirations, he took the book of the Life of the Holy Fathers and the remarkable institutes of the Abbas" (ch. 11). The first book was undoubtedly one of the then-circulating Latin accounts of the Egyptian Fathers; the second book was certainly St. Cassian's *Institutes*. With these, and his exposure to monasticism in practice under the Abba Sabinus, he had all the theoretical basis he needed for the monastic life.

He set out, not for any distant place, but for the wilderness close to his own home. What did he hope to achieve by this? Why did he not stay in an established monastic community, or seek out one with more renowned elders, such as Lerins? Everything in the Life of St. Romanus seems to indicate that he had no religious "romanticism" whatever: he did not dream of far-away lands, "ideal monasteries," or "holy elders." He thought of only one thing: how, on the solid foundation of the ABC's of spiritual life and strict monastic practice, to save his soul and prepare for the heavenly kingdom. His simple Christian upbringing had prepared him for this: "He was not particularly educated, but, a rarer merit, he was endowed with purity, with an unequalled loving kindness, to such a degree that one does not see him in childhood giving himself over to childish pranks, nor in mature years becoming enslaved to human passions and to the bonds of marriage" (ch. 5). This simple village boy from the mountain provinces, once his heart had been inflamed in mature years with the ideal of Christian perfection and he had learned the basic principles of monastic life, had no thought but to go and practice what he had learned in the nearest suitable place. And so it was that, "in about his 35th year, attracted by the solitudes of the desert, after having left his mother, his sister and his brother, he penetrated into the forests of the Jura near to his home" (ch. 5). In fact, the place where he finally settled is about 20 miles as the crow flies from his native town of Izernore — close enough to be found out later by venturesome spirits like himself, but far enough away to be quite remote from and inaccessible to the world.

"Going about in all directions through these forests, which were suitable and favorable for his way of life, he ended by finding, farther on, amidst valleys bordered by cliffs, an exposed place suitable for tilling. There, the abrupt sides of three mountains turn aside a little the one from the other, leaving between them a flat place of some extent. Since the beds of two courses of water come together in this place, the site which thus constituted a unique river-bank was soon popularly called Condadisco" (ch. 6). Condadisco ("Condat" in French, derived from a Celtic word meaning "confluence") is the present town of St.-Claude (named after a 7th-century abbot-bishop of the monastery), located at the confluence of the Bienne and Tacon rivers (tributaries of the Rhone); it lasted as a monastic community until the 18th century.

"The new lodger, seeking a dwelling corresponding to his ardent desire, found on the eastern side, at the foot of a rocky mountain, a most densely-growing fir which, arranging its boughs in a circle, covered the disciple of Paul as before the palm had covered Paul himself" (ch. 7). In recalling the palm which,

The way into the Jura

Cascade des Planches — a waterfall of the Jura

Le Bayard and Le Chabaud — the two striking cliffs above Condadisco

The river Bienne just below Condadisco

in Blessed Jerome's *Life of Paul the First Hermit* (ch. 5), was the dwelling place of the first monk of Egypt, and in calling St. Romanus the "disciple of Paul," the author of the *Life of the Jura Fathers* shows the Eastern roots of the desert-dwellers of Gaul; and the forest fir, as opposed to the desert palm, reveals the different Western locale of the same monastic struggle. The "rocky mountain" is the one presently known as "Le Bayard," which towers over the town of St.-Claude.

"Thus the fir furnished him, against the heat of mid-summer and the coldness of rains, a roof continually green. . . In addition, there were several wild bushes that provided their berries, sour for pleasure-lovers, no doubt, but sweet for those whose senses are at peace. . . If anyone should decide, with an audacious boldness, to cut across these trackless solitudes, not to mention the density of the forest and its heaps of fallen trees, the very high ridges where deer lived and the steep ravines of the bucks would scarcely permit such a man, even if robust and agile, to make the journey" (chs. 8, 9).

In this wild and inaccessible place St. Romanus settled down for the monastic life of struggle, determined never to leave. Being practical and not a "dreamer," he did not hope to gain his daily food entirely from what the forest could provide, but brought with him the minimum necessary for a small garden. "Having brought seeds and a pickax, the blessed one began in this place, while devoting himself assiduously to prayer and reading, to satisfy the needs of a modest existence by manual labor, according to the monastic institution. He was in great abundance, for he had need of nothing; he gave enough, for he had nothing to put away for the poor; he did not set foot beyond his retreat; he returned no more to his home; as a true hermit, he labored so as to provide his own living" (ch. 10).

What a lesson, and what a wealth of inspiration for the monastic aspirants of the 20th century! With modern means of communication, the very idea of *losing oneself from the eyes of the world* has been all but forgotten, and to live in one place for one's whole life is almost unheard of. Later St. Romanus did travel, on monastery business, throughout the Jura Mountains and as far as Geneva and beyond (journeys of no more than a hundred miles); but his disciple, St. Eugendus, provided a perfect example of monastic stability: from the time when he came to Condadisco at the age of seven, to his death more than fifty years later, he never once left the monastery (ch. 126). If we are helpless to imitate such stability today, let us at least understand its importance: Christianity in practice, and monasticism above all, is a matter of *staying in one place and struggling with all one's heart* for the Kingdom of Heaven. One may be called to do the work of God elsewhere, or may be moved about by unavoidable circumstances; but without the basic and profound desire to endure everything for God in one place without running away, one will scarcely be able to put down the roots required in order to bring forth spiritual fruits. Unfortunately, with the ease of modern communications one may even sit in one spot and *still* concern oneself with everything but the one thing needful — with everyone else's business, with all the church gossip, and not with the concentrated labor needed to save one's own soul in this evil world.

In a famous passage of the *Institutes,* St. Cassian warns the monks of his time to "flee women and bishops, for neither the one nor the other will allow one any more to have repose in one's cell, or to be occupied with the thought of God, to behold holy objects with pure eyes" (XI, 17). Women, of course, tempt by means of the flesh, and bishops by means of ordination to the priesthood and in general by the vainglory of acquaintance with those in high positions. Today this warning remains timely, but for the monks of the 20th century one can add a further warning: Flee from telephones, travelling, and gossip — those forms of communication which most of all bind one to the world — for they will cool your ardor and make you, even in your monastic cell, the plaything of worldly desires and influences!

"In this place, the imitator of Anthony the ancient hermit took delight for a long time in an angelic life and, apart from heavenly vision, enjoyed the sight of nothing but wild beasts and, rarely, hunters. But then his venerable brother Lupicinus, younger than he by birth but soon his equal in sanctity, informed at night by his brother in a dream, abandoned for the love of Christ those whom the blessed Romanus had already abandoned, his sister and mother, and with warm desire reached the dwelling of his brother and adopted his way of life. . . In this humble nest, in this remote corner of the desert, these two conceived, by inspiration of the Divine Word, a spiritual posterity and distributed a little on all sides, to the monasteries and churches of Christ, the fruit of their chaste childbearing" (ch. 12). Thus, with the arrival of the second brother, a community was formed, and the news of this began to attract others. The first to join them were two young clerics (probably from the lower orders, Readers or Sub-deacons) from Nyon (near Geneva), and already the "cradle of the saints," the fir tree, was found to be too small for their life and prayer, and the first buildings had to be erected. "They established themselves not far from the tree, on a sort of small hill with a gentle slope where now is to be found, as a remembrance, the oratory reserved for monastic prayer; after having hewn with an axe and polished with the greatest care some pieces of wood, they constructed huts for themselves and prepared others for those who would come" (ch. 13). The site of this oratory is now occupied by the 14th-century cathedral in the town of St.-Claude.

From this time on the community began to grow rapidly, and people from the world also began to come on pilgrimage. "Crowds of believers fled the world in order to follow, for the Lord, the vocation of renunciation and perfection. Some came there to behold the marvels of the new institution and to report, when they returned home, the good gift of its example. Others brought there people tormented with demons so that the prayer of the saints, joined to their own faith, might heal them; the insane and paralytics were also brought. Most of these sick ones, after recovering their health, returned home; but others remained in the monastery. . . Issued from the two founders, the holy community . . . developed in the unity of faith and love . . . Not only the remote regions of the province of Sequanie (the Jura region), but many distant lands also, were filled by the holy propagation of this divine race, with monasteries and churches" (chs. 14-16). We know of one of the pilgrims to the Jura from the letters of the celebrated bishop of Clermont (the birthplace of St. Gregory of Tours), Sidonius Apollinaris. Writing to a certain Domnulus in about the year 470, he indicates in a passing reference the renown which the Jura monasteries then enjoyed in Gaul: "And now, unless the monasteries of the Jura keep you, where you love to ascend as if in foretaste of a celestial habitation, this letter ought to reach you. . ." (O.M. Dalton, *The Letters of Sidonius*, Oxford, 1915, Book IV, 25).

I N THE YEAR 444 (the only precise date in the *Life of the Jura Fathers*), St. Hilary of Arles (himself a disciple of St. Honoratus of Lerins) travelled to Besancon at the edge of the Jura in connection with the famous dispute mentioned earlier in this Introduction (the author of the *Life* takes the side of Pope St. Leo in this dispute). Having heard of the renown of Sts. Romanus and Lupicinus, "he summoned the blessed Romanus, not far from the town of Besancon, through clerics sent for this purpose. Exalting, in a magnificent eulogy, his initiative and his way of life, he conferred on him the honor of the priesthood and let him return, heaped with honor, to the monastery" (ch. 18). This was perhaps some fifteen years from the time of St. Romanus' undertaking of the hermitic life, when he must have been about fifty years old. Roman Catholic scholars generally assume that there must have been already a number of priests in the flourishing community, having in mind the later Latin practice. But we must remember that the monastic inspiration of the Jura Fathers comes from the East, where there were many monasteries without any priests at all; the celebrated monastery of St. Sabbas the Sanctified, for example, had over 150 monks before having a single priest, and St. Sabbas himself, a younger contemporary of St. Romanus, is called the "Sanctified" or "Consecrated" because, possessing the priestly rank, he was a notable *exception* among the ranks of monks and even abbots. (Like St. Romanus, he was about 50 when his bishop compelled him to receive ordination as the first priest in his community.) Some forty years later, St. Eugendus, even after becoming abbot, was stubbornly to resist being raised to the priesthood: "Often he would tell me in confidence that it was much better for an abbot, because of the ambition of the young, to direct the brothers without being clothed in the priesthood, without being bound by this dignity which should not be sought by men vowed to renunciation and withdrawal. 'Besides,' he added, 'we know also that many fathers, after having practiced to perfection the humility of their state, have been deeply and secretly filled with pride by the priestly ministry. . ." (chs. 133, 134). St. Lupicinus never received the priesthood, even after the death of St. Romanus, when he was abbot over the brethren for some twenty years. It is more than likely, then, that St. Romanus, in full accord with Eastern tradition, was the first priest of the community, and that before his ordination the Liturgy would be served in the oratory (chapel) only on the fairly rare occasions when a parish priest would visit. St. Eugendus himself was the son of perhaps the nearest parish priest during the lifetime of St. Romanus, at Izernore (ch. 120). (Priests in the world in the West at this time, it should be noted, could be married, while bishops were required, if married when elected, to cease living with their wives after ordination.)

"St. Romanus, then, clothed with the priesthood, returned to the monastery; but remembering his original profession, he attached so little importance, in his monastic humility, to the prestige of the clerical office that although at the time of the solemnities the brothers would be able to require him properly to occupy a higher place than they for the sacrifice, on the other days, monk among monks, he would not allow to appear on his person any sign of the eminent dignity of the priesthood" (ch. 20). This passage also would seem to indicate that the Liturgy, in the tradition of the Eastern lavras, was not celebrated every day at Condadisco, but only (perhaps) on Sundays and feast days.

With the increase of the brethren, several new monasteries were founded, all of them jointly under the direction of the two brothers. "The site of the

The church at Romainmoutier — St. Romanus' monastery

community of Condadisco from this time on had difficulty in providing support, not only for the crowds who came there, but even for the brothers. Hanging on hills or leaning against slopes, in the midst of rocky projections and humps, ruined by frequent coursings of water over a stony soil, agriculture is limited and difficult, as much by the scantiness of the fields as by the poorness of the harvests and the uncertain yield. If, in fact, the rigors of the winter not merely cover but rather bury the countryside under snows, in spring, on the other hand, and in summer and autumn, either the soil, overheated by the reflection of the heat off the nearby cliffs, is on fire, or else the overwhelming rains carry off in torrents not only the land made ready for agriculture, but often also the uncultivatable and hard terrain itself, together with the grass, the trees and shrubs . . . Thus, in their desire to avoid this scourge to a certain extent, the most holy Fathers, in the neighboring forests, which were not at all deprived of places with less slope and more fertile, cut down firs, uprooted stumps. . . and made fields, so that this land, suitable for agriculure, might lessen the poverty of the inhabitants of Condadisco. Each of the two monasteries was submitted to the authority of the two Abbas. However, Father Lupicinus lived more especially and more usually at Laucone — the name which this place bears — and at the death of blessed Romanus there were left not less than 150 brothers, whom he had formed following his own discipline" (chs. 22-24). This, the second monastery of the Jura, several miles west of Condadisco, where the same river Bienne emerges from a deep gorge into a fertile plain, is the present-day village of St.-Lupicin, where the relics of St. Lupicinus are still to be found. St. Gregory, in his Life of the two saints, mentions another monastery founded by the brothers "in the territory of Alamannia"; this is usually interpreted as the monastery of Romainmoutier (in Latin, *Romani monasterium*, "Romanus' monastery") in

127

Switzerland some 45 miles northeast of the original monastery. In addition to these main monasteries, there were numerous cells and hermitages scattered throughout the mountains, making of the Jura a kind of "Thebaid of the Gauls" (or a Mount Athos), even though the population of monks never reached Egyptian proportions, being numbered in hundreds rather than thousands.

In the midst of all this fresh monastic activity, women too began to be attracted by the desert and by the example of the brother-saints; the first to come was the saints' sister, Yole. As Sts. Anthony and Pachomius for their sisters (and later St. Caesarius of Arles for his sister Caesaria), so now the monastic founders of the Jura had to establish a monastic community for their sister and the women who followed her into the wilderness. "Not far from there, on a high cliff, dominated by a natural rock and bounded by a stone arch which concealed vast caverns within, the saints, according to tradition, established — being guided in their choice by parental affection — a Mother for a community of virgins, and assumed in this place the governance of 105 nuns. . . Here the blessed Fathers constructed a basilica, which not only received the mortal remains of the virgins, but had the honor also to contain the tomb of the hero of Christ, Romanus himself. So great was the strictness of the observances of this monastery that every virgin who entered there for renunciation was never again seen outside, unless it be when she was carried to her tomb" (chs. 25-26). This convent, known as "La Balme", is not heard of later, and evidently it disappeared amid the barbarian raids of the 5th and 6th centuries. It was perhaps the first western community for women in the "desert," earlier convents having been established in or near cities. Later a community of monks was established nearby, and presently the site (about three miles southwest of St.-Lupicin, also on the river Bienne) is near the town of St.-Romain-de-Roche, where the relics of St. Romanus are indeed still kept in the parish church. In later centuries there was another community of nuns in the Jura, at Neauville-les-Dames, which was dependent on Condadisco; perhaps it was a successor to St. Yole's convent.

The rest of the Life of St. Romanus — the first of the three parts of the *Life of the Jura Fathers* — is devoted to the Saint's miracles, to the devil's attacks against the brethren, and to the weaknesses and murmuring of some of the brethren, once they came to accept the marvellous monasteries of the Jura as part of the church "establishment" and therefore something to be taken for granted. All of this is described in terms very familiar to readers of the Lives of the Eastern Fathers, and some of it is related by St. Gregory of Tours in his Life of the brothers, although it is evident, because of many differences, that he did not have this *Life* as his chief source, if indeed he knew it at all.

The gorge of the river Bienne

The cliffs of St. Yole's convent — showing the later monastery

Salins — the salt-producing town of the Jura where the monks often travelled

The town of St.-Lupicin — site of the monastery of Laucone

La Balme -- the cliffs on which St. Yole's convent was built

The cliffs of St. Yole's convent as they look today

The present-day abbey below the cliffs

In one passage of the *Life of the Jura Fathers,* when one of the elder monks is described as complaining to St. Romanus that he is admitting too many aspirants into the community and not making a careful selection of them, the author takes the opportunity, in giving St. Romanus' reply, of describing something of the monastic spirit which St. Romanus imparted to the brethren, and also something of the monastic trials the brothers underwent. St. Romanus replies to the elder: "Tell me, O you who desire for us so small a community: are you capable, among all the brothers whom you see about you in our community, of making the sorting and the division in order to form the two groups of which you speak, as if, in examining one after the other, you could separate perfectly, before their death, the tested saints from the careless ones?. . . Have you not seen here in our community some monks devote themselves with fervor to a rule of life which, later on, after a slow decline from lukewarmness to lukewarmness, they trampled underfoot? How many times, also, brothers have left the community under the blow of a contrary impluse! And among these latter, how many times have we seen one or the other abandon the world again and return to us, once, twice, three times, and in spite of that, finding his courage again, persevere unto the palm of victory in the profession which he had abandoned so long before! Some, also, without incurring reproach, return, not to their vices, but to their land of origin and observe there our rule with such love and zeal that, being raised to the priesthood by the love and the election of the faithful, they direct with great dignity monasteries and churches of Christ. . . And did you not see, quite recently, in our own monastery, what happened to Maxentius? After having imposed on himself an asceticism and privations unheard of in Gaul, with continual vigils after having shown an untiring diligence in reading, — persuaded by the vice of pride, he became the prey of the most impure of the demons, and his folly and rage surpassed by far that of those he had only lately taken care of, when he had been mighty in the fruit of his merits: bound with straps and ropes by those whom he had long before healed by the virtue of the Lord, he was finally delivered from the deadly spirit by anointment with holy oil. Therefore, acknowledge that it is the same pride, inspired by the devil, that secretly instigates you, and that your case is not very different from that of Maxentius" (chs. 29, 32-34).

The *Life of the Jura Fathers* — like St. Gregory's Life — shows the two brothers as different but complementary in their virtues: "The two Fathers surpassed each other in complementary qualities which are indispensable in the art of directing and governing. For if the blessed Romanus was very merciful towards all, with a perfect calmness, his brother was more severe, both in correcting and directing others, and first of all towards himself. Romanus, when all hope of pardon had been lost, would spontaneously make use of indulgence toward the guilty ones; while the other, fearing lest small sins, repeated, should end in great ones, gave reproaches with great vehemence. Romanus would impose on the brothers no more privations than their own will would accept; while Lupicinus, offering his own example to all, permitted none to avoid what the help of God made possible" (ch. 17). The austerities of St. Lupicinus are described in rather greater detail (chs. 63-67) than in St. Gregory's life.

Toward the end of his life St. Romanus made the longest journey recorded in his Life — a pilgrimage to the site of the martyrdom of St. Maurice and the Theban Legion in the third century. "In the ardor of his faith, he decided to go to Agaunum to the basilica of the saints — I should rather say, to the camp of the martyrs —, according to the testimony furnished by the account of their passion" (ch. 44). The first account of the martyrdom of these saints is that of St. Eucherius of Lyons, which St. Romanus had apparently read. On this journey, near Geneva, occurred the incident with the lepers mentioned by St. Gregory. The organizaion of an actual monastery at Agaunum (as distinct from the cells of individual monks around the basilica, such as existed at the time of St. Romanus) dates from the early years of the 6th century, when the *laus perennis* (continual chanting of the psalms) was introduced there from Constantinople; the monastery of Condadisco at that time sent 100 monks to form one of the nine choirs that alternated in the psalm-singing.

The death of St. Romanus occurred in the convent which he had established, where he had gone to bid farewell to his sister (ch. 60); this was about in the year 460. St. Gregory, in his Life of the brothers, does not mention the convent, perhaps because it no longer existed in his day; but he does mention the burial of St. Romanus outside the monastery, where women would have access to his relics.

Among the brothers who were being trained in monasticism by the two saints, there reigned above all an absolute *oneness of soul* based on self-sacrifice — a concept which is at the heart of Orthodox monasticism, whether of East or West. "According to the custom of apostolic times, absolutely no one would say, 'This is mine.' The difference between one person and another resided solely in the possession of his name, and not in consideration of his fortune or nobility. Content with their destitution, they practiced oneness of soul *(unanimitas)* in love and faith with such fervor, that if a brother, having received an order to do some task, should go out in cold weather, or if he should have just returned all soaked by a winter rain, everyone would eagerly abandon his most comfortable and driest garment or would take off his footwear the sooner to warm and comfort the body of his brother, rather than to think of himself" (chs. 112-113).

St. Lupicinus governed the monasteries some twenty years after the death of St. Romanus and finally reposed in extreme old age, practicing the severest austerities to the end (refusing in the last moments of his final illness the consolation of a little honey with water). He was buried in the monastery of Laucone, where in 1689 a part of his relics were uncovered with perhaps his original tombstone, and where they remain to this day in the parish church of St.-Lupicin.

THE THIRD OF THE GREAT Jura Fathers, St. Eugendus, is not treated by St. Gregory, but he should be mentioned here for his historical importance in the development of monasticism in the West. He was offered by his father, a parish priest, to the monastery during the lifetime of St. Romanus and, as has been said, remained there without leaving it until his death at the age of over sixty, in about the year 513.

In the monastery "he acquired a solid knowledge, not only of Latin works, but also of Greek eloquence" (ch. 126). If St. Eugendus actually knew the Greek language, it would be a rare thing for late 5th-century Gaul; but in any case it is clear that the tie with the Greek East was still very strong in the Jura monasteries at this time, even if the Eastern Fathers were more probably read in Latin translations. We know that the daily reading in the refectory at Condadisco (a custom introduced by St. Eugendus, "following the ancient Fathers" and in particular St. Basil (ch. 169); in the time of Sts. Romanus and Lupicinus the traditional silence of the Egyptian monasteries was maintained) included "the institutions promulgated of old by the holy and eminent Basil, bishop of the capital of Cappadocia, or those of the holy Fathers of Lerins, or those of Saint Pachomius the ancient abba of the Syrians, or those which most recently the venerable Cassian has formulated" (ch. 174). If St. Romanus had begun his monastic life with only two books, it is clear that his successors had a well-equipped Patristic library!

In his asceticism St. Eugendus kept up the strict standard of his predecessors; his vigils were remarkable, and he ate but once a day, "sometimes at noon, with all the community, when he was tired, and sometimes in the evening, with the monks who took a second meal" (ch. 131). He had only one garment, which he would wear until it was worn out (ch. 127), and his footwear was "solid and rustic, in the fashion of the ancient Fathers. His legs were bound with leggings, and his feet in bands. But for the office of Matins and that of Lauds he never had around his naked feet, even in the most severe frosts or when there was much snow, anything but wooden overshoes in the Gallic manner. It was with this footwear also that, very often, in the morning hours, he would walk far in the snow in order to go to the cemetery of the brethren and pray there" (ch. 129). Like Sts. Romanus and Lupicinus, he was a miracle-worker, and his fame was widespread, so that for centuries the town that sprang up around Condadisco bore his name *(Saint-Oyend* in French). There were so many pilgrims that they "seemed almost to exceed in number the multitude of monks" (ch. 147).

St. Eugendus directed the monks with the utmost prudence and wisdom: "He took all care to assign to each monk the functions or tasks for which he found him more particularly endowed by the gifts of the Holy Spirit. Thus a brother who was peaceable and gentle would be given a service and a post where the advantages of his gentleness and patience would not be at all altered by the heat of an agitated companion. Did he find others, on the contrary, marked by the blemish of pride or vanity? He would not permit them to live apart, out of fear that, puffed up by an injurious feeling of their personal superiority, they might fall lower, into more serious faults, no longer even realizing their sins and vices, in spite of repeated public reprimands. Did he learn, in the meantime, that certain brothers, suffering the condition of human weakness, were the prey of the biting of a devouring sadness? He would come unexpectedly, deliberately show such supernatural pleasantness and joy, warm the heart of the unfortunate ones by words so holy and sweet, that the latter purified of the most harmful venom of sadness, would find themselves healed of their bitter pessimism as by the anointment of a healing oil. But the monks whose conduct was too free, those who were light-minded, found always in the Abba more of roughness and severity" (chs. 149-150).

THERE WAS ONE EVENT during St. Eugendus' governance of the monasteries that marks a whole change of epoch in Western monasticism. Occurring about the year 500, it is a kind of watershed between the less organized, semi-hermitic, lavra-type monasticism of the 4th and 5th centuries, which was very dependent upon the personal qualities of the great monastic founders (St.

Martin, St. Honoratus, Sts. Romanus and Lupicinus), and the more strictly coenobitic monasticism of the 6th and later centuries. This event was the total destruction by fire of the monastery at Condadisco. "As it was built of wood, and
not only was composed of a block of cells bound together one to the other by
their frame, but had also been doubled by a well- arranged second story, it was
so suddenly reduced to ashes that, the next morning, not only did nothing remain
of the buildings, but the fire itself was already almost entirely extinguished"
(ch. 162). There were so many monks then in the monastery that, even apart
from the fire, the Eastern lavra ideal of monks in separate cells had become
impractical; the cells, rather than being a certain distance apart (a stone's throw,
in the later description of the skete ideal by the Russian St. Nilus of Sora) were
actually joined to each other. Therefore St. Eugendus, when rebuilding the monastery, introduced a strict coenobitic rule rather in the spirit of St. Pachomius
than in that of most of the other monastic Fathers of the East. "Refusing to follow on this point the example of the oriental archimandrites, he did a more
useful thing in subjecting all the monks to the common life. After the destruction of the small individual cells, he decided that all should take their repose
with him in a single shelter: those whom a common refectory had already united
for a common meal, he wished to unite also in a common dormitory, only the
beds being separate. In this place there was, as in the oratory, an oil lamp which
gave its light the whole night long" (ch. 170).

One cannot but regret the disappearance of the early monastic "infor-
mality" of the West; but the dominance of the coenobitic Rule was actually unavoidable. St. Martin with his 80 monks could live in the isolation of Marmoutier like the "oriental archimandrites" with the brethren in their lavras; perhaps
even a few hundred brothers could live like that in the remote Jura Mountains.
But when there came to be multitudes of monastic aspirants (perhaps as many
as a thousand), a strict regulation of them was obviously required. This need
had been felt also in the East, as may be seen in the coenobitic establishments
of Sts. Pachomius in Egypt and Theodosius in Palestine with their thousands of
monks; but the lavra or skete ideal remained alive in the East and was never
simply replaced by the coenobitic ideal.

In the West, the 6th century is the century of the great writers of monastic coenobitic Rules (St. Caesarius of Arles, St. Benedict of Nursia, St. Columbanus of Luxeuil and Bobbio, the Irish monk who settled in Gaul and then
Italy). Condadisco also had its own Rule, suited to "the climate of the country
and the necessities of labor" as well as to "Gallic infirmity" (ch. 174); unfortunately, this Rule has not come down to us. Thanks to such Rules, a particular

way of monastic life could spread farther and have more lasting influence than could the example of a single monastic founder. This is particularly noticeable in the spread of the Rule of St. Columbanus in the 7th century, especially in Gaul, and even more noticeable in the spread of the Benedictine Rule throughout the West in the 7th and later centuries. By Carolingian times (9th and 10th centuries) the Rule of St. Benedict was supreme even in individualistic Gaul. Thus monasticism survived and was in relatively good order; but the freshness and "non-establishment" character of the young monastic movement was thereby largely lost. With monasticism such a small and fragile phenomenon in the Orthodox world today, it is no wonder if we are drawn more to the early "unorganized" phase of it in the West rather than to the later "organized"

The church of St. Hymetiere,
where relics of the
6th-century saint are kept

phase. Sixth-century Gaul, with few exceptions, still retained the early, individualistic character of monasticism; this is really the only kind to be seen in the *Life of the Fathers*, which, apart from bishop-ascetics, deals mostly with hermits and desert-dwellers, whether in the wilderness or in cities.

In the 6th and later centuries, still other monastic communities were established in the Jura by monks from Condadisco; at such sites as Grandvaux and the Lac de Bonlieu there are still ruins of these monasteries. At the village of St.-Hymetiere, near the town of Antre, may still be seen one of the oldest surviving churches of the Jura region; built in the 7th or 8th century, it houses the relics of St. Hymetiere, a 6th-century monk of Condadisco who founded a hermitage there.

The author of the *Life of the Jura Fathers* was a disciple and intimate of St. Eugendus, and thus he is able to relate about him something of his hidden spiritual life. In particular, he tells of five visions which St. Eugendus had and described to him in detail. These are: a childhood vision of Sts. Romanus and Lupicinus showing him his spiritual posterity (chs. 121-124); his installation as abbot by the two saints, which occurred just before he was in fact made abbot (chs. 135-136); the visit of the Apostles Peter, Andrew and Paul, who announced the arrival of pieces of their relics from Rome (chs. 153-154); the vision of St. Martin of Tours (who was held in the highest veneration in the Jura monasteries), who informed St. Eugendus that he was watching over two travelling monks of the monastery (ch. 160); and the final appearance of Sts. Romanus and Lupicinus, five days before his death, carrying him to the oratory for his funeral while his own monks protested (chs. 176-177).

The longest and most detailed of these visions is well worthy of comparison with similar visions in Eastern hagiographical literature (for example, the vision of the birds, signifying his spiritual posterity, in the Life of St. Sergius of Radonezh): "The holy child, in a vision, was carried by two monks and placed before the entrance of his father's house, in such a way that he could behold with an attentive gaze the eastern region of the sky and its stars, as before the Patriarch Abraham beheld his numerous posterity. And already he was also told, in a sort of figurative language: 'Such will be your seed' (Gen. 15:5). A little after this, one person appeared here, a second there, another in a different place, until the growing crowd of them became numberless; they surrounded the blessed child and the holy Fathers — without any doubt, Romanus and Lupicinus — who had spiritually raised him up. . . It was as if an enormous swarm of bees, resembling a honey-flowing cluster, came together around them and

enclosed them. And suddenly, from the side towards which his gaze was directed, Eugendus saw as it were a vast door open in the heights of heaven and a
path of gentle slope descend from the summit of heaven to him, surrounded by
light and resembling a slightly-inclined staircase with steps of crystal, and choirs
of angels clothed in white and brightly shining, coming towards him and his
companions: they joyfully exulted in the praise of Christ, and yet, despite the
ever-increasing number of persons, the sacred fear of the Divinity, which struck
them with amazement, did not allow any of them to move his lips to speak or his
head to make a sign. Little by litle, with care, the angelic multitude mixed with
the mortals; the angels gathered these earthly beings, joined them to themselves,
and singing all the same song, mounted again towards the sacred abodes of heav-
en as they had come.

"Among the modulations of this hymn, the holy child understood only
one phrase, a phrase of the Gospel, as he learned about a year later when he
entered the monastery. Here is what the alternate choir of the angelic multitude said, in antiphonal manner (I remember it very well, because Eugendus
himself had the kindness to relate it to me): 'I am the Way and the Life and the
Truth' (John 14:6). Then the immense crowd retired; having been long beheld,
the region of the heavens filled with stars also closed; the child, seeing himself
alone in this place, awoke with a start and, struck with terror by this vision,
immediately related the event to his father. And the holy priest recognized
at once to whom supremely such a holy son should be consecrated. Without de-
laying, he taught him the rudiments of knowledge, and at the end of the same
year Eugendus was offered to St. Romanus . . . In him, truly, converged the
double profusion of graces accorded to the blessed Abbas who had spiritually
transported him outside his earthly dwelling, so that the generation which immediately followed that of these Abbas already hesitated, asking whether in
Eugendus it beheld the image of Lupicinus or that of Romanus" (chs. 121-125).

In this striking description of Jacob's Ladder (Gen. 28:12) — the same
image which St. Eucherius had used in his *Praise of the Desert* to describe the
"unseen visitation" of "rejoicing angels making watchful call upon the desert
expanse" (ch. 38) — the author of the *Life of the Jura Fathers* well indicates
the spiritual offspring of Condadisco and monastic Gaul in general. St Gregory's
Life of the Fathers will give us in some detail the quality of this monastic movement which was still so powerful in his own day, a century after this vision.

A Pilgrimage to the Jura Mountains

The following account is that of an American soldier,
a convert to Orthodoxy, stationed in Germany.

O N THE FEAST DAY of the Prophet Elias, July 20/August 2, 1976, I began my pilgrimage to the Orthodox holy places of Eastern France and Switzerland. It began in Wiesbaden at the church of the Righteous Elizabeth. I had come to Wiesbaden for the weekend, as I often do. On this day Father Mark celebrated the Vigil and Divine Liturgy for the holy Prophet, and then read a prayer for me for the beginning of my journey. From Wiesbaden I went to the nearby U.S. Air Force base at Frankfort, where I rented a car. I wasn't too pleased at the prospect of traveling alone, but, asking for God's blessing, I started off by myself.

The next morning I began the first leg of my journey. Traveling in Germany is very convenient since there are many spots along the way where one can rest and eat. Once into the Swiss countryside, the terrain begins to climb, and the scenery becomes more picturesque. After passing through Bern, the freeway (autobahn) ended, and a pleasant drive began on small country roads through the Swiss countryside. There are lots of farm villages, all built in a distinctive Swiss style. The weather was warm and clear, making for a very pleasant drive. After passing through Lausanne, I continued on around Lake Geneva, toward the upper Rhone Valley. The first Orthodox holy place I wished to visit was St. Maurice (the ancient monastery of Agaunum).

Ouside of Lausanne I stopped to give a traveler a ride, which was very fortuitous. He turned out to be an American who had been studying in Thailand,

141

but for the previous six months had been making his way slowly overland through Asia and Europe. He was on his way to Paris for a flight home to Indiana. Of course I was very glad to meet a fellow-countryman. He was going toward Chamonix in France, and since St. Maurice was on the way he was glad to get a ride. His name was David.

The road from Lausanne to St. Maurice curves around the northeast side of Lake Geneva and then continues up the Rhone Valley. It is a very beautiful drive along the lake shore. The mountains are quite spectacular and the river valley is dotted with farms and villages. Soon we reached the town of St. Maurice. It is located next to steep cliffs; most of the surrounding countryside is farmland. We didn't have much difficulty finding the abbey with its prominent bell tower. After parking the car, we entered a building adjacent to the church and inquired whether anyone there could speak English. The porter who answered spoke only French, and with my poor French we didn't get very far. He directed us to the church, and there we found a young man apparently preparing for evening service. He was able to speak some English and was very helpful. It turned out that he was a young priest of the community of Augustinian canons which had inhabited the site since 1128, when the canons took over the Abbey. As a result of the reforms in the Roman church, the members of the community for the most part wear lay garb, except during their church services.

We had arrived too late for the last tour of the "Treasury," but the young priest was kind enough to see that we were able to view the relics and treasures. The relics of St. Maurice, as well as those of other saints, along with many ancient artifacts, are kept in a specially constructed vault. Unfortunately, everything is displayed like items in a museum rather than as holy relics. I boldly asked about the possibility of venerating the relics (which are kept behind glass), but they said it was impossible. Apparently, the relics are removed from the vault only once or twice during the year. Although there wasn't much time, I did manage to address a prayer to St. Maurice before his relics and I remembered your Brotherhood.

We were informed that one of the priests of the community was English, but he wasn't there at the time and would only be there the next day. I wanted to see more, but it was getting late and I had to think about where to spend the night. David (the American student) was heading for Chamonix, just over the border in France, and since he had information on inexpensive places to stay, I decided to go there for the night.

From St. Maurice we drove to Martigny and then began climbing into the mountains. It is a very steep and spectacular drive, especially the ascent from the Rhone Valley. We crossed the border into France and shortly thereafter came to Chamonix, where we ate supper and found an inexpensive place to spend the night.

We awoke the next morning in the shadow of Mont Blanc, which dominates majestically over the area. I planned to head back to St. Maurice, hoping to find the English priest and get some information from him about the abbey. From there I planned to travel on to Geneva. David agreed to go with me. I was glad to have the company.

A brief word about David. He was a young man about 21 years old, of medium height, with long blond hair in the style currently fashionable among young people. He had had some very interesting experiences during the course of his travels. I can't say that he was particularly religious, but he was open to religious ideas and he asked many questions of me during the time we were together. His background was Protestant, and he didn't have many firm beliefs other than some basic concepts about Christianity. Unfortunately he had acquired a few ideas — probably through his American educational experience — which would have to be labeled "liberal," and we had some lively discussions a couple of times.

We returned from Chamonix to St. Maurice and were able to find the English priest, Father Fox. He was an older man, although still energetic. He had definitely accepted aggiornamento and spoke somewhat deprecatingly of the French Archbishop Lefebre who has been defying the Pope about the Latin Mass and other reforms enacted at Vatican II. I did catch a note of regret, though, when Father Fox mentioned that the office in the abbey was now sung in French instead of the Latin which had been used for the previous 15 or so centuries.

Father Fox was very friendly. I explained to him why I had come, told him something about *The Orthodox Word,* and told him of your plans to publish some of the writings of St. Gregory of Tours. At this he became quite interested and immediately went to the abbey's library and pulled off the shelf an old volume of Migne's Latin Patrologia containing St. Gregory's works. Later he read to us a portion of the Saint's writings in which the abbey is mentioned.

Father Fox directed us to a pathway up the side of the cliff to a chapel where once there was a hermitage founded by a St. Amatus in the 6th century. The climb is rather steep, but the path is in good condition and has even been built up in spots. Apparently services are held there regularly and pilgrims go there often; when we reached the chapel, a nun was there praying. Nearby is a tiny house, indicating that perhaps even in recent times someone had been living there.

When we climbed down from the cliff, we met again with Father Fox, and he showed us the abbey church. The present church is old, but it is not the original one. The original church (apparently the basilica which St. Romanus visited) was built right up against the cliff; all that remains of it are the foundations and a crypt underneath. Father Fox told us that in excavating the crypt, they uncovered an ancient fresco which vanished within a matter of hours, apparently from being exposed to the air — but not before they were able to photograph it.

The highlight of my whole visit to the abbey was seeing the actual spot in the crypt where the relics of St. Maurice and other martyrs had lain. I asked Father Fox for a piece of stone from the tomb where the relics had lain, and although he hesitated at first, he finally gave me a piece of rock from the actual spot where St. Maurice's relics had been, and another piece from a spot a few feet away where other relics had been.

As we left St. Maurice, we stopped to see the parish church of St. Sigismund, a pious king of the Burgundians in the 6th century. He helped to found the abbey and introduced the *laus perennis* there; his relics lie beneath the altar in the parish church. I was able to offer brief prayers here also. We continued our journey along the southern shore of Lake Geneva, crossing into France and then back into Switzerland just before reaching the city of Geneva.

Geneva is a bustling metropolis and very international in character. I first wanted to find our Russian Orthodox Cathedral and also Archbishop Anthony, with the hope of getting a place to spend the night. We found the cathedral but could not locate the Archbishop. I found out later that he was visiting in Germany at the time. Since David had some information about inexpensive lodging, we made some calls and found a place located right near the Palace of the Legion of Nations. The next day we returned to the Russian Cathedral in order to see the interior. The exterior is very impressive, the interior less so. I lit a candle in memory of Bishop Leonty of Geneva, the brother of the present Archbishop, and then we left, driving toward the French Jura. David had decided to accompany me into France.

The Jura are not far from Switzerland. They are not as impressive as the Alps, but they do have their own beauty and are quite rugged. After the initial climb into the mountains, we came upon a very pleasant valley where I made a wrong turn. We travelled quite a few kilometers before I discovered my mistake, but it was nice driving through the countryside, where mostly farms and small villages were to be found. Once I got going in the correct direction, we

A view of the Jura

A depiction of the martyrdom of St. Maurice, which occurred in the 3rd century in the town of Agaunum (now called St. Maurice).

The cathedral of the town of Saint-Claude, constructed in the 15th century on the site of a little oratory which Sts. Romanus and Lupicinus had built a thousand years earlier and had dedicated to the Apostles Peter, Paul and Andrew.

eventually came to St. Claude. It is a busy town, and it seems to be somewhat of a resort too. Because my French is so poor, I searched diligently for someone who could speak English, but in the local tourist office and the cathedral they could speak only French. It was very discouraging, especially since I had so many questions to ask.

The cathedral, built on the site of St. Romanus' monastery, dates from the middle ages, but is not really outstanding in any particular way. The town itself is dominated on one side by steep cliffs (LeBayard). Inside the cathedral is a chapel to St. Claude, who was an abbot and also bishop in the 7th century. The incorrupt relics of the saint were destroyed by revolutionaries during the French Revolution, and all that remains is a finger of the left hand. I was able to pray before this relic and light candles too.

Since I was having such a difficult time finding anyone with whom to talk about St. Romanus and his monastery, I decided to travel on to some of the other nearby sites that you wrote me of. The next stop was the village of St. Lupicin.

It seems that the site of St. Romanus' monastery was not particularly suitable for farming, and as the brotherhood increased it was necessary to find other places to raise food. One of these spots was the present village of St. Lupicin, named after the brother of St. Romanus. St. Lupicinus lived mostly at this monastery established to provide food for the main monastery. The village is not far from St. Claude, but there is a difference in terrain, and the area around St. Lupicin appears to be definitely more suitable for farming.

St. Lupicin is a sleepy village. The main building is the church, which seems to be fairly old, although I wouldn't want to guess just how old. The front door is below street level. There is nothing spectacular about the church itself, but I was very pleased to find that the relics of St. Lupicinus were there, resting beneath a side altar. I was able to offer prayers before these relics also.

Not far from the church, down a side street, is the house of the village priest. I think that the buildings of this house were once part of the monastery. I managed to find the priest, and we were able to converse because he spoke some German. He was very pleasant. I explained why I was there and what I was looking for, and he gave me directions on how to find the village of St.-Romain. He also told me about the grotto of St. Anne, which is located near St.-Claude. This priest (who was also dressed in lay garb) made one comment which I thought was quite accurate. He said that there was very great veneration for saints in the Orthodox Church, while among Protestants there was hardly any at all; as for the Roman Catholics, he said that they were somewhere in between. This priest mentioned that very soon a pamphlet about the church of St.-Lupicin was due to be published and would have pictures.

From St.-Lupicin we drove about five kilometers to the village of St.-Romain. Outside of the village, on a cliff overlooking the river valley, there is a small chapel. The chapel is right on the edge of some steep cliffs. It is completely bare, and besides the altar there is only the reliquary, containing the relics of St. Romanus, which is on the altar. I went around to the back of the altar to see if the reliquary could be opened, and sure enough, there was a small door. Inside, there was a glass case with the relics of St. Romanus. It was truly a great blessing to have been deemed worthy to see the Saint's relics and pray before them.

From St.-Romain we returned to St-Claude, mainly so I could find the grotto of St. Anne. I was directed to follow a path leading up into the cliffs. On the way I took a cone and branch from one of the fir trees, as you requested. I managed to find the grotto, but it was just a large cave, and there was no indication of anything religious about it. Apparently it had served as the dwelling of a hermit in the ancient past. About half-way up to the grotto was an old house which was abandoned.

We now headed towards Grandvaux. Our road took us north, out of the high mountainous region and into the beautiful countryside dotted with lakes and rolling hills. The lake of Grandvaux is very beautiful. At one time there was a monastery on this lake, one of those founded by the monks of the Jura after the time of St. Romanus; but now all that remains is a village and a parish church. The church was closed, so I didn't see the interior. We also visited the Lac de Bonlieu, which is more isolated than Grandvaux. A plaque near the lake mentions a Carthusian foundation that once existed on the spot. A short distance away from the lake I noticed several buildings which appeared to be a monastery of some kind, but I really wasn't able to tell for sure.

In the morning we were on the road again, heading now towards Germany. Along the way we stopped in Romainmoutier, which is southwest of the Lake of Neuchatel. This is the site of a monastery founded by St Romanus. The village, situated in a lovely, peaceful valley, is quite old and picturesque. The church is quite old — about a thousand years or so — and has been nicely restored. The interior is now very plain, in the style of a Protestant church, as it has been since the Bernese imposed their rule and Protestant religion on the town during the Reformation. Originally there were frescos on the walls, but the Protestants whitewashed them. Some of the frescos have been restored, although they are pretty faint. At present the church is in Protestant hands; there are two

The town of Saint-Claude — site of the ancient Condadisco

The Monastery of Agaunum, showing
the foundation of the ancient Basilica

Church of St. Lupicinus,
where his relics are kept

Chapel of St. Romanus, where his relics are kept

Reliquary of
St. Lupicinus

Relics of St. Romanus

The grotto and hermitage of St. Anne, on the mountain above Condadisco

The fir forest around Condadisco

Roumainmoutier — ancient church of St. Romanus' Monastery in Switzerland

Protestant sisters who take care of it, assisted by two Roman Catholic sisters, with whom, in "ecumenical" fashion, they say their prayers together.

From Romainmoutier we made our way back to Basel and on into Germany, eventually arriving at my home. Thus the pilgrimage ended. In a few short days I covered quite a few miles and saw many interesting and inspiring things. I would have liked to have spent more time, but it just wasn't possible. I was able to see the relics of many saints and visit the places sanctified by their holy lives, for which I am grateful.

It is all very hidden, however. These saints are, with the exception of some local veneration, unknown and uncared for. What is worse is that undoubtedly there are many other places in the West similar to the sites I visited which are just as neglected. One no longer finds pilgrims — only tourists. The various holy places have endured much over the years; they have suffered from wars, from the Reformation, and from revolution. But now, in the 20th century, these wonderful places have been turned into tourist attractions. It seems to be the ultimate blasphemy. All that one takes away from such museums is coldness and a feeling of regret for that which is lost.

I attempted to explain to David about saints and their importance for Orthodox Christians. It wasn't easy, since the concept has fallen into such disuse in the West. And yet, the concept is such a profound one. Really, the saints are the key to Orthodoxy. They are not ideas and theories which scholars and pseudo-scholars banter about, but rather they are theology in practice, they are living bearers of Orthodoxy, they are what we must become. And the glory of the Orthodox Church is that the saints are alive and real and present, leading the way for us and helping us along by their examples and teachings and prayers. If the saints are not what they should be for us, it is because we have departed from them and forgotten and neglected them. What is terrifying for us is that we too are in danger of losing the saints, just as the West lost them before us. It is only by struggles and diligent effort that we can hold on to the saints.

Archbishop John, by merely showing interest in the saints of the West, has given the impetus for us to strive to know and love the saints of the West as truly our own. And to whom else do they belong, if not to us?

I thank you with my whole heart for suggesting this pilgrimage to me and also for your suggestions and advice on what to see. May God bless you in your efforts to kindle in the Orthodox Christians of these last days the fire that shone so brightly and continues to shine for those who have the eyes to see, in the saints of the West.

3

Orthodox Monasticism Today in the Light of Orthodox Monastic Gaul

WHAT HAS ALL THIS to say to us today? Is there a still-living message for us in the examples of Sts. Romanus and Lupicinus, in the words of the great Western Fathers of monasticism, in St. Gregory's monastic Gaul of the 5th and 6th centuries? Let us look for a moment at our own situation.

Orthodox monasticism is coming to the West today also as something new and fresh, and it is attracting increasing interest especially among converts to the Orthodox Faith. The Orthodox mission in the West up to the mid-20th century did not produce a monastic movement, but in the last 20 years or so, as serious monastic literature has become available, especially in English, there has been a definite manifestation not only of interest in Orthodox monasticism, but of the practice of it as well. Parallel to this manifestation in Western Europe and America, there has been also a noticeable monastic "revival" in Greece and Mt. Athos. Often, and most logically, this monastic movement (although it is perhaps too early to call it that) is bound up with the preservation of Orthodox tradition in general, as against the general religious current of modernism and renovationism, and it has already been responsible for something of a revival of the ancient standards of Orthodox piety — the veneration of saints and holy relics, the serious reading of Lives of Saints and basic Patristic texts on spiritual life, love for the fullness of the Orthodox Divine services, and the like. Today— in sharp contrast to the situation only a quarter-century ago — it is quite possible for an Orthodox convert to undertake the monastic path with some hope of success.

The aspirant who wishes to undertake the monastic life today finds before him three general types of monastic situation:

1. A long-established institution with a definite place in the church "organization." Here the emphasis is usually on the institution itself, which continues to exist without change no matter who comes or goes. The monastic authorities in general mistrust any idea of change or "renewal," and the "zealotry" common in young novices is viewed as being bound up with a spiritual immaturity which can only be outgrown by long experience. Such institutions perform an immense and difficult — and usually thankless — labor in handing down the Orthodox monastic tradition as well as possible in a world that is profoundly hostile to it; these monasteries are actually citadels of Orthodoxy in a foreign world. Monastic aspirants today, however, are easily disillusioned by such monasteries, looking at their faults (both real and imagined) with an overly-critical eye, and regarding them as "idiorhythmic" and as having departed from pure monastic traditions; those who do stay in such monasteries can find it a heavy burden, due most of all to the immense disharmony between the Orthodox spiritual life and the life of the contemporary world. But the unbroken connection with the past in such communities, and the very suffering required to remain in them, continue to produce spiritual fruit. Those who can remain in them without falling into apathy, carelessness, or discouragement can attain to a high spiritual state; but very often the young aspirant will leave them in order to seek something more "correct" or "perfect".

2. An individual struggler, usually a convert, inspired with the highest monastic ideals (often skete or hermit life), "opens a monastery" and begins to live according to his idea or adaptation of the great monastic strugglers of the past, sometimes attracting a few disciples. This is the most dangerous of the monastic paths open today. Its great temptation is over-reliance on oneself; its great pitfall is loss of contact with the age-old monastic tradition. The 20th century has already had a rich experience of eccentric "elders" whose ultimate authority is their own opinions. Prof. I. M. Kontzevitch, in his classic work on the institution of elders or *startsi* in the Orthodox Church (*Optina Monastery and its Epoch,* Jordanville, 1970, in Russian), felt compelled to write a special section (pp. 10-13) on the "false elders" who cripple and ruin so many souls in their spiritual pretentiousness; among converts this is an especially dangerous temptation. Even when they do not go far astray, such "elders" are seldom able to offer the monastic aspirant anything more than their own inexperienced human opinions of what monastic struggles should be. Often, in such monastic

attempts, spiritual wounds remain unhealed through a lack of mutual trust between spiritual father and spiritual child; thus deeply-rooted sins and inclinations may remain unconfessed and untreated. (This can happen in the "established" monasteries also, but usually with less serious spiritual consequences, since the authentic monastic environment itself can at least partially compensate for any personal deficiencies.) Sometimes also, unknown to the aspirant himself, the energy for struggles comes more from the passions, especially from hidden pride and vainglory, than from a genuine thirst for God. Numerous examples from the past, to be sure, show that such a path is a *possible* one; but the conditions of today's world render the probability of success and spiritual soundness in such an undertaking rather small. When his own spiritual energy and resources are exhausted, the individual struggler on such a path often collapses and gives up spiritual struggle (and sometimes Orthodoxy) altogether. The Life of St. Romanus of the Jura (as also many other Lives of Saints, such as that of St. Sergius of Radonezh) gives us some of the basic necessities for success in a monastic path outside an already established monastery: deep roots in Orthodoxy since childhood, with a childhood experience of the simplicity and difficulty of daily life, a balanced character and long experience in acquiring virtues, a basic spiritual training and knowledge, a resolute determination to suffer everything for Christ, physical difficulties accepted as a matter of course, a lack of "publicity" and a desire to be "lost to the world," the absence of any desire to "be somebody" or do such an important thing as "open a monastery," and deep humility and distrust of oneself. Those who venture on this path without at least most of these necessities: *beware!*

3. More often in recent years: a group of two or more young strugglers rediscovers the ancient traditions of monasticism and begins to struggle together, usually in the coenobitic way of life. Traditional monastic phenomena (seldom emphasized in the older monastic institutions) are spoken about and sometimes strictly followed: 'hesychasm,' 'elders,' 'confession of thoughts,' strict obedience, and the like. Special attention is paid to a conscious spiritual life, usually with frequent Holy Communion. Such groups open new monasteries or move into old monasteries and "renew" them, and often they have notable success, especially if their leader has personal "charisma"; they can be formed either of native Orthodox or largely of converts, and they generally have access to the monastic sources in one of the languages where they are most plentiful (Greek or Russian). The leader is characteristically Orthodox "by blood," not a convert, although the group as a whole may seem (especially to monks of one of the

older, "conventional" monasteries) to have definite "convert" characteristics. Such groups have a rather good chance of relative stability and outward success, but they face special dangers which should not be underemphasized. Among the chief temptations to such groups, especially if they are very successful, are: outward success can blind them to inward deficiencies, community solidarity and well-being can cause them to become inflated with a false sense of their own importance, and the appearance of "correctness" can produce spiritual smugness and disdain of those outside the group who are not so "correct". If these temptations are not overcome, a deadly "group pride" can take the place of individual pride and lead the whole community on a fatal path which none of its members can recognize because it is not his *personal* doing; the "renewed" community can become so much out of harmony with the "unrenewed" rest of the Church as to form a virtual "jurisdiction" of its own, and even end in a schism brought about by its own exaggerated feeling of "correctness." The more such groups stay out of the limelight of publicity and church disputes, and the less a point they make of emphasizing their "correctness" and their differences from the older institutions, the better chance they have for remaining spiritually sound.

In view of these contemporary monastic situations, all of them with their particular dangers and temptations, it would not be an exaggeration to state that Orthodox monasticism as a whole in the late 20th century, despite a few appearances of outward prosperity, is weak, fragile, shallow-rooted and mostly immature (at least in the sense of "under-ripe" — not yet sufficiently formed and tested). Any of the three paths that have been described (and other paths as well, for these are only generalities) *could* produce sound monastic fruits; but the probability of failure, as well as of spiritual fakery, is greater than ever before, and it would be foolish, especially for the monastic aspirant himself, not to keep this well in mind.

Monasticism, despite its other-worldly goal, is still in the world, and its state cannot but reflect the state of the world contemporary to it. The pampered, self-satisfied, self-centered young people who form the vast majority of those who come to monasticism today (at least in the free world) cannot but bring with them their worldly "baggage" of attitudes and habits, and these in turn cannot but affect the monastic environment. With a fierce and conscious battle against them, their influence can be minimized; without this constant battle, they can come to dominate even the best-organized monastery, often in hidden ways.

True Orthodox monasticism by its very nature is hostile to the principle of modern *comfort*. The constant activity of the monk is not giving ease to himself, sacrificing himself, giving himself over heart and soul to something above himself; but this is exactly the opposite of the first principle of modern life, which is based on the chiliastic dream of making life easy on earth. To commit oneself to a conscious battle against the principles and habits of modern comfort is a rare and dangerous thing; and thus it is no wonder that our monasticism is so weak — it cannot but reflect the feebleness of Orthodox life in general today.

In the convert lands of the West, the earlier generation of 20th-century monastic aspirants depended much upon its own strength and its own opinions; there was little chance for it to enter into fruitful contact with genuine Orthodox monastic tradition. Numerous converts, with little or no guidance and with insufficient grounding in spiritual knowledge and monastic practice, have tried to struggle on their own (even to the extent of undertaking long fasts, praying long prayer-rules with prostrations, wearing chains, etc., or even to "open monasteries." All of these attempts have met with an almost uniform lack of success; apart from other failings, these attempts have been too personal and peculiar, too little in the tradition of Orthodoxy.

Now, however, the general atmosphere has changed; there are more monasteries, more books, more teachers, and thus Orthodox monasticism has become something more normal and less peculiar in the West. Few would now venture to try the monastic path on their own, without some kind of guidance and basic knowledge. Outwardly, at least, Orthodox monasticism is now known in the West, and all but the freshest of monastic aspirants knows that he must find a spiritual father, not undertake the monastic life (and especially "open a monastery"!) without a blessing and direction from some recognized monastic teacher, and must beware of spiritual deception. The teaching of recent Fathers of Orthodox monasticism — in particular, Bishop Ignatius Brianchaninov and Bishop Theophan the Recluse — has had a sobering effect on many who might otherwise be carried away by a monastic "romanticism"; the reading of spiritual books especially addressed to the Orthodox Christians and monks of modern times *(Unseen Warfare, The Arena)* has had the effect of bringing "down to earth" those monastic aspirants who have been a little too exalted by the more advanced teachings of such Fathers as St. Isaac the Syrian and St. Simeon the New Theologian. One may see a greater balance in the monastic interest of today.

Unfortunately, the awareness of Orthodox monasticism and its ABC's remains largely, even now, an outward matter. There is still more *talk* of "elders," "hesychasm," and "prelest" than fruitful monastic struggles themselves. Indeed, it is all too possible to accept all the outward marks of the purest and most exalted monastic tradition: absolute obedience to an elder, daily confession of thoughts, long church services or individual rule of Jesus Prayer and prostrations, frequent reception of Holy Communion, reading with understanding of the basic texts of spiritual life, and in doing all this to feel a deep *psychological* peace and ease — and at the same time to remain *spiritually* immature. It is possible to cover over the untreated passions within one by means of a facade or technique of "correct" spirituality, without having true love for Christ and one's brother. The rationalism and coldness of heart of modern man in general make this perhaps the most insidious of the temptations of the monastic aspirant today. Orthodox monastic *forms,* true enough, are being planted in the West; but what about the heart of monasticism and Orthodox Christianity: repentance, humility, love for Christ our God and unquenchable thirst for His Kingdom?

In all humility let us admit the poverty of our Christianity, the coldness of our love for God, the emptiness of our spiritual pretensions; and let us use this confession as the *beginning* of our monastic path, which is a path of correction. Let us, the monks of the last times, realistically aware of our failings and of the pitfalls before us, not lose courage at the sight of them, but let us all the more strenuously offer to God our humble entreaty that He might forgive our sins and heal our wounded souls.

Orthodox monastic Gaul shows us that the monastic path is not something merely "Eastern"; rather, it is *universally Christian* and, indeed, it has been tried before in the West, and with great spiritual success. The teaching of the Orthodox monastic Fathers of East and West is one and the same, and it offers nothing less — for those with ears to hear it — than the shortest path to Christ's Kingdom.

Again, the Orthodox monasticism of Gaul is always close to its roots and aware of its aim, never bogged down in the letter of its disciplines and forms. Its freshness and directness are a source of great inspiration even today.

Finally, Orthodox monastic Gaul reveals to us how close true monasticism is to the Gospel. St. Gregory's *Life of the Fathers* is particularly insistent on this point: each of the Lives begins with the Gospel, and each saint's deeds flow from it as their source. No matter what he describes in Orthodox Gaul — whether the painting of icons, the undertaking of ascetic labors, the veneration of a saint's relics — all is done *for the love of Christ,* and this is never forgotten.

The monastic life, indeed, even in our times of feeble faith, is still above all *the love of Christ,* the Christian life par excellence, experienced with many patient sufferings and much pain. Even today there are those who penetrate the secret of this paradise on earth — more often through humble sufferings than through outward "correctness" — a paradise which worldly people can scarcely imagine. May this book help increase their number and fill all with a greater love of God Who is truly glorified in His saints.

IV

VITA PATRUM

OR

A BOOK OF THE LIFE OF CERTAIN BLESSED ONES

by St. Gregory of Tours

Early Monastic Sites of the Auvergne

↖ *Tours (120 km.)*

Paris (210 km.) ↑

Treves (350 km.) ↗

Loire R.

Rhône R.

● Columbarium

🏛 Monastery of St. Portianus

⌐ Cell of St. Patroclus ●

Forest of Ponticiacus
St. Emilianus

● Lipidiacus
Hermitage of St. Lupicinus

🏛 Monastery of Manatense
St. Bracchio

— Limoges (60 km.) —

St. Illidius
St. Gallus
St. Quintianus

● Clermont —

Monastery of St. Cyricus·
St. Abraham

Monastery of St. Martius ←

● Lyons
St. Nicetius

🏛 Monastery of Melitum
St. Caluppa

0   10   50 km.
Scale ⊢┅┅┄─┼────┤

FRANCE
● Paris
☐ Clermont

THE PROLOGUE OF
SAINT GREGORY

I HAD RESOLVED to write only of what has been divinely accomplished at the tombs of the blessed martyrs and confessors; but as I have recently found out certain things about those men whom the merit of their blessed sojourn here below has elevated to heaven, and as I thought that their mode of life, which is known from some accounts, could edify the Church, I do not wish — since the opportunity presents itself — to put off recounting something about them, for the reason that the life of the saints not only makes known their resolve, but also incites the souls of the hearers to imitation.

There are those who ask whether we should speak of the *life* of the saints or of their *lives*. Agellius* and several other philosophers wished to speak of the *lives*. But the author Pliny**, in the third book of his *Art of Grammar*, expresses himself thus: "The ancients spoke of the *lives* of each of us; but the grammarians do not believe that the word *life* has a plural." Therefore, it is manifestly better to say the *Life of the Fathers* rather than the *Lives of the Fathers*, because although there is a diversity of merits and virtues among them, nevertheless one life of the body sustains them all in this world.

I have written, to be sure, in my book on the Confessors, some brief details of what certain ones have done while in the body, even though things great by the power of God are thus rendered small by the writing. Now, in this work, which we wish to call the *Life* of the Saints, we presume, despite our inexperience and ignorance, to speak of such matters at greater length, entreating the Lord that He, Who has often opened the mouth of the dumb for its original use, might vouchsafe to give the word to our mouth, so that from my lips there might flow salutary things for my hearers and readers, things worthy of the holy Fathers. And those things which He inspires to be written about the Saints, may He regard as chanted to His praise.

---

*Aulus Gellius, 2nd-century writer and grammarian (rather than "philosopher," a term St. Gregory uses in a very broad sense), author of *Noctes Atticae*, "*Attic Nights*."
**Pliny the Elder, 1st century, author of *Natural History*.

1

Saints Romanus
and Lupicinus

DESERT-DWELLERS OF THE JURA MOUNTAINS

Commemorated February 28 (†460) and March 21 (†480)

T HE TEXT OF the evangelical teachings informs us that the money entrusted to us by the generosity of the Lord, being committed to bankers can, with God's favor, obtain a just and fruitful increase, and that it should not remain uselessly buried in the earth. Rather, increased by wise use, it serves for the gain of eternal life, so that when the Lord shall inquire concerning the sum He has loaned, upon receiving with satisfaction twice the amount, He will say *Well done, good servant; since thou hast been faithful over a few things, I will set thee over many things; enter thou into the joy of thy Lord* (Matt. 25:21). Indeed, it belongs to the elect to accomplish these things with the help of God; it belongs to those who from the cradle — as we read about many of them — have merited to know the Lord, and having known Him have never withdrawn from His commandments nor, after the sacrament of Baptism, have ever soiled by shameful acts that precious robe of regeneration white as snow. It is these who properly *follow the Lamb wherever He goeth* (Apoc. 14:4), whom the unequalled brightness of the Lamb Himself has crowned with lilies of glory which no heat of temptation can cause to fade.

It is by means of such crowns, then, that the right hand of the Divine Majesty arouses those who begin, aids those who succeed, adorns the victors whom He has marked beforehand with the seal of His Name, whom He draws

165

On the way to the town of Saint-Claude along the river Bienne —
site of the ancient Condadisco, where Sts. Romanus and Lupicinus
founded a monastery.

away from the groanings of the earth and raises up, glorious, to the joy of Heaven. In the number of these elect ones white as snow, I do not doubt, are also those men who, traversing the dark places of the wilderness of Jura, have not only merited to become temples of God themselves, but also have set up in many souls tabernacles of the grace of the Holy Spirit — that is, Lupicinus and his brother Romanus.

1. Lupicinus, then from the beginning of his life sought God with all his heart; having learned his letters, when he came of age, being compelled by his father, he was joined in the bond of marriage, although his soul did not consent to it. Romanus, however, was still a youth, and desiring also to consecrate his soul to the work of God, refused marriage. When their parents departed this world, both with common consent thirsted after the wilderness; together they went into the solitudes of the desert of the Jura, between Burgundy and Alemannia and near the region of Avenches; there they fixed their abode, and, prostrate on the earth, each day entreated the Lord with the singing

of their psalmody, seeking food from the roots of plants. But because the jealousy of him who fell from Heaven has the habit of setting snares for the human race, he likewise armed himself against the servants of God and by his agents endeavored to turn them away from the path which they had undertaken. In fact the demons did not cease for one day to overwhelm them with stones, and each time they would bend the knee to pray to the Lord, immediately a rain of stones hurled by the demons would fall upon them, so that often they were injured and endured terrible sufferings.

Then, in their immature years, they began to fear the daily attacks of the enemy, and, unable to endure any longer their sufferings, they decided to abandon the wilderness and return home. What things does the hatred of the enemy not compel one to do? But when, after leaving this abode which they had gone to seek out, they reached inhabited towns, they entered the house of a certain poor man. The wife inquired where the soldiers of Christ were coming from. They replied, not without confusion, that they had left the wilderness, and they revealed to her in detail what had turned them away from their undertaking. Then she replied: "You ought, O men of God, to have fought manfully against the snares of the devil, without fearing the hatred of one who has so often been overcome by the friends of God. For he is jealous of holiness, fearing lest the human race, ennobled by faith, should achieve the heights whence it fell through his faithlessness." Whereupon, touched to the heart, they said to one another, apart from the woman, "Woe to us who have sinned against God by renouncing our intent! See now how we are convicted of indolence by a woman. And what henceforth will be our life if we do not return to the place from which we have been driven away by the malice of the enemy?"

2. Then, armed with the sign of the Cross, staff in hand, they returned to the wilderness. Upon their arrival, once again the treachery of the demon began to overwhelm them with stones; but, persisting in prayer, they obtained from the Lord's mercy to be delivered from temptation and to persevere freely and without hindrance in the service of the Divine worship. Thus, while they devoted themselves to prayer, crowds of brothers began to come to them from all parts to hear the preaching of the word from them. Since the blessed hermits, as we have said, had now become known to people, they founded for themselves a monastery which they wished to be called Condadisco. In this place, the forest once hewn down and levelled, they sought their food from the labor of their own hands. And so much fervor of love for God inflamed those of neighboring regions that the multitude which came together for the worship of God could not all dwell together; thus they founded yet another monastery wherein they installed a swarm from the blessed hive. But the new swarm so

increased thereafter, with God's help, that they established a third monastery in the territory of Alemannia. By turns these two Fathers would go there to visit their sons, whom they had imbued with the divine teachings, preaching in each monastery what pertained to the formation of the soul.

Lupicinus, however, held the rule of abbot over them. He was very sober, abstaining from food and drink to the point of often partaking of them only every three days. When thirst would overpower him, out of the need of the human body, he would have a vessel of water brought, in which he would immerse his hands for a long time. And, O wonder! His flesh would so absorb the water it was placed in that one would have said that he took it by mouth; and thus the heat of thirst would be extinguished. He was most severe in the discipline of the brethren, nor did he permit anyone either to act or even to speak improperly. He carefully avoided both speaking and meeting with women. Romanus, on the other hand, had such simplicity that women did not leave a deep influence on his soul; but to all equally, men or women, he gave the asked-for blessing after invoking the Name of God.

3. It happened, when Abbot Lupicinus had insufficient means wherewith to feed so large a community, that God revealed to him a place in the wilderness where a treasure had long before been hidden. To that place he betook himself alone, and he carried back to the monastery all the gold and silver he could load upon himself; having bought provisions with it, he fed the multitudes of brethren he had gathered for the service of God. He did the same each year. But to none of the brethren did he make known the place which the Lord had vouchsafed to reveal to him.

Now it came to pass that once he visited the brethren assembled, as we have said, in the regions of Alemannia. Toward noon, when the brethren were still in the fields, he entered the house in which the food was being cooked for the meal; there he saw a great preparation of various dishes and a multitude of fish gathered together, and he said within himself, "It is not proper that monks, whose life is one of solitude, should make use of such inappropriate sumptuousness." And immediately he ordered a large cauldron prepared. When, placed on the fire, it began to boil, he threw in together all the dishes they had prepared, fish as well as vegetables and herbs — everything that was intended for the monks' meal — and said, "Let the brethren take their meal now from this pottage instead of abandoning themselves to delicacies which hinder them in the divine work." When the monks learned of this, they took it very ill. Finally, twelve men, having taken counsel together, left that place in the heat of anger and went away, wandering through the solitudes in pursuit of worldly delicacies.

These actions were immediately revealed to Romanus in a vision, for the Divine mercy did not wish to hide from him what had happened. Therefore, when the abbot returned to the monastery, he said to him, "If you had to go in order to disperse the brethren, it were better that you had not gone to them!" Lupicinus answered him, "Be not troubled, most beloved brother, over what has happened. Know that the Lord's threshing-floor has been cleansed: only the wheat has been put in the granary, while the straw has been cast out." "May it not be," replied Romanus, "that any of them depart! But tell me, I pray, how many of them have left?" "Twelve men," answered Lupicinus, "pretentious and proud, in whom God does not dwell." Then Romanus said in tears, "I believe, in light of the Divine mercy, that He will not separate them from His treasury, but that He will gather them and regain those for whom He has deigned to suffer." And having prayed for them, he obtained their return to the grace of Almighty God. The Lord, in fact, touched their hearts and, doing penance for their defection, they each gathered together a community and founded for themselves monasteries which, until today, continue to praise God. As for Romanus, he persevered in simplicity and good works, visiting the sick and healing them by his prayer.

4. Now it happened once, while he was on the way to visit the brethren, that, overtaken by dusk, he turned aside into a little hospice for lepers. There were nine men there. Being welcomed by them, immediately, full of the love of God, he ordered water to be heated, and with his own hands he washed the feet of them all; then he had a spacious bed prepared, in order that all take their rest together in one couch, not fearing the ugly blemish of leprosy. When this had been done, as the lepers slept he kept vigil, chanting psalms; as he was so doing, he stretched out his hand and touched the side of one of the sick men, and he was at that moment cleansed. Repeating this health-giving touch, he touched another, and that one also was immediately cleansed. When they perceived that their health had been restored, each touched his neighbor in order that all might be awakened and ask of the saint their own purification. But when all had been touched in turn, they also were cleansed. When morning came, seeing them all with shining, healthy skin, Romanus gave thanks to God, bade them farewell, giving each a kiss, and went away, ordering them always to keep in their hearts and to practice in their deeds those things which were of God.

5. Once Lupicinus already old, betook himself to the King Chilperic, who at that time ruled over Burgundy, having heard that he was then in the city of Geneva. When he entered the door, the chair of the king, who at that hour was seated at a banquet, trembled. Seized with fear he said to his men,

"There has been an earthquake." Those present replied that they had felt no shock. Then the King said: "Run as quickly as possible to the door, lest perchance there be some enemy there who desires our kingdom or wishes to harm us; for not without reason has this seat been shaken." Running with haste, they found an old man clothed in animal skins; when they told the King of him, the latter said: "Go, bring him before me, that I may know what sort of man he is."

Being brought right away, Lupicinus stood before the King, as once Jacob stood before Pharoah (Gen. 47:7). Chilperic asked him, "Who are you, and where do you come from? What is your occupation? And what necessity makes you come to us? Speak up!" Lupicinus replied: "I am the father of the Lord's sheep; although the Lord arranges that they are given spiritual food by His constant aid, food for the body they sometimes lack. Wherefore we ask Your Majesty to grant them some necessities of food and clothing." Hearing these words, the King said: "Accept fields and vineyards, by which you will be able to live and satisfy your needs." But Lupicinus answered, "We will not accept fields or vineyards, but, if it please Your Majesty, assign us something of their revenue. For it is not fitting for monks to be exalted by worldly abundance, but rather to seek in humility of heart the Kingdom of God and His righteousness." When the King heard these words, he gave an order that each year they receive three hundred measures of wheat and as many of wine, in addition to one hundred gold pieces to buy clothing for the brethren. Until now, it is said, these are given over by the treasury.

6. After this, when they had become old and advanced in years — Lupicinus the abbot, that is, and Romanus his brother — Lupicinus said to his brother, "Tell me, in what monastery do you wish your tomb to be prepared, that we may repose together?" He replied, "It is impossible that I have my tomb in a monastery to which access by women is forbidden. You know indeed that, despite my unworthiness and without merit on my part, the Lord my God has granted me the gift of healing and that many, by the laying on of my hand and by the power of the Cross of the Lord, have been delivered from diverse sicknesses. Many will come to my tomb when I shall have left the light here below. That is why I ask to lie at a distance from the monastery." For this reason, when he died he was buried on a knoll ten thousand steps from the monastery. Afterwards, there was built over his tomb a large church where every day an enormous crowd gathered. And indeed many miracles are manifested there in the Name of God: the blind receive sight there, the deaf hearing, and paralytics the power of walking.

As for Abbot Lupicinus, at his death he was buried within the monastery basilica, and he thus left behind for the Lord talents multiplied from

the money loaned (Matt. 25: 16-17), that is, blessed communities of monks
devoted to His praise.

NOTES

A much fuller anonymous Life of these Saints, together with that of
their successor, St. Eugendus, has come down to us from about the year 520,
some seventy years before St. Gregory's Life *(Vita Patrum Jurensium,* Latin
text and French translation in Francois Martine, *Vie des Peres du Jura,* Sources
Chretiennes, No. 142, Paris, 1968).

St. Romanus died about 460 and is commemorated on February 28 —
the same day as St. John Cassian (in non-leap years), whose *Institutes* he
brought with him into the wilderness. St. Lupicinus died about 480 and is
commemorated on March 21.

St. Gregory's Life differs in some details from the *Vita Patrum Jurensium.* In particular, the latter states that St. Lupicinus was never married.
Perhaps St. Gregory's emphasis of St. Lupicinus as the chief abbot is owing to
the reputation which the latter acquired as sole abbot for some twenty years
after the death of St. Romanus.

The second monastery which the Saints founded is that of Laucone,
where St. Lupicinus more often resided; the third monastery is generally
thought to be Romainmoutier in Switzerland.

King Chilperic is probably the King of the Burgundians who reigned
in Geneva in 476-477; his daughter was St. Clotilde, wife of King Clovis.

The monastery of Condadisco flourished for many centuries after its
foundation. In the Middle Ages it was a wealthy landowner, and its abbots
occupied important positions in the feudal society of the West. The monastery
was secularized in the 18th century, and its holy things were desecrated in the
French Revolution. It is presently the mountain resort town of Saint-Claude.
(For its history see Paul Benoit, *Histoire de l'Abbaye et de la Terre de Saint-
Claude,* Montreuil-sur-Mer, 1890, 2 vols.)

St. Romanus was buried in the convent which the Saints established
for their sister, St. Yole (not mentioned in this Life); the site, several miles
from Condadisco, is now the village of St.-Romain-de-roche. St. Lupicinus was
buried in Laucone (now the village of St.-Lupicin). Their relics may still be
venerated in these places.

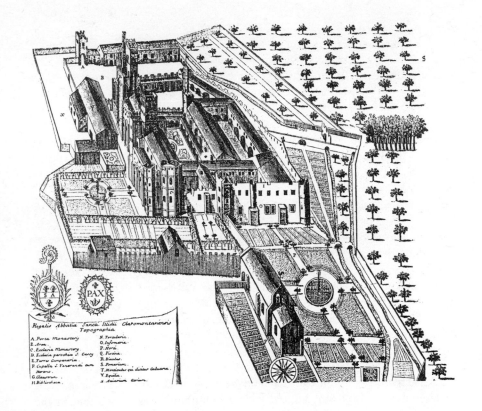

The Monastery of St. Illidius in Clermont
(destroyed in the French Revolution).
16th-century engraving from the *Monasticon Gallicorum*

2

Saint Illidius the Bishop

WONDERWORKER OF CLERMONT

Commemorated June 5 (†385)

AMONG THE SEEDS of eternal life which the heavenly sower, in the field of an untilled soul, irrigates with waters flowing from the divine source by His precepts, and which He makes fertile by His doctrine, is the one in which He tells us: *He that doth not take his cross and follow after Me, is not worthy of Me* (Matt. 10:38). And elsewhere He says: *Except a grain of wheat fall into the earth and die, it abideth by itself alone; but if it die, it beareth much fruit. He that loveth his life loseth it; and he that hateth his life in this world shall keep it unto life eternal* (John 12:24-25). Moreover, has not the Apostle Saint Paul, that vessel of election, said: *Always bearing about the body the death of Jesus, that the life also of Jesus may be manifested in our body* (II Cor. 4:10)?

Therefore, the confessors of Christ whom the time of persecution had not thrown into martyrdom, became their own persecutors in order to become worthy of God, having recourse to various crosses of abstinence; and in order to live with Him alone, they mortified themselves in their members, concerning which the Apostle says: *It is no longer I that live, but Christ liveth in me* (Gal. 2:20). And again, citing this verse of the 43rd Psalm: *For Thy sake we are killed all the day long; we were counted as sheep for the slaughter* (Rom. 8:36). For they beheld with the eyes of their inward mind the Lord of Heaven descending to earth, not brought low by humility, but humbling himself by His mercy for the redemption of the world; they beheld hanging on a cross, not the glory of the Diety, but the pure victim of the body He had assumed, of which John had foretold a little while before: *Behold the Lamb of God, that taketh away the sin of the world* (John 1:29). They had in themselves the fastening of the nails when, crucified by fear of Him and filled with terror at the Divine judgments,

173

they bore in the dwelling of their bodies nothing unworthy of His Almightiness, following these words written in Psalm 118: *Nail down my flesh with
the fear of Thee, for of Thy judgments am I afraid.*

In them also shone that brilliant light of the Resurrection, with which
the angel was resplendent when he removed the stone from the tomb, about
which mention is made in the sixteenth chapter of Mark: *And entering into
the tomb, they saw a young man sitting on the right side, arrayed in a white robe;
and they were amazed* (Mark 16:5). So Jesus also shone when He entered unexpectedly, the doors being shut, into the midst of the gathering of the Apostles, and when, after filling them with the words of life, He was raised to the
heavenly throne.

Among such ones, the blessed confessor Illidius had all things so well
placed in the tabernacle of his heart that he also was worthy to become the
temple of the Holy Spirit. Being thus about to write something on his life, I
ask the indulgence of my readers. Indeed, I have made no study of grammar, and
I have not been formed by the learned reading of the authors of the world; but
I have obeyed the entreaties of the blessed father Avitus, bishop of Clermont,*
who urged me to write works for the Church. Even though the things which I
have heard from his preaching or which he obliged me to read have not formed
my judgment — since I do not know how to fulfill them — it is he who, after
the songs of David, introduced me to the words of the preaching of the Gospel,
and then to the histories and epistles which recount the virtue of the Apostles. It is from him that I was able to acquire the knowledge of Jesus Christ, the
Son of God, Who came for the salvation of the world, and to learn to honor
with respect worthy of them His friends who took up the cross of an austere
way of life and followed the Bridegroom. And so, revealing all the boldness of
my ignorance, I am going to recount as well as possible what I have learned
concerning the blessed Illidius.

1. Saint Illidius, then, when he had commended himself by the sanctity of his perfect life and united in himself the diverse free gifts which God
had bestowed, merited — something which until then had been lacking to his
sanctity already so high — to be chosen by the God-inspired people as bishop
of the Church of Clermont and shepherd of the Lord's sheep. The renown of
his holiness, ascending by various graces, spread not only through all parts of the
territory of Auvergne, but it even passed beyond the borders of neighboring
cities. And so it happened that the report of his glory came to the ears of the

* The chief of St. Gregory's teachers in his youth; lived 517-594. See the Life of St.
Gregory above, ch. 6.

emperor at Trier,** whose daughter was possessed by an unclean spirit and suffered greatly. No one could be found who could deliver her from it, until the public rumor pointed out the blessed Illidius. Immediately the emperor sent messengers, who promptly carried out his orders and brought into the above-mentioned city the saintly old man, who was received with much respect by the prince, who was greatly grieved by the unfortunate state of his daughter. With true faith in the Lord, the bishop prostrated himself in prayer, and when he had passed an entire night in sacred hymns and spiritual songs, he placed his fingers in the young girl's mouth and expelled the evil spirit from her tormented body. The emperor, seeing this miracle, offered the holy bishop immense sums of gold and silver. The latter refused them but obtained that the city of Clermont, which was paying tribute in wheat and wine, might pay it in gold, because it was with great labor that duties in kind were transported to the public treasury. The saint, having fulfilled the time of this present life, died, as it is said, on this same journey in order to go to Christ. Borne up by his own people, he was buried in his city.

2. And perhaps — as men are very often wont to murmur — someone will babble, saying, "It is impossible that for the working of a single miracle this man should be numbered among the saints." Yet if one weighs well what the Lord has said in the Gospel — *Many will say to Me in that day, Lord, Lord, did we not cast out demons by Thy name, and do many miracles? And then I will profess unto them, I never knew you* (Matt. 7:22-23) — then surely one will say that the virtue that comes forth from the tomb is more praiseworthy than that which one has brought forth while alive in the world; for the latter may have some blemish by the continual hindrances of worldly occupations, whereas the former is free from all stain.

Since, then, as we believe, the things done by Saint Illidius before that time have been given up to oblivion and have not come to our notice, we shall recount what we have seen with our own eyes, what we have put to the test, or what we have learned from persons worthy of credence.

At the time when Bishop Gallus* governed the Church of Clermont, he who writes these things was still young and fell gravely ill; he was often visited by the bishop, who loved him dearly, being his uncle. His stomach was filled with a great quantity of liquid, and he was seized with a high fever. Then there came to the child a desire, which I believe came from God, to have

---

** Trier (or Treves) in the north of Gaul, was known as the "Rome beyond the Alps," the second city of the Empire in the West and the frequent residence of the Roman emperors in the 4th century. The emperor in question here was Maximus, who ruled in the West from 384.

* His life is chapter six of *Vita Patrum.*

himself carried to the basilica of blessed Illidius. And when he had been carried on the arms of servants to the saint's tomb and had prayed with tears, he felt himself better than when he had come; but upon returning to his house, he was seized anew by the fever.

Now one day, when he began to be worse and the fever was afflicting him more than usual, to the point where it was doubted that he would recover from it, his mother came to him and said, "Today, my sweet son, I shall have a sad day, since you have such a high fever." And he answered, "Do not think, I beg you, of any sadness, but send me back to the tomb of the blessed bishop Illidius; for I believe, and it is my faith, that his virtue will gain for you joy, and for me health." Then, having been carried to the saint's tomb, he made a prayer prostrate to the Lord that if he were delivered from his illness by the intercession of His bishop, he would become a cleric, and that he would leave there only if his prayer obtained its object. No sooner had he spoken thus than he felt the fever leave him immediately, and calling the servants, he asked to be taken back home. There he was placed on a bed, and while they were at table, he had a great nosebleed, and the fever came to an end with the flow of blood: which certainly happened by the merits of the blessed confessor. Recently, also, a servant of Count Venerandus, after having been blind a long time, kept vigil near the saint's tomb and returned from it healed.

3. As for what took place on the subject of his relics, here is what the above-mentioned writer** saw with his own eyes. In the first year of his episcopate (573 A.D.), he had dedicated, below the episcopal residence in Tours, an oratory in which he placed some relics of this holy bishop together with those of other saints.* Many days after the dedication, he was advised by the abbot to visit the relics which he had placed in the altar-table, lest by the dampness of the new building they be given over to corruption. Having found them damp, he took them up from the altar-table and began to dry them by the fire. Then he put them back in their own containers and came to the relics of the blessed bishop Illidius. As he held them before the fire, the thread by which they were held, because it was too long, fell on the glowing coals, and like copper or iron began to glow from the fire's heat. And although he took little notice what became of the thread by which the holy relics had been held, thinking it already to have been reduced to ashes, he discovered it whole and unharmed, because it had served a little while before as a bond for the glorious hierarch.

** That is St. Gregory himself.
* For a description of this event, see the Life of St. Gregory, ch. 25.

4. There was an infant about ten months old who was accepted as being — and it was recognized as true — a great-grandnephew of the blessed one himself; this infant was afflicted with the approach of a grievous sickness. His mother was weeping, not as much over the death of her child, as that he had not yet received the Divine sacrament of Baptism. Finally, having taken counsel, she betook herself to the tomb of the blessed confessor, placed on the stone the sick child who had scarcely a breath left in him, and did not cease to keep vigil and pray over the tomb.

Now when the bird that announces the light had chanted more loudly than usual, flapping his wings, the infant who had remained stretched out and nearly dead regained his strength. Showing by a smile the joy of his heart, he opened his mouth by means of the Divine assistance and calling his mother said, "Come here." But she, filled with fear and joy — for she had never before heard her son's voice — stood dumbfounded. "What do you want, my sweetest child?" He answered, "Run as fast as you can and bring me a cup of water." But she remained unmoving in prayer until the coming of day, giving thanks to the holy bishop and consecrating her son to him; then she returned home. The infant drank the water offered to him, and delivered from all infirmity, fully recovered his health. Then, returning to the first cries of infancy, he could no longer speak until he had attained the age at which infants' tongues are usually loosened for speech.

I do not think I ought any longer to pass over in silence what happened at the time when an oven was lit to bake the lime for the basilica. The lintel, which held solidly in place the entrance of the oven, broke while those who were there together with the abbot of the place were sleeping. Immediately there appeared to the abbot a bishop who said to him, "Hasten to wake up those who are sleeping, lest the ruin of the house which is threatening overtake them. The lintel which holds the mass of the stones is on the point of falling with the fire." The abbot awoke, made everyone run from the entrance of the oven, and the mass of stones fell on both sides without injuring any of those present — which would not have occurred, I think, wihout the bishop's intervention. Then the abbot, after making prayer over the saint's tomb, had the lintel repaired and the stones replaced, and they could finish, thanks to the bishop's help, the work which had been begun.

The blessed body of the confessor was of old buried in a vault, but since the building was narrow and difficult of entry, Saint Avitus, bishop of the city, had an apse made in circular form and of admirable workmanship, and having gathered the blessed limbs which he found in a coffin made of wood, he enclosed them according to custom in a sarcophagus. In that place reposes one who was Justus (just) both by merits and name, who is said to have been the glorious hierarch's archdeacon.

5. There are reported of the same saint many other miracles which I have judged too long to recount, thinking what I have said to suffice for a perfect faith; for many things will not be of use to him for whom this little does not suffice. Indeed, at his tomb the blind see, demons are cast out, the deaf recover their hearing, and the lame the use of their limbs, by the grace of our Lord Jesus Christ, who promises to those who have faith that He will grant them all that they ask for without doubt in the success of their prayers.

NOTES

St. Illidius (*Allyre* in French) was the fourth bishop of Clermont. He died probably in 385, on June 5, on which day his feast is celebrated.

The tomb of the daughter of Emperor Maximus was preserved in the Abbey of St. Illidius at least until 1311, in which year it was uncovered by the (Roman Catholic) bishop of the city together with an inscription which testified to her healing by St. Illidius.

The Abbey of St. Illidius in the city of Clermont-Ferrand, where the saint's relics were kept, was destroyed in the French Revolution.

3

Saint Abraham the Abbot

N O ORTHODOX CHRISTIAN, I think, is ignorant of what God says in the Gospel: *Verily I say unto you, that whosoever shall say unto this mountain, Be thou removed and be thou cast into the sea, and shall not doubt in his heart, but shall believe that those things which he saith will come to pass, he shall have whatsoever he saith* (Mark 11:23-24). Thus, there is no doubt that saints can obtain from the Lord what they ask, because the faith which is in them is firm, and they are not shaken by the wave of hesitations. And for that faith, not only have they been exiles within their own land, because they desired to arrive at the heavenly life, but they have gone as well into foreign lands across the sea, in order the more to please Him to Whom they have vowed themselves.

Such in our time was the blessed Abraham the Abbot, who, after many temptations of the world, entered the territory of Auvergne. And it is not without reason that he is compared for the greatness of his faith to that ancient Abraham to whom God once said: *Depart from your own land and your kindred and go into the land which I will show thee* (Gen. 12:1). Hence he left not only his own land, but even the life of the old man, and he put on the new man, which was formed according to God in justice, holiness, and truth. That is why, when he was found perfect in God's work, he did not hesitate in his faith to seek what he had confidence to obtain by a holy life; and through him the Maker of heaven, sea, and land vouchsafed to work miracles, few in number, it is true, but worthy of admiration.

179

1. This Abraham, then, was born near the banks of the Euphrates where, advancing in the work of God, he conceived the desire to betake himself to the solitudes of Egypt to visit the hermits. On the way he was seized by pagans and put in bonds, receiving a great number of blows for the name of Christ. He was in irons for five years with much joy until he was freed by an angel. Also wishing to visit the lands of the West, he came to Clermont and there established a monastery near the basilica of Saint Cyricus. By a wondrous power he cast out demons, gave light to the blind, and was a most powerful healer of other maladies.

Thus, when the feast of the above-mentioned basilica had come, he told the steward to prepare in the courtyard, according to custom, the vessels full of wine for the refreshment of the people who had come to the solemnity. The monk excused himself, saying, "Behold how we have to receive the bishop with the duke and the citizens, and scarcely four amphoras of wine remain to us. How are you going to satisfy them all with so little?" And he answered: "Open the cellar for me."

This done, he went in, and like a new Elias, he raised his hands to heaven in prayer, and with eyes full of tears said: "O Lord, I pray Thee that the wine fail not in this vessel until all be served from it in abundance." And being filled with the Holy Spirit, he said: "Thus saith the Lord: The wine will not fail in the vessel, but it will be given freely to all who ask for it, and there shall remain some."

And according to his word, it was served freely to the whole people, who drank it with joy, and there remained some left over. Since the steward had measured the vessel beforehand, and found that there were but four palms in it, he measured it again the next day, after seeing what had taken place, and found in the vessel as much as there had been the day before.

Thus was made manifest to the people the virtue of the Saint, who at length died, full of days, in that monastery, where he was buried with honor. At that time Saint Sidonius was bishop, and the duke was Victorius, who was ruler over seven cities by leave of the Gothic King Euric.

The blessed Sidonius wrote the epitaph of the Saint, wherein he speaks of some of the things we have just related:

"Abraham, worthy to stand beside the celestial patrons whom I shall not fear to call thy colleagues, since they are gone before on the path which thou shalt follow; a share in the martyrs' glory gives a share in the Kingdom of Heaven. Born by Euphrates, for Christ thou didst endure the prison, chains, and hunger for five long years. From the cruel king of Susa* thou didst fly, escaping alone to the distant land of the West. Marvels born of his holiness followed the steps of the confessor; thyself a fugitive, thou didst put to flight the spirits of evil. Wherever thy footsteps passed, the throng of Lemures cried surrender; the exile's voice bade the demons go forth into banishment. All sought thee, yet didst thou yield to no vain ambition; the honors acceptable in thy sight were those that brought the heaviest burdens. Thou didst shun the tumult of Rome and of Byzantium, and the walls of the city that warlike Titus breached (Jerusalem). Not Alexandria held thee, not Antioch; thou spurnedst Byrsa (Carthage), the famed home of Dido. Thou didst disdain the populous lands of Ravenna by the marshes, and the city named from the wooly swine (Milan). But this corner of earth was pleasing to thee, this poor retreat, this hut roofed with reeds. Here didst thou rear a sacred house to God, thou whose own frame was already itself His temple. Here ended thy wanderings, here thy life's course; now thy labors are rewarded by a twofold crown. Now dost thou stand in Paradise amid the thousands of the Saints, with Abraham for thy fellow wanderer. Now art thou entered into thine own land, from which Adam fell; now lies thy way clear to the sources of thy native stream."**

Several of those sick of fever have been healed at the tomb of blessed Abraham by the aid of heavenly remedies.

NOTES

St. Abraham died in 477, on June 15, when his memory is kept.

The funeral inscription by St. Sidonius, Bishop of Clermont, as quoted above has been taken from *The Letters of Sidonius,* translated by O. M. Dalton, Oxford, 1915, vol. II, pp. 134-5. This same letter of St. Sidonius contains his instructions to his friend Volusianus (later bishop of Tours) concerning the good order of St. Abraham's monastery after his death:

"With these lines I have paid, as you desired, the last observance due to him who is now laid to rest. But if it is the duty of those who yet live, of brothers, friends and comrades, to obey the commands of brotherly affection, I shall make you a request in my turn: I would beg you to use the principles with which you are so eminently endowed for the consolation of the dead man's fol-

---

*The Persian Sassanian King Yezdegerd, whose great persecution began in 420 and lasted for thirty years.
**I.e., the river Euphrates, traditionally one of the rivers of Paradise.

lowers; confirm by the discipline of Lerins or of Grigny* the shaken rule of a brotherhood now cast adrift without a leader. If you find any insubordinate, see to it in person that they are punished; if any obedient, give them praise from your own lips. The holy Auxanius is presumed to be their head; but he, as you well know, is too infirm of body and of too diffident a character, and more fitted to obey than to command. He himself insists that you should be called in, that in succeeding to the headship of the house, he may have the support of your overheadship; for if any of the younger monks should treat him with disrespect, as one lacking alike in courage and experience, thanks to you, a joint rule would not be slighted with impunity. I say no more. If you would have my wishes in a few words, they are these: I desire brother Auxanius to be abbot over the rest, and you yourself to be above the abbot. Farewell." *(The Letters of Sidonius, p. 136.)*

It may well be assumed that St. Abraham's monastery, in view of the "Eastern" orientation of Gallic monasticism in the 5th century, and especially of the Saint's own Eastern origin and travels, was modelled on the eremetic lavras of the East, just as was the monastery of Condadisco founded by St. Abraham's contemporaries, Sts. Romanus and Lupicinus (see chapter one). St. Sidonius' description of the Saint's "poor retreat, this hut roofed with reeds," indicate a monastery of separate huts, like Condadisco or St. Martin's monastery near Tours. The above instructions of St. Sidonius probably represent the beginning of the tendency towards "Western" organization and coenobitism which also transformed Condadisco into a coenobitic monastery early in the 6th century.

The Monastery of Saint Cyricus (named for a martyr of Antioch — *Saint-Cirgues* in French) remained as a priory until 1793, when it was sold as public property by the Revolutionary government.

The tomb of St. Abraham was preserved in the basilica of St. Cyricus until the 10th century, but then was forgotten. Its site was rediscovered in 1684, when miracles again began to flow from prayers to the Saint. In 1761 the stone tomb itself was uncovered, and in 1804 the skeleton of St. Abraham was transferred to the parish church of St. Eutrope. Part of the walls of the ancient basilica still remain as part of the marketplace located between the rues Saint-Cirgues, Fontgieve, and La Place Fayolle, in the city of Clermont-Ferrand, less than half a mile southwest of the site of the basilica of St. Illidius (chapter two).

*The early monastery located at Grigny on the Rhone river near Vienne.

4

Saint Quintianus the Bishop

EXAMPLE OF CHRISTIAN CONSTANCY AND LOVE
IN A TIME OF CONFUSION

Commemorated November 13 (†525)

E VERYONE WHO KNOWS that he possesses a body of earthly mat-
ter must so conduct himself as not to give himself over to those things which he
knows to be earthly and sweet to the flesh, because, according to the Apostle
Paul, *the works of the flesh are manifest* (Gal. 5:19) as being full of impurity
and iniquity, fit to make the man who seeks them soiled and dirty, and at last
to give him over to eternal weeping. Now the fruit of the Spirit is all that which
is profitable and flourishing in God, all that which in this age, by the mortification of the flesh, rejoices the soul and assures it of eternal joys for the future
age.

For this reason, we who are now in the body ought to consider for ourselves what God has accomplished in His saints, in whom — as in a tabernacle
adorned with various flowers of virtue which their merits make to shine with a
vivid brilliance, establishing His abode and stretching forth the majesty of His
right arm in them — He has vouchsafed in His mercy to accomplish what they
have asked, as we may see in blessed Quintianus, about whom we are now going
to speak. He was a man of noble mind and remarkable for generosity, in whom
the Lord has accomplished the works of His justice. So then, let not the following of the flesh lower us and draw us to earthly things after the manner of cat-
tle, but rather, after the example of the saints, wisely understanding the
things of God, let the Spirit raise us toward heavenly and eternal works; neither
let our mind be conquered by impure acts, but let victorious wisdom reign and
for our deeds gain the throne of eternity.

183

1. The most blessed Quintianus, an African by nation, and, as some say, a nephew of Bishop Faustus, who, it is related, resurrected his mother — this Quintianus was endowed with sanctity, resplendent with virtues, fervent with the fire of Christian love, and adorned with the flowers of chastity. He was elected to the bishopric of Rodez and was ordained. In this episcopate his virtues underwent a new growth, and, as he was always advancing in the works of God, he had the holy body of the blessed bishop Amantius brought into the church he had built in his name; but such a deed did not please the Saint. Whereupon it happened that he appeared to him in a dream and said: "Because you have done this brazen thing and displaced my bones which were resting in peace, behold, I will remove you from this city, and you will be an exile in another land; nevertheless, you will not be deprived of the honor which you enjoy."

And in fact, not long after that a scandal arose between the citizens and the bishop, and the Goths who were then in the city conceived the suspicion that the bishop wished to submit to the authority of the Franks; having taken counsel together, they had the thought of slaying him with the sword. When this was made known to the holy man, he rose during the night, and leaving the city with his most faithful servants, he came to Clermont in the Auvergne. There he was received by the holy Bishop Eufrasius, who had succeeded the late Bishop Aprunculus, and who gave him houses, fields, and vineyards. He was treated with the greatest respect by that bishop and by the bishop of Lyons. He was indeed a venerable old man and a true servant of God.

Now when Saint Eufrasius died (515 A.D.), the people elected in his place Saint Quintianus. Alchima and Placidana, the wife and sister of Apollinaris,* went to Saint Quintianus and said: "It should be enough for you in your old age, holy prelate, that you have already been appointed to one bishopric. Won't you, who are so pious, allow your servant Apollinaris to occupy the episcopate here? If he does gain this high honor, he will obey your command in all things. You will give orders, and he will execute your wishes. Please listen sympathetically to this humble proposal of ours."

"What can I do for you," asked Quintianus, "I who have no control whatever over this election? I certainly ask nothing more than that the Church should give me enough to eat each day, so that I may devote myself to prayer."

When they had heard this reply, the two women sent Apollinaris to King Theoderic.** He took many gifts with him, and he was given the bishop-

---

*The son of St. Sidonius Appollinaris, who had been Bishop of Clermont from 472 to 488.
**A Frank, one of the four sons of King Clovis who divided the latter's kingdom on his death in 511.

ric. When he had been bishop for only four months, he died.***

When this was made known to King Theoderic, he ordered Saint Quintianus to be bishop in place of Apollinaris and all the authority of the Church to be given over to him, saying, "It was because of the zeal of his love for us that he was cast out from his own city."

Messengers were sent to Clermont. The local bishops and the townsfolk were called together, and they elected Quintianus to the bishopric of the city, where he was the fourteenth prelate to rule the diocese.*

After this, when Saint Quintianus was bishop in that city, a certain Proculus, who had been ordained priest for money, gave him many injuries, and taking away from him all power over the Church's goods, scarcely left him enough for his daily needs. But when the bishop entreated the wiser citizens regarding this, all his authority was returned to him, and he kept such snares at a distance from him. Remembering, nevertheless, the injuries he had received, as aforetime the Apostle Paul regarding Alexander, so also Quintianus whenever speaking of Proculus said, "Proculus the publican did me much harm; the Lord will requite him according to his deeds" (compare II Timothy 4:14). This indeed came to pass in what followed.

2. The blessed man was assiduous in prayer, and he loved his people so much that when Theodoric came with his army to besiege the city (525 A.D.), the Saint of God spent the night in psalmody, going about the walls; and in order that God would quickly vouchsafe to succor the land and its people he prayed earnestly with vigils and fasting. The king Theodoric, just when he thought to throw down the city's walls, was softened by the Lord's mercy and by the prayers of His priest whom the king was thinking to send into exile. And during the night, seized with fear, he leapt from his bed and strove to flee alone by the public highway. He had lost his wits and no longer knew what he was doing. When his men saw this, they tried to restrain him, and did so only with difficulty, exhorting him to fortify himself with the saving sign of the Cross. Then Hilpingus, one of his dukes, drew near to the king and said, "Listen, most glorious king, to the counsels of my littleness. See, the walls of that city are very strong, and great fortifications defend it. And in order that Your Majesty recognize this more fully, I need only to speak of the churches of the saints which are about the city's walls; further, the bishop of this place is great before God. Do not do what you have in mind; do no evil to the bishop, and do not

---

***These three paragraphs have been added from *The History of the Franks* (III, 2), where St. Gregory speaks of these things in greater detail than in *The Life of the Fathers*.
* This paragraph has also been added from *The History of the Franks*, III, 2.

destroy the city." The king received this counsel favorably and gave the order that no one be harmed within eight miles of the city. No one doubted that this was granted by the prayer of the holy Bishop.

Then too, when the walls of the fortress of Vollore were broken by the incoming troops, the priest Proculus was hacked to pieces by the sword before the altar of the church, and the Lord thus requited him according to his deeds, as the bishop was wont to say. I should not be surprised if it were Proculus' fault that the fortress was allowed to fall into enemy hands, for until then it had always been inviolate.*

3. After the massacre and desolation of Clermont, Hortensius, one of the senators who was acting as count of the city, had one of the Saint's relatives, Honoratus by name, unjustly detained in the street. This was immediately made known to the blessed man. Through his friends he requested the count to grant an audience and to order him released, but he gained nothing. Then the blessed old man had himself taken to the place where Honoratus was being held, and when he was announced he begged the soldiers to let him go; but they, full of fear, dared not obey the Bishop. "Then quickly take me to the house of Hortensius" — for he was very old and could not walk. His servants carried him to the house of Hortensius, where he shook off against it the dust from his sandals, saying, "Cursed be this house, cursed also forever those who dwell in it; may it become deserted, and may there be no one to live in it." And all the people said, "Amen." And he added, "I ask, O Lord, that no one of this family, which has not obeyed its bishop, be raised to the episcopal dignity."

And as soon as the bishop had retired, all those of the family who were in that house were stricken with fever, and after being sick for a short time they gave up the ghost. When this had lasted for three days, Hortensius, seeing none of his servants survive, feared lest he perish himself, and went in mourning to the holy man and cast himself at his feet, begging his pardon with tears. The Saint granted it to him indulgently and sent holy water to the house; when it was thrown on the walls, immediately the sickness went away and great power appeared there. Those who had been afflicted were healed, and those who were healthly did not become sick later.**

At that time there was a local official called Lytigius who kept plotting against Saint Quintianus. The holy bishop went so far as to demean himself at

---

*This last sentence has been added from St. Gregory's words in *The History of the Franks,* III, 13.

**However, St. Gregory notes in another place that "the pronouncement which God had made through the mouth of St. Quintianus could not be changed," and no one of this family was ever made bishop, even when they were considered for this position. (See *The History of the Franks,* IV, 35.)

this man's feet, but even then Lytigius showed him no respect. In fact, he once went so far as to make fun of the Bishop to his wife. She had more sense than her husband. "Quintianus may be humbled today," she said, "but that will never do you any good." Only three days later messengers arrived from the king's court. Lytigius was bound and dragged off with his wife and children. He disappeared and was never seen again in Clermont.***

4. This holy bishop was very learned in ecclesiastical writings, and also generous in almsgiving. Indeed, whenever he would hear a poor man cry out, he would say, "Help, I beg you, this poor man and give him everything needful. For you do not know, O heedless ones, whether this is not the very One Who has commanded in His Gospel that He be taken care of in the person of the least of the poor ones" (Matt. 25:40).

He also cast out demons, who would confess their evil actions. Having come into the monastery of Canbidobrinse (in the diocese of Clermont), he found there a possessed man who was prey to horrible convulsions, and he sent priests to lay their hands on him. But when their exorcism was unable to cast out the demon, the Saint of God drew near, and having put his fingers in the man's mouth, he delivered him. The blessed man performed many other miracles, and by his prayers he often obtained what he asked for from the Lord.

Once a severe drought laid waste the fields of Auvergne, and, as the grass was dried up, there was no forage for the stock. At this time God's Saint was devoutly celebrating the Rogations before the Ascension of the Lord. On the third day, as the procession was already approaching the city gate, he was asked to intone the antiphon, with these words: "Blessed hierarch, if you devoutly intone the antiphon, we have such confidence in your holiness that we believe the Lord will immediately in His clemency vouchsafe to grant us an abundant rain." The holy Bishop prostrated himself on his hair-shirt in the middle of the road and prayed for a very long time with tears. Then he arose and intoned with all his strength the antiphon which they had requested, the words of which were drawn from the prayer of Solomon, as follows: *If heaven is shut and there is no rain because of the sins of the people, and turning to Thee they pray unto Thee, hear, O Lord, and remit the sins of Thy people, and give rain to the earth which Thou hast given to Thy people for an inheritance* (II Chronicles 6:26-27). And when they began to sing most devoutly, the humble prayer of the confessor penetrated even unto the ears of the Divine Majesty; and behold, the heavens grew dark and were covered with clouds, and before they had arrived

***This paragraph has been added from *The History of the Franks,* III, 13.

at the gate of the city, there fell a heavy rain on all the land, so that all wondered and said that this was due to the blessed man's prayers.

5. Finally the priest of God grew old, to the point where he had not the strength to spit on the ground, but put a handkerchief to his mouth to wipe it. Even so, his eyes were not darkened, and his heart did not abandon the ways of God. He never turned away his face from the poor; he never feared the mighty man; but he always had in everything a holy liberty, so that he received a poor man's cloak with as much respect as if he had received an illustrious senator's toga. He died perfected in holiness and was buried in the basilica of Saint Stephen, to the left of the altar. Frequently, even now, at his tomb those with quartan fever are helped and their sadness alleviated.

NOTES

Saint Quintianus died about the year 525, on November 13, on which day his feast is kept. He signed the Acts of the Councils of Agde (506) and Orleans (511) in Gaul, as Bishop of Rodez (*Rutena* in Latin).

The historical background of St. Quintianus' life is set forth by St. Gregory in *The History of the Franks,* Book II, chapters 35, 36, and 37, and Book III, chapters 11, 12, and 13. At this time there was intense rivalry between the Franks under the newly-baptized King Clovis, and the Goths under Alaric II. The Franks defeated the Goths in many battles, and in the battle of Vouille near Poitiers (507) Clovis gained a great victory and killed Alaric. St. Quintianus, living under Gothic rule, was suspected of being friendly with the Franks, all the more in that he, like Clovis, was Orthodox, while the Goths were Arians.

With the advance of Frankish power, St. Quintianus came into favor with the Frankish King Theodoric, son of Clovis. Later, however, Theodoric evidently forgot this friendship when he was besieging Clermont. The conflicts of this time were largely inspired by the rivalries of the various still-barbarian kings; only gradually was the land of Gaul enlightened by Orthodox Christianity, whose roots became very deep.

The "Rogations" mentioned in this Life were first instituted by St. Mamertus, Bishop of Vienne (near Lyons) in the 5th century, at a time when, during Great Lent and the season of Pascha, the city was shaken by earthquakes and the attacks of wild beasts. They consisted of fasting, almsgiving, and special prayers with a religious procession (see *The History of the Franks,* II,

34). This custom quickly spread to the rest of Gaul, where it was celebrated just before the Feast of the Ascension.

The Church of St. Stephen, where St. Quintianus' body was placed, was built outside the walls of Clermont in the middle of the 5th century by the widow of Bishop Namatius of Clermont. In *The History of the Franks* (II, 17), St. Gregory describes how she had this church adorned with iconographic frescoes. The relics of St. Quintianus were later transferred to the church of St.-Symphorien-et-Saint-Genes, where they were still venerated as late as the 17th century. They have not been heard of since the French Revolution.

ST. POR-
TIANUS

5

Saint Portianus the Abbot

EARTHLY SLAVE WHO INHERITED
THE HEAVENLY KINGDOM

Commemorated November 24 (†527)

WHAT GOOD THINGS Almighty God grants in His name to those who faithfully consecrated themselves to His service in good works! He promises them great rewards in heaven, but often, too, He lets them know in this life what they will receive. For often He sets slaves free and makes those who are free glorious, as was said by the Psalm-writer: *Who raised up the poor man from the earth, and from the dunghill lifted up the pauper, that He may seat him with the princes of His people* (Ps. 112: 6-7). About this, Hannah the wife of Elkanah said, *They that before were full have hired out themselves for bread, and they that were hungry have ceased to hunger* (I Sam. 2:5—I Kings in the *Septuagint*). And concerning this the Virgin Mary, the very Mother of our Redeemer, said, *He hath put down the mighty from their seats, and exalted them of low degree* (Luke 1:52). And the Lord Himself said in the Gospel: *The last shall be first and the first last* (Matt. 20:16). Thus, may the Divine mercy shine forth with His love upon the poor, so that it may make great ones from the little, and that from the weak it may make co-inheritors with His Only-begotten Son. For it exalts the poverty of this world to heaven, to which the earthly kingdom cannot rise, so that the rustic comes to the place where he who wears the purple does not merit to come.

Such was the case with the blessed abbot Portianus, whom the Lord not only freed from the burden of worldly bondage, but whom He also glorified with great virtues and whom He established in eternal repose after the affairs and afflictions of this life, placing him among the choirs of angels, from which the prince of this world was expelled.

191

1. The most blessed Portianus, then, from the beginning of his life, always sought after the God of Heaven, even in earthly servitude. And in fact, they say that he was the slave of a certain barbarian, and that several times he took refuge in a monastery so that the abbot might stand on his behalf before his master. In the end he took to flight; his master followed in his track and began assailing the abbot of the monastery, accusing him of enticing his servant and withdrawing him from his service. And when, according to custom, he pressed the abbot with accusation to give him back, the abbot said to Portianus: "What do you want me to do?" "Have me pardoned," he replied.

When he was pardoned and his master wished to take him back to the house, he became so blind that he was no longer able to recognize anything. Feeling himself to be afflicted by great pains, he called the abbot and said, "I beg you, entreat the Lord for me, and take this servant for your own service; perhaps I shall regain the light I have lost." Then the abbot called the blessed one and said, "Lay your hands, I beg you, on that man's eyes." And when he refused, the abbot so begged him that he made the sign of the Cross over his master's eyes, and immediately all darkness was dissipated and the pain was eased, and he was returned to his former health.

Thereafter the blessed Portianus was made a cleric, and he displayed such virtue that when the abbot died he succeeded him. It is said of him that during the summer, when the sun's brightness sapped the strength of all by the power of its heat, and even fatigued the bodies of those who from food and drink were more robust, Portianus, who as a result of fasting no longer had moisture in his mouth, would chew salt, which would moisten his parched gums for a little while. And, although he moistened his dry palate by this, nevertheless he added to his bodily torment by increasing his thirst. For as everyone knows, salt increases the burning of thirst rather than extinguishes it; but, by God's gift, he was delivered from it.

2. In those days Theoderic came into the territory of Auvergne and was destroying and ravaging everything. When he had encamped in the fields of the village of Arthone, the blessed Portianus, an old man, hastened to come before him in order to intercede for the people. And coming into the camp in the morning, while the king was still sleeping in his tent, he went to the tent of Sigivald, who was Theoderic's aide-de-camp. And when he pleaded for the release of the captives, Sigivald implored him to wash his hands and take some wine with him, saying, "The Divine mercy will have granted me today a great joy and benefit, if having entered my tent you will deign to drink my wine after praying." For he had heard of that man's

holiness, and that is why, out of respect for God, he had shown him this honor. But the Saint excused himself in various ways and said that this could not be, because the proper hour for eating had not come, because he had not presented himself before the king's majesty, and, most importantly, because he had not yet chanted the Psalms he owed to the Lord. But Sigivald, disregarding all that, constrained him, and when a cup was brought, he bade the Saint to bless it first with his hand. When he raised his hand to make the sign of the Cross, the cup broke down the middle and the wine spilled on the ground together with a huge snake.   Those who were present were filled with fear and cast themselves at the blessed man's feet, licking his footsteps and kissing his feet. All wondered at the old man's virtue; all marvelled at having been divinely preserved from the venom of the serpent. The whole army ran to see such a miracle, and the whole crowd of them surrounded the blessed man, each one wishing only to touch with his hand the fringes of his garment, if he could not honor him with a kiss. The king leapt from his bed and ran to the blessed confessor, and, without waiting for him to say a word, freed all the captives he had asked for and all the others he might wish thereafter. Thus, by the grace of God, he received a double benefit, rescuing some from death and others from the yoke of bondage. Truly, I believe, and it is my faith, that in a manner of speaking he brought back from the dead those who were saved from danger.

3. I do not wish to pass over how the devil, trying to deceive him by various machinations, but seeing he could not harm him, marched against him in open combat. Thus, one night, when he was sleeping, suddenly he awoke and saw his cell as if it were all on fire. Rising in fright, he sought the door. Not being able to open it, he prostrated himself in prayer; then when he had made before and around him the saving sign (of the Cross), the phantom flames which had appeared immediately vanished, and he knew that this was a deception of the devil. This was immediately revealed to the blessed Protasius, who was then a recluse in the monastery of Canbidobrense and who sent in all haste a monk from his cell to his brother in order to exhort him and to say, "You must, most beloved brother, manfully resist the devil's attacks and fear nothing of his knavery, but overcome all he sends against you with continual prayer and the sign of the Cross, because he always tries to conquer God's servants with temptations of this kind."

The blessed man grew old, and having fulfilled his course of good works, he departed to the Lord. His tomb is still glorified often with Divine power. This much we know of the holy man, but we do not judge those who know more about him, if they wish to write something in his praise.

NOTES

Saint Portianus (*Saint-Pourcain* in French) died about 527 and is commemorated on November 24.

The Monastery of Saint Portianus formed the beginning of the town of Saint-Pourcain, about forty miles north of Clermont. The monastery survived until the French Revolution; the Romanesque church of the Holy Cross is all that remains of the monastery today.

The incident when the blessed hermit Protasius (also commemorated on November 24) sent word of exhortation to St. Portianus concerning the deceptions of the devil recalls an incident in the 14th-century life of St. Paul of Obnora, when his spiritual father, St. Sergius of Nurma, told him that the seeming destruction of his cell was not a reality, but only a deceptive phantom of the demons (see *The Northern Thebaid*, St. Herman Brotherhood, 1975, p. 40).

———————————

6

Saint Gallus the Bishop

A SENATOR'S SON WHO FORSOOK THE WORLD
AND GAINED THE HEAVENS

Commemorated July 1 (†551)

THOSE WHO ARE at the summit of worldly nobility always aspire ardently for that which can satisfy their passions: they rejoice in honors, are puffed up with prosperity, agitate the courts with legal actions, live by theft, take pleasure in slanders, avidly desire gold which tarnishes—and when they have a little of it they are inflamed with the desire to amass more, and the more they accumulate the more their thirst increases, as Prudentius* says "For the hunger for gold is increased by gold."

Whence it happens that while they rejoice in the pomps of this world and are charmed by vain honors, they keep nothing in mind of those worthwhile things which are to endure, and they do not consider the things which are not seen, as long as they possess to their harm those things which they think can satisfy their souls. But there are those who, like birds escaping from a trap and rising up on high, have freed themselves by the disposition of a more animated spirit. Forsaking and despising earthly goods, they have turned with all their might toward heavenly things.

Such a one was Saint Gallus, an inhabitant of the city of Clermont, who could be turned away from the worship of God neither by the splendor of his birth, nor by the height of the senatorial rank, nor by his immense wealth; who could be separated from the love of God neither by the affection of his father, nor by the tenderness of his mother, nor by the love of those who had nursed him, nor by the obedience of his servants. But considering all

---

* The 4th-century Christian poet.

these things as nothing, and scorning them as dung, cherishing God and vow-
ing himself to His service, he submitted to the monastic rule; for he knew
that the flames of ardent youth could not be overcome except by submission
to lawful reprimand and the severest discipline. He knew also that he had to
raise himself from the baseness of the world to higher things and to attain by
patience to the height of glory, which later came to pass.

1. Saint Gallus was devoted to God from childhood; he loved the
Lord with all his soul and cherished all those things he knew to be beloved
of God. His father's name was Georgius, and his mother's Leocadia, of the
lineage of Vectius Epagatus, who suffered martyrdom at Lyons, according to
Eusebius in his *History (of the Church)*.* Hence they were among the
principal senators, so that no one was found in Gaul more generous or nobler.
And although his father wished to look for a daughter of some noble senator
for him, he went away with a young servant and retired to the monastery of
Crononense, six miles from the city of Clermont, humbly asking the abbot
that he would deign to tonsure him. This abbot, seeing the prudence and
comeliness of the youth, asked his name, his family, and his country. He
answered that he was called Gallus, a citizen of Clermont, and was a son of
the senator Georgius. When the abbot found out that he belonged to the first
family of the city, he said: "You desire well, my son, but first this matter
must come to your father's notice, and if he consents to it I will do what you
desire." Then the abbot sent to his father to ask him what he commanded to
be done regarding his son. His father, a little saddened, said, "He was my
first-born son, and therefore I wished him to be joined in marriage; but if the
Lord has vouchsafed to join him to His service, may His will be done rather
than mine." And he added, "Do whatever the boy asks of you by the inspiration of God."

2. Then the abbot, learning these things from those whom he had
sent, made the boy a cleric. He was perfectly chaste, and even as he had no
unseemly desires when older, so then also he abstained from youthful exuber-
ance. His voice was of a marvellous sweetness; he sang pleasingly, continually
applied himself to his studies, delighted in fasting, and abstained much from
food. When the blessed bishop Quintianus came to that same monastery and
heard him sing, he did not allow him to remain there longer, but took him
with himself to the city and brought him up, like a heavenly father, in the
sweetness of spiritual life.

---

* Book V, 1; Vectius Epagatus was martyred in 177 A.D.

After his father had died, since his voice improved more and more with the coming of each day and he enjoyed the greatest esteem among the people, King Theoderic was informed of him, and he had the youth brought right away and took such a liking to him that he loved him more than his own son. The queen also cherished him with a similar love, not only because of the beauty of his voice but also because of his bodily chastity. At that time King Theoderic took from Clermont many clerics, whom he ordered to the service of the Lord in the church of Treves; and there he never allowed the blessed Gallus to be separated from him.

Thus it happened that when the king went to Cologne, Gallus went with him. Now there was a temple in that city filled with various ornaments, where the barbarians of the region would make offerings and gorge themselves with food and wine until they would vomit. There too they worshipped idols as gods and would place likenesses of human limbs which they sculptured in wood when some part of their body was stricken with illness. As soon as Saint Gallus learned of this, he immediately hastened there with one other cleric, and having kindled a fire, he burned down the temple while none of the ignorant pagans were present. But they, seeing the smoke from the temple rising in the sky, sought out the maker of the fire, and after finding him pursued him with bared swords. He took flight and hid himself in the royal palace. Knowing what had taken place from the pagans' threats, the king pacified them with soft words and thus calmed their insensate fury. The blessed man had the habit of often recounting this act with tears and would say, "Woe to me who did not remain, that I might have ended my life in this affair." At that time he was fulfilling the office of deacon.

3. Now when the blessed bishop Quintianus passed from this life at the Lord's command, Saint Gallus at that time was living in Clermont. The residents of Clermont gathered at the house of the priest Impetratus, Gallus' uncle, bewailing the bishop's death and inquiring who ought to be put in his place. For a long time they debated this question, and then each went to his own home. After they had departed, Saint Gallus called one of the clerics, and full of the Holy Spirit he said, "Why are these people lamenting? What are they running after? Toward what are they turning their thoughts? Their effort is vain, for I shall be bishop: the Lord has vouchsafed to bestow this honor upon me. As for you, when you hear that I have gone from the king's presence, take my predecessor's horse in harness and come to me. But if you disdain to hear me, beware lest you regret it later."

While he was saying this, he was lying on his bed. Then the cleric was angered against him, and after having reproached him greatly, he injured the Saint's side, striking it against the side of the bed, and left in agitation. After his departure the priest Impetratus said to the blessed Gallus, "My son, listen to my counsel. Do not delay, but go to the king and inform of what has taken place here, and, if the Lord inspires him that you be given this bishopric, we will give great thanks to God for it; if he acts otherwise, at least you will commend yourself to whoever will be ordained bishop."

So he went and told the king what had happened concerning the blessed Quintianus. Then Aprunculus, bishop of Treves, also died. The clergy of that city, having come together before King Theoderic, asked for Saint Gallus as their bishop. The king said to them, "Go back and look for another, for I have reserved the deacon Gallus for something else." So they chose Saint Nicetius and received him.*

As for the clergy of Clermont, they came to the king with the popular approval and many presents. At that time that noxious sprout had already begun to grow whereby a bishopric was sold by the king and bought by clerics. The clergy of Clermont heard from the king that they would have Saint Gallus for bishop. When he had been ordained priest, the king commanded that the citizens be invited to a feast given at public expense, so that they might rejoice in the honor of Gallus, their future bishop; and so this was done. St. Gallus used to say that for his bishopric he had given no more than one-third of a copper coin to the cook who had prepared the feast. After this, the king sent him to Clermont, giving him two bishops to accompany him for his consolation.

As for the cleric (whose name was Viventius) who had injured Gallus' side against the edge of the bed, he hastened to come before the hierarch, according to the latter's word—but not without great confusion—and brought himself together with the horse which the Saint had demanded. When they had both gone to the baths, Saint Gallus reproached him lightly for the pain in the side he owed to the violence of the cleric's pride and caused him great shame by his words, not spoken with anger, but rather cheering him up with a certain spirited playfulness. Then he entered the city, where he was received with much psalmody and was ordained bishop in his church.

4. After he had assumed the bishopric, he conducted himself towards everyone with so much humility and love that he was cherished by all. He had a more than human patience, so that—if one may speak thus—he could be compared to Moses for the bearing of various injuries. And so it happened that if during a meal he were struck on the head by his priest, he would keep

---

*The Life of St. Nicetus of Treves (Trier) is chapter 17 of *The Life of the Fathers.*

himself so calm as to utter no sharp word; but patiently bearing all that came
to him, he would cast it upon the judgment of God, by Whom he sought to be
sustained. Thus, when one Evodius, a priest of a senatorial family, had pro-
voked him with calumnies and outrages at a church meal, the bishop got up
and went out to the place in the city where the holy basilicas were. When
this was made known to Evodius, he quickly ran after him and cast himself
at his feet in the middle of the street, asking pardon and begging that the
bishop's prayer to the Almighty Judge not bring about his condemnation.
But the bishop, raising him up with kindness, generously pardoned him for
everything he had said, only admonishing him for the future not to dare to
attack the Lord's bishops, because he himself would never deserve to receive a bishopric, as later proved to be the case. For when he had already been
elected bishop of Gabalitanus and was already on the episcopal throne, and
all was ready for his consecration, then all at once the people rose up against
him, so that he scarcely escaped alive, and in the end he died a simple priest.

5. In the city of Arles, after the bishop Mark had been accused by
evil men and sent into exile, a large assembly of bishops was gathered by
order of King Childebert. In that synod* the blessed bishops recognized that
all that was entered in complaint against the bishop was without foundation,
and they restored him to his city and see. There was then in Saint Gallus'
service a deacon, Valentinian, who is now a priest and singer. At the time when
another bishop was saying the Liturgy and this deacon wished to sing, out of
vanity rather than in the fear of God, he was forbidden by Saint Gallus, who
said to him, "Leave off, my son. When by God's will we celebrate the solemnities, it is then that you ought to sing. But now let the singing be done
by the clerics of him who is consecrating the Liturgy." But he said he could
sing at the present time too, to which the bishop replied, "Do what you will,
but you will not accomplish what you desire." The deacon, taking no account
of the hierarch's command, went out, but he sang so disagreeably that he was
mocked by all. When another Sunday came, and Saint Gallus was saying the
Liturgy, he ordered the deacon to be present, saying: "Now, in the Lord's name,
you will sing as you wish." Upon his doing so, his voice was so beautiful
that he was praised for it by everyone. O blessed man to whom so much grace
was given that men's voices as well as their souls were put under his authority, to the point of being able either to hinder them from singing or to permit
them to sing!

---

* The fifth Council of Arles, which met in 549.

6. God also performed by him other miracles. When one Julian, first a defense counsel and later a priest, a man of very agreeable character, was seized with a severe quartan fever, he betook himself to the holy bishop's bed where, lying down, covering himself with the bedclothes, and sleeping a little, he was so healed that afterwards he was in no way affected by that infirmity.

Once when the city of Clermont was engulfed by a great fire and the holy man learned of it, he went into the church and for a long time prayed to the Lord with tears before the holy altar-table; then, arising and taking the Gospel, he went out and held it up, opened, before the fire. When he did so, the flames died out at the sight of him, so that not a single spark of that fire remained.

In his time the city of Clermont was shaken by a great earthquake. We do not know why this happened, but we do know that none of the people were hurt.

When that epidemic which they call bubonic plague was raging in various regions and ravaging the province of Arles worst of all, Saint Gallus feared not so much for himself as for his people. And, while he was praying to the Lord night and day in order that in his lifetime he might not see his people devastated, an Angel of the Lord appeared to him in a dream, with hair and garment white as snow, and said to him, "O priest, the Divine goodness regards favorably your supplication for the people. Therefore do not fear, for your prayer has been heard, and see! You will be free from this infirmity with your people, and no one, while you live, will perish in this land from this epidemic. Do not be afraid now, but after the completion of eight years you will depart from this world." Indeed, this came to pass later. Having awakened, and giving thanks to God for this consolation with which He had vouchsafed to comfort him by the heavenly messenger, Saint Gallus instituted those rogations which are performed in mid-Lent as they go on foot to the basilica of blessed Julian the Martyr while singing psalms. There are about 360 furlongs in this route. So then, while the plague was ravaging these parts, as we have said, it did not touch the city of Clermont, through the prayers of Saint Gallus. And I think it no little grace which he merited, that this shepherd did not see his flock devoured by the epidemic, for the Lord protected it.

7. But let us come to the time when the Lord ordered him taken from this world. When he was sick in bed, an internal fever so wasted all his members that he lost his hair and beard at the same time. Having learned

by a revelation from the Lord that he would die in three days, he assembled the people, and having broken the Bread, he distributed (Holy) Communion with a holy and pious will. On the third day, which was a Sunday, and which brought mourning to the citizens of Clermont, as the sky began to grow light, he asked what they were singing in church. They said that they were singing the benediction. And he sang the fiftieth psalm and the benediction and recited the Alleluia with the short chapter and thus finished Matins. At the end of the office he said, "We bid you farewell, brethren." And saying this, stretching forth his limbs, he rendered to the Lord his spirit which had always been directed toward Heaven. He departed in the sixty-fifth year of his age, the twenty-seventh year of his episcopate.

Then, having been washed and vested, he was carried into the church, until the bishops of the province would come to bury him. A great miracle was also accomplished there before the people: the Saint of God drew up his right foot on the bier and turned himself to the side which was toward the altar. When these things had taken place, the rogations were celebrated which occur each year in the Paschal season. He lay three days in the church, with continuous psalmody and a great concourse of people. The bishops arrived on the fourth day; taking him up out of the church and carrying him to the basilica of Saint Laurence, they buried him there.

What mourning there was at his funeral and how many people were present can scarcely be told. The women were there in mourning-dress as if they had lost their husbands, and similarly the men covered their heads as if they were at the funerals of their wives. They were even followed by some Jews, weeping and holding lamps. And all the people said, with one voice, "Woe to us, who from this day will never deserve to have such a hierarch."

And since the bishops of the province, as we have said, being very far away, could not come promptly, the faithful, as was the custom of the country folk, put sod on the Saint's body so that it would not swell from the heat. And after the funeral ceremonies, a certain woman, or rather, as I have learned with care, a virgin most pure and devoted to God, named Meratina, took away the sod which had been removed by others and placed it in her garden. She watered it often, and, as the Lord granted the increase, she kept it alive. The sick who would carry away the growth from this sod and take it in a drink were healed, and even a believer who only prayed over it obtained his request. Later, being neglected after the virgin's death, the sod died.

Many miracles were worked at his sepulchre. Those who were sick of quartan fever and various other fevers recovered their health as soon as they had touched the blessed tomb with faith. The singer Valentinian (of whom we spoke earlier and who is now a priest), when he was serving as deacon, was attacked by quartan fever and was gravely ill from it for several days. It happened that on the day of an attack of this fever, he had decided to visit the holy places and pray there; coming to the Saint's sepulchre and prostrating himself, he said, "Remember me, most blessed and holy priest. By you I was raised, instructed, and encouraged. Remember your own disciple whom you loved with a rare love, and deliver me from the fever which possesses me." This said, he collected the little shoots which had been scattered by the devout in honor of the Saint around his tomb, and, as they were green, he put them in his mouth, ground them with his teeth, and swallowed the juice. The day passed without his being troubled by the fever, and thereafter he was so restored to health that he no longer even had what are commonly called the shivers. I heard this from the mouth of the priest himself. And there is no doubt that it is He Who called Lazarus from the tomb Who causes miracles to come forth, by His power, from the tombs of His servants.

NOTES

St. Gallus, the successor of St. Quintianus (see Chapter Four) as Bishop of Clermont, succeeded him in 525 and died in 551; he is commemorated on July 1.

St. Gallus was St. Gregory's own uncle, the brother of his father, whom St. Gregory knew personally, even though he was only 13 when St. Gallus died.

King Theoderic (Thierry I, d. 534) and King Childebert I (d. 558) were both sons of King Clovis who, on the latter's death in 511, divided his kingdom with two other brothers. Theoderic reigned in the northern part of the realm (including Treves or Trier, Cologne and other parts of present-day Germany), where paganism was still strong in the 6th century. Later chapters of *Vita Patrum* describe some of the Christian missionary work among the pagans there. Theoderic's queen was Suavegotha, daughter of the holy King Sigismund (see *The History of the Franks,* III, 5).

The basilica of St. Laurence, where St. Gallus was interred, was a short distance from the cathedral church of Clermont; it evidently fell into ruins in early times, and the tomb of St. Gallus was lost. The Saint's funeral epitaph was written by the Christian poet Fortunatus (Carmina, I: IV, 4).

7

Saint Gregory the Bishop

INCORRUPT WONDERWORKER OF LANGRES

Commemorated January 4 (†539)

MEN OF PERFECT SANCTITY, whom the palm of perfect blessed-ness has raised from earth to heaven, are those who are bound by the bond of true charity, who are enriched by the fruits of almsgiving, who are adorned by the flower of chastity, who are crowned by the determined combat of martyrdom, or, finally, those whose principal desire, in order to begin the work of perfect justice, was above all to make of their bodies a spotless temple prepared for the Holy Spirit and thus to arrive at the summit of the other virtues. And therefore, having become their own persecutors, while they were destroying the vices within themselves, being tested like the martyrs, they triumphantly finished the course of their lawful combat—which no one would be able to do without God's help, without being pro-tected by the shield and helmet of the Divine assistance, and which one does not achieve himself but imputes to the glory of the Divine Name, according to the Apostle's word: *He that glorieth, let him glory in the Lord* (I Cor. 1:31). It is in this that the blessed Gregory sought all his glory, he who from the high authority of senatorial rank lowered himself to such humility that, disdaining all the cares of this world, he devoted himself entirely to the work of God which he kept in his heart.

1. Saint Gregory, then, who was among the foremost senators and well versed in letters, rose to the dignity of Count of the city of Autun and administered the region for forty years with justice. He was so rigorous

and severe toward malefactors that there was hardly a single one who could escape him. He had a wife named Armentaria, of senatorial lineage, whom he is said to have known only for the begetting of children. God granted him sons, and it never came to him to burn for another woman, as often happens in the ardor of youth.

2. After his wife's death he turned towards the Lord, and after having been chosen by the people he was ordained bishop of Langres. Great was his abstinence, but lest it be imputed to pride, he hid smaller barley loaves under his wheaten loves; then, breaking and giving the wheat bread to others, he would secretly take the barley bread for himself without anyone knowing about it. He did the same with wine: if the cup-bearer presented him with water, in order to conceal this fact he would choose a cup opaque enough to hide the transparency of the water. He was so devoted to and energetic in fasting, almsgiving, prayer, and vigils, that he shone forth as a hermit placed in the middle of the world. Indeed, since he ordinarily abode in the castle of Dijon, and his house was next to the baptistery where the relics of many Saints were kept, he would rise from his bed during the night without anyone noticing and, having only God for witness, would go to pray in the baptistery, whose door would open miraculously, and where he would sing psalms with heedfulness.

But after he had done this for a long period of time, finally he was seen and recognized by a deacon: when the latter saw him act thus, he followed him at a distance and saw what he was doing, without the blessed man being aware of him. And the deacon said that when the Saint of God came to the baptistery door, after he struck it with his hand the door opened without anyone appearing to open it, and that after he went in, there was silence for a very long time, but then there was heard a psalmody of several voices for the space of more than three hours. I believe that since there were in that place the relics of many Saints, they revealed themselves to this blessed man in order to sing psalms to the Lord with him. And when he had finished, he would go back to his bed and lie down with so much care that no one knew anything. In the morning the custodians, finding the door closed, would open it with the key as usual and ring the bell, and the Saint of God would go there again with the others for the Divine Office.

The first day of his episcopate, when the demoniacs were confessing their possession, the priests requested him to agree to give them his blessing, which he emphatically refused to do, lest vainglory assail him, proclaiming himself unworthy to be the minister for the manifestation of miracles of the Lord. Nevertheless, not being able to refuse them for too long, he had the possessed ones brought; then, without touching them, but only employing the word and the sign of the Cross, he commanded the demons to depart. Immediately upon hearing this, they abandoned the bodies which they had bound in malice. Even in his absence, many would stop the demoniacs and expel the demons by making the sign of the Cross with the staff he customarily carried in his hand. Moreover, if a sick person carried away something from his bed, it was a sure remedy for him. His granddaughter Armentaria* was once seized in her youth by a severe attack of quartan fever, and having received no relief from the repeated attention of the physicians, she was often exhorted by the blessed confessor himself to apply herself to prayer. One day she wished to lie down in his bed, and then her fever disappeared so completely that she never suffered from it again.

3. Saint Gregory, having gone to the city of Langres for the holy day of Epiphany, was seized by a slight attack of fever, at the end of which he left this world and went to Christ. His blessed face was so adorned with glory after death that it resembled roses. His cheeks were red, whereas the rest of his body was as white as a lily, so that you would have thought him already prepared for the future resurrection. As they were taking him to the castle of Dijon, where he had ordered himself buried in that plain to the north, right near the castle, the pall-bearers could not hold up the coffin and set it on the ground; and then, after regaining their strength, they picked it up and bore it into the church which is within the city walls.

The bishops having arrived on the fifth day, he was brought from the church to the Basilica of Saint John. Those held in the prison began to cry out to the blessed body, saying, "Have mercy on us, most pious lord, in order that those whom you did not deliver while you were in this world you may free now that, being dead, you possess the heavenly kingdom. Visit us, we beg you, and have mercy on us." As they were crying these and other similar things, the body grew heavy, so that the pall-bearers could not hold it up. Placing the coffin on the ground, they awaited a miracle of the blessed bishop. While they were waiting, all at once the prison doors opened, and the beam to which the prisoners' feet were fixed broke in the middle. The bonds snapped and the chains broke, and all were freed and rushed without hindrance toward the blessed body. The bearers then easily raised the coffin and the prisoners followed it with the others; later they were dismissed by the judge without penalty.

---

* The mother of St. Gregory of Tours.

4. After this, the blessed confessor manifested himself by many miracles. A certain monk said that on the day of his burial he had seen the heavens opened; nor is it to be doubted that after these angelic actions our Saint had been admitted into the heavenly assemblies. A prisoner was brought to the aforesaid castle by the same way by which they had brought the Saint's body from Langres. And as the soldiers, going ahead on horseback, were dragging the prisoner behind their backs, they came to the place where the limbs of the blessed confessor had rested. As they passed by, the prisoner invoked the blessed bishop's name and asked that he would free him in his mercy. While he was thus praying, the bonds fell from his hands. Perceiving himself released, he remained quiet, and since his hands were covered, he was thought still to be bound. But after they had gone through the castle gate and had come before the atrium of the church, he dashed off, holding in his hand the thong with which those who were dragging him had bound him, and he was delivered by the help of Almighty God and by the intercession of the blessed hierarch.

Admirable also is that miracle by which his blessed body appeared glorious when it was being translated after a long time. Since the holy hierarch had been buried in a corner of the basilica, and it was a small space so that the people could not approach it as devotion demanded, Saint Tetricus, his son and successor, took note of this, and seeing miracles being worked unceasingly at his tomb, he knocked down the foundations of that part of the basilica before the altar and there laid out an apse which he constructed in the round with admirable workmanship. When the circular wall was finished, he pulled down the old high wall and built an arch. When the building and its ornamentation were done, he excavated in the middle of the apse a crypt, wishing to place in it the body of his blessed father.

He called together for this office the priests and abbots, who assiduously prayed that the blessed confessor would permit himself to be transferred to the place prepared for him. The next morning, with chanting choirs, they took the sarcophagus from before the altar and transported it into the apse which the holy bishop had built. But as they were arranging the sepulchre carefully, suddenly, by God's command—as I believe—the cover of the sarcophagus fell off to one side, and behold! the blessed face of the Saint appeared, whole and intact, so that you would have thought him to be not dead, but sleeping. Nor was there any deterioration in the vestments which had been put on him. Thus it was not without reason that he appeared glorious after his death, since his flesh had not been corrupted by passions. And certainly, great is the integrity of body and heart which preserves grace in this world and is given eternal life in the future age, of which the Apostle Paul speaks: *Follow peace and holiness, without which no man shall see the Kingdom of God.* (Heb. 12:14).

5. One Sunday a girl was grooming her hair with a comb. Because of the injury—so I believe—she was doing to the holy day, the comb stuck to her hands in such a way that the teeth entered her fingers and the palm of her hand, which caused her great pain. After she had made the round of the basilicas of the Saints, weeping and praying, she prostrated herself at the tomb of the blessed Gregory, full of confidence in his virtue. And after she had begged the blessed confessor's help for a long time, the comb fell out and her hand was restored to its original condition. The possessed, also, confessing his name at his sepulchre, were often cleansed. And several times since his death we have seen that by touching such ones with the staff which he carried in his hand (of which we spoke earlier), they became so fastened to the walls that you would have thought they had been held by large stakes well sharpened on the ends.

6. We know many other deeds of his, but lest they incite fatigue, we have spoken briefly only of a few out of many. He died in the thirty-third year of his episcopate and the ninetieth of his age, this man who often made himself known by manifest miracles.

NOTES

St. Gregory of Langres was born about 450, was Count of Autun from about 466 to 506, was elected bishop of Langres in 506 or 507, and died in 539 or 540. He was the grandfather of St. Gregory of Tours' own mother, Armentaria. He is commemorated on January 4; evidently he died just before Epiphany, on the road to Langres.

St. Tetricus, the son of St. Gregory of Langres and grand-uncle of St. Gregory of Tours, succeeded his father as bishop of Langres and ruled in this capacity from about 540 to his death in 572 or 573. He is commemorated on March 18.

The "baptistery" where St. Gregory prayed secretly at night in Dijon was probably the oratory of St. Vincent, which existed up to the 17th century. The nearby church of St. Stephen, where the Saint was buried, became a cathedral in 1731 but is now a grain exchange.

St. Gregory's relics were later translated to the basilica of St. Benignus the martyr, outside the walls of Dijon.

ST. NICETIUS

8

Saint Nicetius of Lyons

MODEL OF MEEKNESS, FREER OF CAPTIVES

Commemorated April 2 (†573)

THE ORACLES OF HOLY SCRIPTURE often bear witness to those whom the goodness of the Divine foreknowledge destines for His Kingdom, as we learn from these mystical words of a heavenly mouth which said to Jeremiah the great Prophet: *Before I formed thee in the belly I knew thee, and before thou camest forth out of the womb I sanctified thee* (Jer. 1:5). And the Lord Himself, author of both Testaments, when He places at His right hand those whom His joyful generosity has covered with the Lamb's fleece, what does He say to them? *Come, ye blessed of My Father, inherit the Kingdom prepared for you from the foundation of the world* (Matt. 25:34). And the blessed Apostle, that vessel of election, says, *Whom He did foreknow, He also did predestinate to be conformed to the image of His Son* (Rom. 8:29). Thus He predicted of both Isaac (Gen., ch. 17) and John (Luke, ch. 1), how they would be born, how they would live, their names, their works, their merit.

So now also, concerning the blessed Nicetius, that ancient mercy which enriches him who does not merit it, sanctifies the unborn, and disposes and ordains all things before they are created, willed to reveal first to his mother with what adornments of priestly grace he would flourish in this world. A book about his life has come into our possession, whose author I know not, which makes known to us many things about his virtues, but which at the time speaks to us clearly of neither his birth, nor his conversion, nor the order of his miracles. And although we have not researched all the

209

marvels which the Lord vouchsafed to work through him, whether in private or in public, nevertheless we propose to recount in the simplicity of our style those things which did not come to the notice of the first author.

1. Now one Florentius, of senatorial rank, having taken to wife Artemia and having had two children, was asked for as bishop of the city of Geneva. The prince having consented to this, Florentius went back to his house and told his wife what had taken place. Upon hearing this she said, "I beg you, dearest husband, to desist from this matter, and not to seek the episcopate of that city, because I am carrying in my womb a bishop whom I have conceived by you."* Hearing this from his wife, that wise man remained silent, recalling what the Divine voice had commanded aforetime of the father of our Faith, the blessed Abraham: *In all that Sarah hath said unto you, hearken unto her voice* (Gen. 21:12).

At last the time of childbirth came, and his wife brought into the world a child whom she called Nicetius at his baptism, as if to announce that he would be a conqueror of the world.** She had him brought up with the greatest care in ecclesiastical letters. After his father died, Nicetius, although already a cleric, lived with his mother in his father's house, working with his hands among the domestics, for he understood that bodily movements could not be subdued except by labors and pains.

One day, while he was still in the house, a foul blister appeared on his face, and in time it grew larger and inflamed and made the boy despair of life. His mother continually invoked the name of blessed Martin, together with the names of many other saints, and implored him especially for the healing of her son. And when for two days the boy had lain in bed with his eyes closed and had given to his grieving mother no word of consolation, she, wavering between hope and fear, was already preparing the necessities for his funeral; on the evening of the second day he opened his eyes and said, "Where has my mother gone?" Coming immediately, she replied, "Here I am. What do you want, son?" And he said: "Do not fear, mother, for the blessed Martin made over me the sign of the Cross of Christ and ordered me to get up healed." Having said that, he forthwith got out of bed. The Divine power increased the grace of this miracle, both to make known

---

* It was the rule at this time that a married man, if elected bishop, would live separately from his wife; therefore, his wife's conceiving a child obligated him to continue his family life and refuse the bishopric.

** The name Nicetius means "conqueror."

Martin's merit and to deliver from a contagious sickness him who would later be a hierarch. The scar on his face remained as a witness to what had happened.

2. At the age of thirty he was honored with the dignity of the priesthood, but he did not abstain because of this from the work he had been doing before: he always worked with his hands among the domestics, in order to fulfill this precept of the Apostle, which says, "Labor with your hands, in order that you be able to give to those in need" (Eph. 4.28). He saw to it especially that all the children who were born in his house, as soon as they began to speak, were instructed in letters and psalms, in such a way that they could sing them and meditate upon them with the others and thus fill their souls with good things, according as devotion could suggest.

As for chastity, not only did he guard it most carefully, but also he always admonished others to guard the grace of it and to keep themselves from impure touches and improper words. In fact, I remember that in my youth, when I was beginning to know my letters and was in my eighth year, he told me, the unworthy one, to go to his bed, and he took me in his arms with the tenderness of fatherly affection; taking in his fingers the hem of his garment, he so wrapped himself in his tunic that my limbs were never touched by his blessed members. Consider, I pray you, and take notice of the precaution of the man of God, who thus abstained from touching a child's limbs, in which there could be neither the least sting of lust nor the least excitation to impurity. How much more, then, did he flee from any situation where there could be some suspicion of impurity? Indeed, as we have said, he was so chaste in body, so pure of heart, that he never spoke a jesting word, but always he spoke of the things of God. And although he embraced all men by this bond of heavenly love, nevertheless he was so submissive to his mother that he obeyed her as one of the domestics.

3. Sacerdos, bishop of Lyons, took sick in Paris, and as he was loved by the elder Childebert with a great love, the king wished to come to his bedside to visit him in his sickness. At his approach the bishop said, "You have known perfectly, O most pious king, that I have faithfully served you in all your necessities and that I have scrupulously carried out whatever you have commanded. Now I ask you, since the moment of my end has come, that you not leave me to depart from this world with sadness, but freely grant me the one request I make." And the king said: "Ask what you will, and you shall have it." "I ask," said the bishop, "that the priest Nicetius, my

nephew, succeed me as bishop of Lyons. For my testimony of him is that he cherishes chastity, that he loves the churches, that he is very devout in alms-giving, and that he delights, both in his work and in his habits, to do all that is becoming to God's servants." The king answered: "God's will be done." And so Nicetius was ordained bishop of Lyons with the full consent of king and people.

He always showed himself a thorough lover of peace and concord, and if he was offended by someone, he immediately pardoned the offense himself or suggested by someone else that pardon be asked. Once I saw the priest Basil, sent by him to Count Armentarius, who was then governing the city of Lyons with judicial authority; he said to him: "Our hierarch has by his judgment put an end to this matter which nevertheless has come up anew, and he advises you not to occupy yourself with taking it up again." The count, inflamed with anger, replied to the priest, "Go tell him that there are many matters brought into his presence that will be finished by some-one else's judgement." On his return the priest simply reported what he had heard. Then Saint Nicetius was vexed with him: "Truly, you will not receive blessings from my hand, because you have brought to my ears words spoken in anger." He was then reclining at table, and I was nearest to him on his left, then exercising the office of deacon, and he said to me in a whisper: "Speak to the priests so that they might intercede for him." When I spoke to them, they were silent, not understanding the Saint's intention. Seeing this, he said to me: "You get up and intercede for him." I got up trembling. and kissing his holy knees, I made entreaty for the priest. He granted the request, and giving him the blessing said: "I pray you, my beloved brothers, that useless words which are murmured rudely not assail my ears, for it does not befit reasonable men to sustain the impudent words of unreasonable men. Rather, you ought to apply yourselves to confounding with your arguments those who seek to plot against the Church's interest. As for senseless words, not only do I make no case for them, but I do not even want to hear them." May they hear these words who, when offended, do not know how to forgive, but even, calling a whole city to the vengeance, do not fear to use witnesses who by evil reports say: "We have heard such a one saying this and that about you." And so it happens that Christ's poor ones are oppressed by such accusations, to the neglect of mercy.

4. One morning Saint Nicetius arose for Matins and, after waiting for two antiphons to be chanted, he entered the church, where, after he was

seated, a deacon began to sing the responsory psalm. The bishop said in
irritation: "Let him be quiet, let him be quiet, and let not the enemy of
justice have the audacity to sing." And these words were no sooner uttered
than the deacon was silent, with his mouth obstructed. The Saint ordered
him called over and said: "Have I not ordered you not to enter the church
of God? Why have you been bold enough to enter herein? Why have you
dared to join your voice with the sacred chants?" All those present were
astonished, knowing nothing evil of the deacon, when the demon in him
cried out and admitted that he was subjected to grievous torments by the
Saint. He had, indeed, dared to chant in the church, but his voice, unknown
by the people, the Saint had recognized, and he abused not the deacon, but
the demon, with the harshest words. Then, having laid his hands on the
deacon and cast out the demon, he restored the man to his right mind.

    5. After having made himself known to the people by these and
other signs, he departed to Christ in the twenty-second year of his episcopate
and the sixtieth of his life.

    While the Saint was being taken for burial, a small child, afflicted
with blindness for a long time, was following with the others, weeping,
being helped by someone who supported him. While he was walking, a
voice was heard at his ear, whispering to him: "Go up to the coffin, and
when you will have gotten under it, you will immediately recover your sight."
The boy asked the man who was conducting him who this was who was
whispering these words in his ear, and the man replied that he saw no one
speaking to him.

    The boy, having heard this voice in his ear a second and a third
time, understood that he was to do something, and asked that he be taken
to the coffin. He drew near, slipped in through the crowd of deacons in
white vestments, and placed himself as the order had been given him; and
as soon as he began to invoke the name of the Saint, his eyes were opened
and he recovered his sight.

    After this event, the child undertook to serve zealously in the Saint's
sepulchre and to light the lamps there. However, some of the leading men
of the city oppressed and persecuted him to such an extent that he could
not even obtain food for himself by charity. As he was often lamenting over
this at the foot of the blessed sepulchre, the Saint appeared to him and said:
"Go to King Guntram and tell him exactly what you have endured; he will
permit you food and clothing and take you from the hand of your enemies."
Finally, reassured by these words, the child went to the king and obtained

what he asked.*

Thus the Divine goodness did not defer glorifying by signs the blessed members of the one whose soul it received into Heaven amid the choirs of angels.

When there had elapsed the days fixed by Roman law for the testament of any deceased person to be read publicly, the testament of this bishop was brought to the public forum, where it was opened and read by the judge in the presence of the people. A priest of the basilica, puffed up with rancor because the Saint had left nothing to the church where he was interred, said: "Many are always saying that Nicetius was poor in spirit; now it is seen very clearly, since he has bequeathed nothing to the basilica in which he is buried." But the next night he appeared to the priest in radiant apparel with two bishops, Justus and Eucherius,** to whom he was saying: "This priest, well-beloved brethren, covers me with blasphemies by saying that I have bequeathed nothing to the temple where I repose, and he ignores the fact that I have left it what I have that is most precious, the dust of my body." And they replied: "He has done ill to detract a servant of God." The Saint then turned toward the priest and struck him with fists and palms on the throat, saying: "Sinner who ought to be trampled under foot, leave off speaking foolishly." The priest woke up and felt his swollen throat seized with such pains that he had great difficulty just to swallow his saliva. Whence it came about that he kept to his bed for forty days with the most acute suffering; but having invoked the confessor's name, he was returned to health, and thereafter he dared not utter such words as he had earlier presumed.

The bishop Priscus, whom we knew always to have been a strong adversary of the Saint, gave a certain deacon a mantle of Nicetius. It was ample, for the man of God was stout of body. The garment's hood was wide and sewn, as was the custom for the white mantles worn on the shoulders of priests during feasts of Pascha. Now this deacon went about with this vestment and took little notice of the use to which it had been put. He wore it in bed and in the forum, without thinking that its fringes could give health to the sick if one's faith were strong. Someone said to him: "O deacon, if you knew the power of God and what was he whose vest-

---

* This incident has been added from St. Gregory's other account of St. Nicetius in *The Glory of the Confessors,* ch. 61.
** Earlier bishops of Lyons.

ment you are wearing, you would use it with greater caution." He answered: "I tell you truly that I use this mantle to cover my back, and since it is too big in the hood for me, I am going to have slippers made of it." At once the wretch did as he had said, and he had to submit immediately to the vengeance of Divine judgment. As soon as he had undone the hood and made himself slippers from it, which he put on his feet, he immediately fell to the ground, seized by a demon. He was then alone in the house, and there was no one who could help the wretch. And while he was spitting from his mouth a bloody froth, having stretched out his feet to the hearth, the fire burned his feet together with the slippers. And this is what I have to say concerning vengeances.

6. Agiulf our deacon, coming back from Rome, was bringing us blessed relics of saints. On the way he went aside for the sake of prayer to the place where the Saint reposed, and having gone into the temple, he was looking over the register of miracles which had taken place there, when he saw an immense crowd of people near the tomb who were gathering like swarms of bees about their hive. Some were taking from the priest who was standing there bits of wax which they carried away for a blessing; others, a little dust; some were getting hold of some threads drawn from the covering of the tomb—all carrying away the same grace of healing for different cases. This the deacon full of faith beheld with tears, saying: "If the devotion of my bishop had me traverse the fluid masses of the sea in order for me to go visit the sepulchres of the martyrs of the East and bring back relics of them, why shall I not take those of a confessor of the Gauls, by which I shall preserve the health of me and mine?" And straightway drawing near, he received some of the herbs which the people's devotion had put around the holy tomb,* and which the priest gave him from his hand, wrapped in linen. He carried them home and put them away with care, and right away the working of miracles justified the man's faith. For when he had shredded some of the herbs and given them with a drink of water to those with chills, they returned to health as soon as they drank, as did many others later. In telling us this, he said that already four people had thus been made well from this sickness.

---

* A common custom in 6th-century Gaul. In *The History of the Franks,* VII, 12, St. Gregory writes of herbs placed on the altar of a church. One might compare the present Orthdox custom of taking as a blessing the flowers which have touched a wonder-working Icon.

John our priest, returning from the city of Marseilles with the goods of his trade, went to make his prayer at the Saint's tomb; then, rising up from there, he noticed the broken shackles and chain links which had held the necks and legs of the guilty, and he was full of wonder. And even this visit was not devoid of miracles: when he came back to us, this priest affirmed on oath that three blind men had recovered their sight there in his presence and had gone home healed.

While the Saint's relics were being carried with honor, to the singing of hymns, to Orleans, a city of the Gauls, the Lord granted so many graces to appear that, humbly venerating the relics, the blind recovered their sight and the lame walked straightly. Nor could anyone doubt that the confessor was present when one saw so many gifts of healing granted to the infirm.

7. A sedition arose somewhere and the crowd in a furor made the stones and torches fly, and procured arms without restraint. One man armed with a bared sword struck another a great blow; and a few days later the brother of the one who had been killed did likewise to the murderer. Having learned this, the judge of the place had this man put in prison, saying, "He is worthy of death, this scoundrel who, by his own will and without awaiting the judge's decision, had the temerity to avenge his brothers death." While he was held in custody, the prisoner, after having invoked the names of various saints in order to excite their compassion, turned especially to the Saint of God and said: "I have heard of you, Saint Nicetius, that you are powerful in works of mercy and generous in delivering captives who cry before you. I pray you now to deign to visit me with that excellent bounty which you have often shown in the deliverance of those who were in bonds." A short time later, while he was sleeping, the blessed one appeared to him and said: "Who are you who invoke the name of Nicetius? And whence do you know who he is, since you do not stop supplicating him?" The man gave him a detailed account of his offence and added: "Have mercy on me, I beg you, if you are the man of God I am invoking." The Saint said to him, "Get up, in Christ's name, and walk free. You will be stopped by no one." Having awakened at these words, he was full of astonishment to see his chains broken and the beam snapped. Right away, without anyone stopping him, he betook himself without fear to the Saint's tomb. Then, the judge having freed him from the sentence which he had incurred, he was released and went to his own home.

8. It is pleasant to add to these miracles the one which he performed by a lamp near his bed, for these things which this Saint, who abides in Heaven, does now upon the earth are truly great. The bed, then, in which the Saint was accustomed to sleep, and which had been made with the greatest care by Aetherius, now a bishop, was often adorned with illustrious miracles. Not without reason was it regarded with the greatest devotion, since those with fever were often healed of fever and shivering by being placed under it, and other sick persons were relieved as soon as they cast themselves on it. It is covered with a beautiful drapery, and lamps burn before it continuously. One of these continued burning for forty days and forty nights, as the sacristan assured us, without anyone doing anything to maintain it—neither papyrus for the wick nor a drop of oil. Rather, left in the same state in which it had been first put, it remained shining with light.

Gallomagnus, bishop of Troyes, came with devotion to look for relics of the Saint, and while they were being carried with psalmody, the eyes of the blind were opened by their virtue, and those sick with other ailments were granted to receive healing. We were also brought an ornamented handkerchief which the Saint had on his head the day of his death, and which we received as a heavenly gift. Now it happened that several days later we were invited to bless a church in the parish of Pernay in the diocese of Tours. I went there, consecrated an altar, pulled out some threads from the handkerchief, and placed them in the temple. Then, after I had celebrated Liturgy and prayed, I retired. Some days later, those who had invited us came to find us and said, "Rejoice in the name of the Lord, priest of God, over the virtue of the blessed bishop Nicetius; know the great miracle which he wrought in the church you consecrated! In our country there was a blind man long held in the dark night of blindness, to whom there appeared in a dream a man who said to him: 'If you wish to be healed, go prostrate yourself in prayer before the altar of the basilica of Saint Nicetius, and you will recover your sight.' When he had done so, the darkness dissipated, and the Divine power gave him light back." I acknowledge that I have placed portions of these relics in other church altars also, and the possessed there confess the Saint, and often prayer full of faith obtains its effect.

The servant of Pronimius, bishop of Agde, was struck with the onset of epilepsy, to the extent that he fell frequently, foaming at the mouth and tearing his tongue with his own teeth. By taking various remedies from the physicians, for several months he was not affected by the sickness; but later he again fell into his sufferings and found himself worse than before. His master, seeing such great miracles wrought at the tomb of blessed Nicetius, said to him: "Go and prostrate yourself before the Saint's tomb, praying to him to deign to help you." After he had carried out this order, he came back healed, and thereafter his sickness did not affect him. It was seven years after the servant's healing that his bishop presented him to us.

9. During the Saint's lifetime a poor man had obtained from him a letter bearing his signature, with which he went to beg alms in the houses of the devout. After the Saint's death he was still using this letter, taking from charitable men no little sums, thanks to the memory of the Saint. Each one desired to see the latter's signature and gave something to the poor man. Seeing this, a certain Burgundian, who neither honored nor venerated the Saint, followed the poor man at a distance, and seeing him enter a forest, threw himself on him, took from him six gold coins together with the letter, and trampled him underfoot, leaving him half dead. But he, in the middle of the kicking and ill-treatment, cried out: "I beg you by the living God and the virtue of Saint Nicetius, at least leave me the letter, for if I lose it, I will have no other means of existence." The Burgundian threw the letter on the ground and went away; the poor man picked it up and went to the city, where Priscus was then bishop, of whom we spoke earlier. The poor man went to him and said, "Behold the man who beat me harshly and stole from me six gold coins which I had received by showing the letter of St. Nicetius." The bishop reported these matters to the count. He, as judge, had the Burgundian summoned and asked him what he had to say to that. He denied the deed before everyone, saying, "I never saw that man, nor did I take a thing from him." The bishop, looking at the letter, saw the Saint's signature, and turning towards the Burgundian, said: "See here on this letter Saint Nicetius' signature. If you are innocent, draw near and swear while touching with your hand the writing which he himself set down. For we believe in his virtue, either that he will convict you this day of the crime, or that he will let you go away innocent beyond doubt." Without scruple he went forward toward the hand of the bishop, who was holding the open letter, and as he raised his hands to pronounce the oath, he fell backward; eyes closed and foaming at the mouth, he seemed on the point of expiring. At the end of about two hours, he opened his eyes and said, "Woe to me, for I have sinned in taking this poor man's property." And

immediately he told in detail how he had done injury to that man. Then, when he had obtained pardon from the judge and returned to the poor man as much as he had stolen, adding two coins more for the blows he had given to him, both parties went out together from the judge's presence.

10. As for how many prisoners the Saint has freed, how many chains he has broken—that heap of iron which is seen in his church today is witness, gathered from the above-mentioned offerings. Recently, in the presence of King Guntram, I heard Syagrius, bishop of Autun, recount how, in one night, the blessed man had appeared in seven towns to the prisoners, how he had delivered them from their prisons and let them go free, and how after that the judges dared not do anything against them. If anyone with fever or chills or suffering from other illnesses took some of the dust from his sepulchre and drank it in water, immediately he received his health; which, doubtless, is the good deed of Him Who said to His saints, *What things soever ye desire when ye pray, believe that ye receive them, and ye shall have them* (Mark 11:24).

11. There was in the borough of Precigny, in the diocese of Tours, a church recently built but not yet having relics of the saints. Since the residents of the locality were often asking that we bless it with the ashes of some saints, we placed in the holy altar the above-mentioned relics. Since then, the power of our Lord has very often manifested itself in that church through the blessed hierarch. Most recently, women coming from the country of Berri, three in number and tormented by a demon, betook themselves to the basilica of Saint Martin and entered the church. Immediately clapping their hands, while crying out that they had been tormented by the virtue of Saint Nicetius, spitting I know not what fluids mingled with blood, they were delivered immediately from the spirits which possessed them.

Waddo, one of those countrymen who took part in the great expedition against Comminges,* and who was in danger of death several times, vowed that if he returned home safe and sound he would give in honor of St. Nicetius, for the adornment of the above-mentioned church, some of the property he had acquired. Then, when he was on his way back, he obtained two silver chalices, and en route made a new vow to deliver them to the church, if he would arrive home safely. But when he arrived, he gave only one, and kept the other deceitfully, giving instead a Sarmatian drapery

* The city where the pretender Gundovald was besieged by King Guntram; Waddo at first supported Gundovald but later betrayed him. The siege is described in detail by St. Gregory in *HF*, VII, 34-42.

to cover the Lord's altar with the offerings. Then the blessed one appeared
in a dream to this man and said: "How long will you hesitate and neglect
to fulfill your vow? Go, and give the church the other chalice you promised
for it, lest you and your family perish. As for the drapery, since it is thin,
let it not be placed on the Gifts of the altar, because it cannot adequately
cover the Mystery of the Body and Blood of our Lord." Whereupon Waddo,
in fear, hesitated no longer and promptly fulfilled his vow.

That man's brother came to the vigils of the Nativity of the Lord
and spoke to the priest, saying, "Let us keep vigil together in God's church
and let us entreat devoutly the virtue of blessed Nicetius, that by his intercession we may pass the course of this year in peace." Hearing this, the
priest joyfully had the signal given for the vigils. But when that was done
and the priest had come with the clergy and the rest of the people, the man,
who was subject to gluttony, delayed his arrival, and the priest sent for him
several times. He answered, "Wait a little; I am coming." And what more?
The vigils were ended and morning came, and he who first had spoken of
them was not present at all. As for the priest, having completed the office
he hastened in irritation to the man's dwelling in order to suspend him from
communion. But the latter, seized with fever, was burned by a Divine fire,
as also by the wine he had drunk, and as soon as he had seen the priest,
he begged him with tears that a penance be imposed upon him. And as the
priest was reproaching him and saying, "Rightly you burn by the virtue of
Saint Nicetius, into whose church you neglected to come for vigils," in the
middle of these words the man gave up the ghost. Then, at the third hour,
when the people had assembled for the celebration of the Liturgy, the dead
man was carried into the church. No one could doubt what had been done
by the holy bishop's power. The priest himself told it to us. We could speak
of many other things which we have known from our own experience or by
the account of credible persons, but we think that would be too long.

12. However, since an end must be put to this account, we will
report one marvel relating to the book written on his life of which we spoke
above. The Divine virtue, having gone out from this book, far from leaving
Nicetius without glory, manifests how glorious he is by demonstrating the
virtue of its marvellous accounts. A deacon of Autun, afflicted with a painful blindness of the eyes, learned of what God, the glorifier of His saints,
was doing at the Saint's tomb, and he said to his family: "If I go to his
tomb and take something of his relics, or if at least I touch the mantle by

which his holy limbs are covered, I will become well." And when he repeated this and similar things to his friends, there was a cleric there who said, "You are right to believe that, but if you wish to strengthen your opnion about these miracles, here is a parchment volume written about them, so that you may believe more easily those things which have come to your hearing." But the deacon, even before having the desire to read it, said by the inspiration of a Divine piety: "I believe that God has the power to work miracles through His servants." And at the same time he put the volume on his eyes. Immediately the pain and darkness were dissipated, and by the virtue of this volume he recovered his sight with so much clarity that, reading with his own eyes, he learned of these narratives of miracles. Thus it is the Lord alone Who works all these things and Who is glorified in His saints, whom He makes glorious by illustrious miracles. To Him be glory and dominion unto the ages of ages. Amen.

NOTES

St. Gregory was the nephew of St. Nicetius and served as deacon under him. The original Life of St. Nicetius of which he speaks still exists in Latin, but seems to have no more information on the events of his life than St. Gregory's account.

St. Nicetius was born in 513, became bishop of Lyons in 551, and died in 573. Bishop Priscus succeeded him as bishop of Lyons and continued his hostility to the Saint's memory, finally calling the wrath of God upon himself, as described by St. Gregory in *The History of the Franks,* IV, 36. Bishop Aetherius, who made the Saint's bed, was his disciple; he succeeded Priscus as bishop of Lyons in 586 and established the veneration of Nicetius as a saint.

Childebert I, son of King Clovis, divided his father's kingdom with his three brothers. He died in Paris in 558. King Guntram was the grandson of Clovis and son of Lothar.

The journey of St. Gregory's deacon Agiulf to Rome is set forth in *HF,* X,1, where the election of St. Gregory the Dialogist as Pope of Rome (590) is described and the text of St. Gregory's address to the people of Rome concerning the plague of that time is given.

9

Saint Patroclus the Abbot

DESERT-DWELLER OF BOURGES

Commemorated November 19 (†577)

WHEN, following the precept from the mouth of the Lord Himself, the remarkable wisdom of the Prophet Moses prepared to build a tabernacle to Divine Providence and to accumulate quantities of material under this charge, since he did not have all those things which were necessary, he ordered that there be made known to the people what the Lord had commanded him on the mountaintop, so that each one should come forward to offer according to his means some gift from God, without constraint, but rather freely (Ex. 25:2). Thus they offered pieces of gold and silver, bronze, iron, beautiful shining gems, double skeins of fine linen, and double cords of purple. Some brought ram skins tinted red, and fleeces.

But as the teachers of the Church have handed down to us that all these things are allegorical and that they signify different kinds of graces, even comparing our words of praise with those fleeces, we, who are devoid of vision, unused to study, and negligent in deed, offer neither gold nor silver nor gems nor double skeins or cords. But at least let us give fleeces, that is, let us set forth those accounts which make known the miracles of the saints and friends of God in the Holy Church, so that those who read might be induced to follow the way by which the saints were worthy to mount up to Heaven. Thus, since an account recently given to us teaches us several things about the life of blessed Patroclus, I have thought it best not omitted but told; and despite a poor style, I have nevertheless not thought to hide what God has accomplished by His servant.

223

1.   The most blessed Patroclus, an inhabitant of Bourges, was the son of Aetherius. When he was ten years old he was appointed to tend the sheep, since his brother Anthony was given over to the study of letters. He was not, it is true, of the high nobility; even so, he was of a free state. One noontime they had both come to take their meal in their father's house, the one coming from the school and the other from the fields where he was watching the flock. Anthony said to his brother, "Stand off a little, peasant. It is for you to pasture the sheep, and for me to exercise myself in letters. The care of such an office ennobles me, whereas that service of watching flocks makes you low." Hearing this, and regarding this reproach as sent from God Himself, Patroclus left the sheep in the field and betook himself in haste and with resolve to the school for children. Upon being taught the fundamentals and then all that is necessary for the study of children, he learned so rapidly, thanks to his memory, that he surpassed his brother both in knowledge and in quickness of spirit, assisted therein by Divine help. Thereafter he was recommended for study to Nunnonius (who formerly enjoyed great favor with Childebert, king of the Parisians). He was brought up by him with the concern of the highest love, and Patroclus showed himself so modest and submissive to all, that everyone cherished him with the tenderness of a parent.

Returning home after the death of his father, he found his mother still living. She said to him, "Now that your father is dead, my sweetest son, I am living without solace. So I am going to look for a pretty young girl, of a free state, for you to marry, and you will be able to provide solace to your mother in her widowhood." But he answered, "I will not join myself to a wife in the world, but I will carry out what my spirit has conceived with the Lord's will." And when his mother, who did not understand him, asked him what he meant, he did not want to explain, but went to find Arcadius, bishop of the city of Bourges, and begged him to tonsure him and admit him to the rank of the clerics; which the bishop, by the Lord's will, did without delay.

A little later, exercising the office of deacon, he gave himself over to fastings, loved vigils, and occupied himself in reading, and so plunged himself in continual prayer that he did not come with the other clerics to take his meal at the table, as the rule was. Hearing of this, the archdeacon was angry at him and said, "Either you take your meal with your brothers, or you are certainly going to go away from us. For it is not seemly that you refuse to eat with those with whom you are reckoned to fulfill the ecclesiastical office."

2.   God's servant was not disturbed in soul by these words, seeing that he already ardently desired to retire into the solitude of the wilderness. Thus, having gone out from Bourges, he came to the village of Neris, and there he built

an oratory, consecrated by the relics of Saint Martin, where he began to instruct children in the study of letters. The infirm also came to him, and they were healed, as well as the possessed, who were delivered after having confessed his name.

But he had not yet found the solitude he was looking for, and the people made his virtues known everywhere. Therefore, to receive a sign, he wrote out little slips which he placed on the altar, keeping vigil and praying for three nights, in order that what the Lord ordered him to do He would vouchsafe to reveal to him clearly. But the great mercy of the Divine goodness, which knew in advance what he would be, had resolved that he be a hermit, and caused him to take the slip which would hasten his way into the wilderness.

Accordingly, he gathered virgins and established a women's monastery in that cell where he had been living, carrying away when he left nothing from all he had amassed there by his labor except a rake and a double-bitted axe. And having entered into the deep solitude of the forests, he came to the place called Mediocantus, built himself a cell there, and continuing the work of which we spoke above, gave himself over to God.

And because in that location he rendered of sound mind many of the possessed and cast out the demons with the imposition of his hand through the sign of the Cross, there was brought to him a ferocious man who, with his mouth open wide and his teeth bloody, tore with his own teeth all that he could get hold of. Having prostrated himself in prayer for three days for this man, he obtained the authority from the Divine mercy to make the man's fury abate, to free him from the danger of death, and to restore him to health by placing his fingers in the man's mouth, casting out the deadly, vicious spirit. Truly the imposture of the wicked seducer had no power against him.

And just as he cleansed those who were possessed, so he also repulsed by the power of the most holy Cross those things which the wicked author of crime prepared in secret. During the *inguinarium* plague of which we have already spoken, the devil, in the appearance of St. Martin, had wickedly brought to a woman called Leubella the offerings which he said would save the people. But soon as they had been shown to Saint Patroclus, not only did they vanish by a revelation of the Holy Spirit, but the frightful perpetrator of evil appeared to the Saint and confessed to him all his evil actions.

Often, it is true, the devil transforms himself into an angel of light (II Cor. 11:14) in order to deceive the innocent with that fraud; and, as he laid out for Patroclus many snares to hinder him from rising up to that place from which he himself had fallen, he sent him the thought of leaving the wilderness and returning to the world. The Saint, feeling the poison creeping into his heart, prostrated himself in prayer, asking to do nothing which was not pleasing to God. Then an angel of the Lord appeared to him in a dream and said to him: "If you wish to behold the world, here is a column, climbing which you will behold all that is happening there." And in this dream there was before him a column of marvelous height which he climbed, and from there he saw the homicides, the thefts, the murders, the adulteries, the fornications, and all the crimes which occur in the world. When he came down he said, "I beg Thee, O Lord, that I not return to these abominations which for a long time I have forgotten in order to confess Thee." Then the angel who was speaking to him said, "Then stop seeking after the world, lest you perish with it, but rather go into the oratory where you will pray to the Lord, and what you find there will be for you a great consolation in your pilgrimage." When he entered the oratory, he found a clay tile on which was the image of the Cross of the Lord; and recognizing the Divine gift, he understood that this would be for him as an impregnable defense against the attractions of all worldly seduction.

3.   After this Saint Patroclus built the monastery of Columbariense, five miles from the cell which he was inhabiting in the wilderness; and there gathering monks, he instituted an abbot who would shepherd the monastic flock, so that he himself might be able to watch over himself more freely in solitude. He spent eighteen years in this wilderness place. Then, after having brought together the brethren to announce to them his passing, he died in a pious old age and in extraordinary sanctity. Finally, his body was washed and placed on a litter, and he was carried to his monastery, where he had ordered when still alive that he be buried.

Then the archpriest of the village of Neris, having assembled a group of clerics, wished to carry off the Saint's body by force in order that it might be buried in the village from which he had come. But while he was coming, filled with enthusiasm, he saw from afar the pall which covered the Saint's limbs and which was of a shining whiteness. And, by God's leave, he was so frightened that he immediately put out of mind what he had improperly and lightmindedly conceived, and joining himself to those who were chanting the office at the Saint's funeral, he, together with the other brothers present, buried him in the monastery of Columbariense.

At the Saint's tomb a blind woman named Prudence and a girl from Limoges, likewise deprived of sight, were granted to receive light as soon as they had kissed the holy tomb. After five years of blindness, Maxonidus went to the holy tomb and also received light. The possessed persons Lupus, Theodulfus, Rucco, Scopilia, Nectariola, and Tachilde were cleansed at the Saint's tomb. There were also two girls from Limoges who, having been rubbed with oil which the Saint had blessed, were delivered from the malignant spirit which beset them. And there every day the Lord, who constantly glorifies His saints, works miracles to confirm the faith of the people.

NOTES

St. Gregory has a short account of St. Patroclus' life in *The History of the Franks* (V, 10), which contains a little more information about him:

"In the neighborhood of Bourges there lived a recluse called Patroclus. He had been ordained a priest and was a man of remarkable holiness and piety, and of great abstinence, too: he was always being plagued with this illness or that through his fasting. He would not drink wine, or cider, or anything else which could intoxicate, taking only water slightly sweetened with honey. He would eat no animal food. His staple diet was bread soaked in water and sprinkled with salt. His eyes were never closed in sleep. He prayed unceasingly, or, if he stopped praying for a moment, he spent the time reading or writing. By prayer he would often cure those suffering from fevers, boils or other maladies. He performed many other miracles which it would take a long time to relate. He always wore a hair-shirt next to his body. He was eighty years old when he died and went to join Christ" (Lewis Thorpe tr., Penguin Books, 1974, p. 265).

He died in 577.

The Bishop Arcadius of Bourges who ordained him to the rank of cleric is known to have attended the Council of Orleans in 538.

The monastery of Columbariense (Columbier in French) became a dependency in turn of several larger monasteries, including the famous Cluny. A romanesque church dedicated to St. Patroclus remains at Columbier, and still has some columns from the 11th and 12th centuries.

The place of St. Patroclus' solitary cell five miles from Columbier is still known by the name of La Celle.

ST. FRIARDUS

THE RECLUSE

10

Saint friardus the Recluse

WHO RAISED HIS COMPANION FROM SATANIC DELUSION

Commemorated August 2 (†573)

THERE are many different ascents by which one can attain heaven, and it is of these, I think, that David spoke: *He hath made ascents in his heart* (Ps. 83:6). These ascents or degrees of different works are received as perfections in the Divine worship, and no one can walk in this way without being called thereto by God's help, as we have said several times. So, in fact, the Psalmist expressed himself concerning that way of perfection when he said, *Except the Lord build the house, in vain do they labor that build it* (Ps. 126:1). And this help has been continually sought not only by the martyrs, but also by all those who have made profession of a holy life and have thus attained to what inflames their spiritual thirst.

And indeed, if the desire for martyrdom is kindled in a heart, the martyr asks for this aid in order to conquer; if one wishes to keep the fast, he asks for it in order to obtain the necessary strength; if one wishes to preserve his members from all attacks against chastity, he prays to be defended by it; if at the beginning of a fault one repents and burns with the desire to be converted, he implores this aid with tears in order to be sustained by it; and if someone tries to accomplish something of all these in order to do well, he asks equally the grace of this assistance. The ascents or steps, then, of this ladder — so difficult, so exalted, so laborious — are very diverse, but by its means one raises himself towards the only God.

That is why one must always ask for this means from Him, one must always seek it, one must always call upon it, in order that what the mind has conceived of good it may accomplish by His aid — concerning which we ought always to say, *Our help is in the name of the Lord, Who hath made heaven and the earth* (Ps. 123:8). Thus did that most blessed man of whom we are about to speak, he who in the midst of different temptations and sorrows of this world always claimed heavenly aid.

1. Near the island of Vindunitta, in the territory of Nantes, there was a man of remarkable sanctity named Friardus, concerning whose life I am happy to make known a little for the sake of edifying the Church, since I do not know if anyone else has written of him. From his infancy he was always devoted to God and very chaste. When he became a grown man, he continually spent his life in the praise of God, in prayer and in vigils. With his own hands he drew from the earth those things needful for his subsistence, and although he surpassed others in work, he never ceased to pray — something which, this being the manner of rustics, was a subject of mockery for neighbors and strangers.

One day, when he was gathering sheaves in a wheat field with the other reapers, there was a swarm of those annoying and mischievous flies commonly called wasps; and as they flitted about the crop, pricking the reapers with their stings, the workmen left to the side the place where the nest was, and mocking blessed Friardus, said to him jokingly, "Let the blessed man come, let the religious man come, who never quits praying and is always making the sign of the Cross on his ears and eyes, who is always showing the sign of salvation on his path; let him reap over the swarm and placate it with his prayer." The Saint, who took these words as a doubt about the Divine power, prostrated himself on the ground while offering his prayer to the Lord, and approaching the wasps made the sign of the Cross, saying, "Our help is in the name of the Lord, who hath made heaven and the earth." As soon as this prayer issued from his mouth, the wasps all went to hide in the hole whence they had come out; and Friardus, in the sight of all the reapers, cut the wheat in that place without suffering any harm, which he could not have done without a miracle intended for the scoffers, since the Lord granted, for their confusion, to strengthen the one who had hoped in Him.

One time, after that, when he had climbed a tree for a certain task, a branch broke beneath his feet and he fell; while he was falling, at each branch he struck he called upon the most blessed name of Christ, saying, "Almighty Christ, save me." When he hit the ground he found himself unharmed, but he always said, "Our help is in the name of the Lord, Who hath made heaven and the earth."

2. Encouraged by these and other miracles, he began to reflect and to say within his heart, "If the Cross of Christ, and the invocation of His name, and the help asked of Him, have so much power that with them one can overcome all difficulties in this world, avoid dangers, dissipate the horrors of temptations, and raise oneself to contempt for all the delights of this world, what have I to do in the world except to abandon all the things which belong to it and to dedicate myself to the service of Him alone Who, when I called upon His name, delivered me from deadly dangers?" And going out from his little dwelling, forgetting his parents and his fatherland, he went in search of the desert, lest his sojourn in the world be a hindrance to his desire for prayer.

So he and Abba Sabaudus, who had formerly been a minister of King Clothaire and who was undertaking penitence, retired to Vindunitta, an island of the territory of Nantes. They also had the deacon Secundellus with them. But the abba, withdrawing his hand from the Lord's plow, went back to the monastery, and shortly thereafter perished by sword for reasons unknown. As for Saint Friardus, he abode on the island with the deacon Secundellus and did not leave it. Each had his own cell apart from the other.

And as they courageously persevered in prayer, the tempter appeared at night to the deacon Secundellus taking the form of the Lord and saying to him, "I am Christ, to Whom you pray every day. Already you are holy, and your name is written in the Book of Life with those of My other saints. So go out from this island and perform healings among the people." Secundellus, taken in by this deception, left the island without saying anything to his companion; and even so, as soon as he laid his hand upon the sick in the name of Jesus Christ, they were healed. But, returning to the island after a long time, he went to find his companion and said to him vaingloriously, "I left the island and worked many miracles among the people." When Friardus, in fear, asked him what he meant, he related simply what he had done. The elder, terror-stricken at this tale, cried with sighs and tears, "Woe to us! For as far as I understand, you have been deceived by the tempter. Go and repent, lest his tricks triumph over you."

Understanding these words and fearing he would perish, the deacon cast himself at the Saint's feet with tears, begging him to intercede for him with the Lord. "Go, and let us together supplicate His almightiness for the salvation of your soul. For the Lord readily has mercy on those who confess their faults, since He has said by His prophet, *I wish not the death of the sinner, but that he be converted and live* (Ezech. 33:11)."

But while they were praying, the tempter again appeared under the same form to the deacon Secundellus, saying to him, "Have I not commanded you, because my sheep are sick and are without a shepherd, to go and visit them and heal them?" He answered, "I have found in truth that you are the seducer, and I do not believe that you are God, Whose appearance you have falsely taken. Nevertheless, if you are Christ, show me your Cross which you have left, and I will believe in you." And when he would not show it, the deacon made the sign of the Cross in his face, and he vanished in confusion. Yet he came back with a multitude of demons and struck the deacon with such force that he could scarcely recover. But finally the devil went away and reappeared no more. The deacon lived thereafter in great holiness and died when his time was fulfilled.

3.   As for blessed Friardus, he shone with brilliant miracles. One day he took up a branch of a tree which the wind had knocked down and which, it is said, he had grafted himself. He made a staff of it for himself, which he carried in his hand. A long time after, he planted in the ground this dried-up staff which, upon frequent watering, put forth leaves and fruits, and after two or three years became a large tree. But this deed was a great miracle in the eyes of the people, and every day an immense crowd ran to see the tree — so that, by the remoteness of the island, the marvel which had been done acquired a still greater renown, and the Saint of God, fearing to fall prey to the dishonor of vainglory, took an axe and chopped down the tree.

Another time, the Saint, seeing a disaster which had struck a tree covered with flowers, which the violence of a storm had knocked to the ground, was moved with pity and prayed, saying, "I pray Thee, O Lord, that the fruits of this tree may not perish, since it is by Thy will that it produced the flowers with which is adorned. But, rather, let it be granted from Thee to raise itself up and grow and have the maturity of its fruits." Having prayed thus, he took an axe and separated the trunk from the roots. Then, having sharpened the trunk on the bottom like a stake, he fixed it in the ground, laying it over the roots which still held. Soon buds formed, although there were no roots, the tree regained its original condition, the flowers which had dried out regained their previous freshness, and the same year the tree gave forth fruits to him who had cultivated it with so much care. This miracle causes me to believe that God's mercy is indeed able to grant resurrection of the dead to him who has obtained by his prayers that dried-up trees regain their first vigor.

4.   The Saint, after having predicted the time of his death several times to his brothers, felt himself attacked by a fever and said to them, "Go to Bishop Felix and tell him of my passing. Say, 'Your brother Friardus has said: See, now the course of my life has come to an end. I am going to depart from this world, and in order that you have complete certitude of my word, know that I will pass away next Sunday in order to go to the rest which God the eternal King has

promised me. Come, then, I beg you, so that I may see you before my departure.' "

But Felix could not come, held up by I know not what reason, and sent to
him, saying, "I beg you, if it is possible, to wait a little for me until I can come
find you after my judicial affairs are finished." His messengers came back and
reported these words to him; although he was already on his bed, he said, "Then
let us get up and wait for our brother." O man of ineffable holiness, who, even
though he was in haste to come to his end and to be with Christ, nevertheless did
not forget his friend and obtained from God to spend one week more in this
world in order to see his brother by spiritual sight. Nor do I believe his merit was
little for the arrival of whom the Lord consented to delay the departure of the
Saint, who immediately felt the fever leave and got up from his bed feeling well.

Much later, the bishop arrived. The Saint, who had right away been taken
with fever, hailed him at his entrance and kissed him, saying, "You made me
wait a long time along the way I must follow, O holy bishop." And when they
had kept vigil together the whole night, which was that of Sunday, as soon as
morning came he gave up the ghost. Immediately the cell was filled with a sweet
fragrance and shook; whence it is certain that the power of the angels was there,
and that to mark the merit of the Saint it perfumed his whole cell with Divine
fragrance. His glorious body was washed and sealed by the bishop in the tomb,
and his soul was received in heaven by Christ, leaving the example of his virtues
to the inhabitants of the earth.

NOTES

St. Friardus died in 573.

The monastery of St. Friardus has been identified with the village of
Besne, on an island near the ocean, north of Nantes in the west of France. The
parish church there (which is all that is left of the monastery) has preserved the
sepulchres of Sts. Friardus and Secundellus; one kilometer away there is also a
chapel and a fountain dedicated to St. Secundellus, who was venerated in the
West as a saint. His life is reminiscent of that of St. Nicetas of the Kiev Caves,
who also worked "miracles" after being deceived by a demon, until he finally
came to his senses and attained true sanctity (see Bishop Ignatius Brianchininov,
The Arena, pp. 31-34).

Felix was bishop of Nantes from 549 to 582. St. Gregory of Tours was his
Metropolitan, but feeling between them was not good, owing to an abusive letter
Felix wrote to him (described by St. Gregory in *The History of the Franks*,
V. 5; see also the present book, p. 88). Thus, St. Gregory's praise of him in the
text above is all the more remarkable for its Christian charity.

ST. CALUPPAN THE RECLUSE

11

Saint Caluppan the Recluse

CLIFF-DWELLER OF THE AUVERGNE

Commemorated March 3 (†576)

THE poverty of this world always opens the door of the heavenly palace, and not only does it dispose for this dwelling those who are attached to it, but it also makes glorious in this world those who are glorified by miracles. So it is that the chains which we carry in this earthly prison open to us the entry-way of paradise, and our soul, which is found in association with the choir of angels, is transported with a holy lightness into eternal rest. Accordingly, let us not pass over in silence what we know for truth about the blessed Recluse Caluppan.

1. From the beginning of his life he always sought the happiness one gains by obedience to the Church, and he found it; having retired to the monastery of Meletense in Auvergne, he conducted himself there with great humility towards his brethren. He observed such an excessive abstinence that, being weakened by it, he could not fulfill the daily work along with the other brethren, and therefore, following the custom of the monks, they reproached him soundly, the superior especially, saying, "He who does not choose to work does not deserve to eat" (cf. II Thes. 3:10). Thus finding himself every day the butt of these reproaches, he cast his eyes on a valley situated not far from the monastery, in the middle of which rose a crag, more than five hundred feet high and completely isolated from the neighboring mountains. A watercourse traversed this valley, gently bathing the foot of the rock.

It was in an opening of this rock, which had formerly served as a retreat from the invasion of enemies, that the holy hermit retired and established his

235

abode, which is now reached by a very steep ladder, for this place is so difficult of access that the wild beasts themselves reach it only with difficulty. There he built a little oratory where, as he was accustomed to relate to us with tears, snakes would often fall on his head and coil around his neck, filling him with fear. Now since the devil passes himself off in the form of this sly animal, it is not to be doubted that it was he who was offering him these snares.

When he remained unmoved despite this and did not stir from the touch of the little snakes, one day two dragons of huge size came towards him and stopped at a certain distance. One of them, stronger than the other, who was to my thinking the chief of all temptations himself, lifted up his breast and raised his mouth even with the blessed one's mouth, as if he had wanted to say something to him. The Saint was so frightened that he became stiff as bronze, not being able at all either to move a limb or to raise his hand to make the sign of the Cross. And after they had both long remained silent, there came into the Saint's mind to say the Lord's Prayer in his heart if he could not move his lips. While he was doing this in silence, his members, which had been chained by the art of the enemy, little by little loosened, and when he felt his right hand free, he made the sign of the Cross against it, saying, "Are you not he who cast the first man out of paradise, who reddened a brother's hand with his brother's blood, who armed Pharaoh to persecute God's people, and who finally stirred up the Hebrew people to persecute the Lord with a blind fury? Depart from God's servants, by whom you have often been vanquished and covered with confusion! For you have been driven away in Cain and supplanted in Esau; you have been brought to the ground in Goliath; you have been hanged in the traitor Judas; and it is in the Cross itself, wherein the virtue of our Lord has shone, that you have been conquered and hewn down with your powers and dominations. So hide your head, enemy of God, and humble yourself under the sign of the Divine Cross, whose heritage is the Kingdom of Christ."

While the Saint was saying these and similar things, and while at each word he made the sign of the Cross, the dragon, vanquished by the power of this emblem, went away in abasement into the depths of the earth. But while these things were taking place, the other serpent insidiously coiled about the Saint's feet and legs. Seeing it about his feet, the holy hermit prayed and ordered it to withdraw, saying, "Go back, satan. In the name of Christ, you can no longer do me any harm." It withdrew to the mouth of the cave, making a terrible racket with its lower parts, and filled the cave with such a stench that it was impossible not to believe that it was the devil. And after that there no longer appeared to the Saint either serpent or dragon.

A cliff of the Auvergne (Orgues de Bort) similar to the one on which St. Caluppan struggled.

2. He was assiduous in the work of God and did nothing else than to read or pray, and even when he took a little nourishment he continued to pray. From time to time — although rarely — he fished in the river, and when he desired it, fish would present themselves immediately by the will of God. For bread, he received only what was sent from the monastery. If some devout person brought him loaves or wine, he sent it all for the feeding of the poor or of those of the monks who asked to receive from him either the saving sign of the Cross or the alleviation of their infirmities; that is to say, to those to whom he had given health by his prayers he also gave to eat, recalling what the Lord said in the Gospel about the crowd he had healed of various maladies: *I will not send them away fasting, lest they faint in the way* (Matt. 15:32).

And I do not think I ought to hide the benefit which the Divine goodness bestowed on him in this place. Since someone had to bring him water from the bottom of the valley, from a distance of nearly ten furlongs, he prayed to the Lord that it would please Him to cause a spring to arise in the very place where his cell was. Then that heavenly power that had formerly made water gush forth from a rock to ease the thirst of a whole people did not fail him, for immediately upon his prayer, a spring, welling up from the rock, spread out on the ground and formed rivulets of water on all sides. The Saint, delighted with the gift, hollowed out in the stone a little basin, which served him as a cistern and which held nearly two gallons, in order to save the water which had been divinely given him and of which he received each day only the amount necessary for himself and for the boy who had been given to serve him.

3. We ourselves came to this place with the Bishop Avitus;* and all these things we have related we take, some from the Saint himself, and others from having seen them with our own eyes. He was ordained deacon and priest by the hierarch we have just named. He gave many healthful remedies to those who suffered from various sicknesses. Still, he never went out of his cell to show himself to anyone, but he would stretch out his hand through a little window in order to give his blessing with the sign of the Cross. And if he was visited by someone, he would approach this window and grant him to pray and speak with him. At last he fulfilled the course of his life in this religious practice, in the fiftieth year of his age, if I am not mistaken, in order to go to the Lord.

---

* Bishop Avitus, St. Gregory's teacher, was bishop of Clermont from 572 to 594.

12

Saint Aemilianus the hermit

AND SAINT BRACCHIO THE ABBOT

Commemorated February 9 (†576)

THE Holy Spirit teaches us by the mouth of the Psalmist how the heavenly discipline communicates itself to those who guard it, and how it must be imposed upon those who do not observe it. "Take hold of discipline lest the Lord be angry and ye perish from the just way" (Ps. 2:12). And of those who are good Isaiah said, "The chastisement (discipline) of our peace will be upon him" (Is. 53:5, Sept.). This discipline, then, brings about the fear of the Lord; the fear of the Lord is the beginning of wisdom; wisdom teaches love of God; love of God raises man above the things of earth, it makes him to mount up to Heaven and places him in paradise, where the souls of the blessed, having drunk of the new wine of the vine of life, are at the banquet in the Kingdom of God.

It is necessary, then, that men desire to drink of the mystery of that vine in order to be able to go to the place of delights of such a pleasing habitation. If the vines which we see now stretching forth their branches, where leaves and grapes intermingle among the vine-branches, are so charming to behold, not only because of the abundant fruits they bear but also for the shade with which they protect us when we are burned by the sun's rays in summer; if, moreover, we see them lose their leaves and dry up after having given fruit in season — how much more ought we to desire those things which are never lacking and never dry up in the summer heat of temptation, which even after this term wherein is no more hope give us all we hope for and make us rejoice in them. Several have desired these things enough not only to abandon their wealth, but even to withdraw into the most uncultivated wildernesses, in order to quench the thirst of their longing for solitary life by the help of prayer and tears of repentance. Thus certainly the blessed Aemilianus did, a new hermit in our days.

1. Aemilianus, then, having left his parents and his possessions, sought solitude in the wilderness and withdrew to the remotest regions of the forests of Ponticiacens in the territory of Auvergne where, chopping down the trees, he made a little field which he cultivated and which furnished him with the food necessary for life. He also had a little garden which he watered with rainwater and from which he took vegetables which he would eat without any seasoning. He had no other consolations than those that came from God, for there were no other inhabitants than the beasts and birds, which would crowd around him every day as around a servant of God. He gave all his time to fasting and prayer, and no worldly care could turn him from them, because he sought only God.

2. There was at that time in the city of Clermont a man named Sigivald, bestowed with great authority, who had in his service a youth named Bracchio, which means in their language "bear cub." The man of whom I have just spoken had charged this young man with hunting wild boar; accompanied by a large pack of dogs, Bracchio went about the forest, and if he took anything, he would bring it to his master. One day, while he was pursuing an enormus boar with the dog pack, the quarry entered the enclosure around the Saint's cell. The baying pack followed it there and came to the entry of the first room, but suddenly they stopped short, not being permitted to go in after the boar.

Seeing this, Bracchio recognized with astonishment that there was something Divine there, and going toward the cell of the Saint, he noticed the boar standing before the door without fear. The elder came to greet Bracchio, embraced him, and invited him to sit down. When they were seated, he said to him, "I see you, beloved son, elegantly dressed and occupied with seeking things which dispose more to the loss of the soul than to its salvation. I beg you, abandon the master whom you serve here below and follow the true God, the Creator of heaven and earth, Who governs all things by His will, Who submits all things to His rule, and Whose very majesty, as you see, renders this beast fearless. May your master's authority — which is nothing — not make you vain and proud. For thus says the Apostle Paul: "He that glorieth, let him glory in the Lord" (I Cor. 1:31), and elsewhere: "If I yet pleased men, I should not be the servant of Christ" (Gal. 1:10). Subject yourself to the service of Him Who said, "Come unto Me, all ye that labor and are heavy laden, and I will give you rest" (Matt. 11:30), worship of Whom gains both present things and eternal life. And thus He said, if anyone renounces all he possesses, he "shall receive a hunderfold, and shall inherit eternal life" (Matt. 19:29).

ST. ᴂMILIANUS   ST. BRACCHIO

While the elder was occupied with these words and others equally worthy of a man, the wild boar withdrew safe and sound into the woods. The young man departed from the Saint, not without admiration from seeing that the wild boar he had begun to hunt became, despite his natural savagery, as gentle as a lamb in sight of the elder. Turning over in his mind various thoughts and asking himself what he should do — whether he should leave the world or continue to serve it — finally, touched by the Divine goodness and (I believe) by the prayer of Saint Aemilianus, he began to look for some secret way to come to the clerical state, for he dared not make it public because of his earthly master.

Meanwhile, although still a layman, he would get up from his bed two or three times during the night and prostrate himself in prayer to the Lord. But he did not know what to chant, because he did not know letters. However, often seeing in the oratory letters written above the icons* of the Apostles and the other saints, he copied them in a book. And since clerics and abbots were continually coming to his master's house, he would approach the youngest of them and ask them the names of the letters; from this he began to learn what they signified, and by the inspiration of God he knew how to read and write before he knew the rest of the letters.

---

* The Latin has the unusual word "iconicas" rather than the more usual "imagines."

After Sigivald had died, Bracchio hastened to the aforesaid elder, and when he had spent two or three years with him, he knew the psalter by heart. In the meantime, his brother, seeing that he did not wish to marry, often had the thought of killing him. Later, other monks joined the elder and himself.

3. Finally blessed Aemilianus fulfilled the measure of days counted for his life: he died about the ninetieth year of his age and left Bracchio as his successor. The latter, having founded a monastery, obtained from Ranichilde, Sigivald's daughter, several parcels of land which he left to this monastery. They were made up of woods from the Vindiacens estate. Having gone forth from this monastery, Bracchio came to Tours, where he built oratories and founded two monasteries.

One day some pilgrims came bearing relics of saints, which they placed on the altar table of the basilica of St. Martin of Tours, since they had to depart the next day. There Abbot Bracchio, who was keeping vigil in the basilica, noticed about midnight a huge ball of fire which went forth from the relics and rose up with a great light to the vault of the temple. This undoubtedly was something Divine, but it was seen only by him among all those present. After that he returned to Auvergne to his first monastery, whence, after having remained there five years, he came back to Tours, where he instituted abbots in the monasteries he had founded; then he returned once more to Auvergne.

When he was residing in his old cell, he was charged with re-establishing in the monastery of Manatense the rule which had been relaxed there through the negligence of the abbot. He led the purest life and courageously forced the others likewise to keep their chastity. His speech was soft, his demeanor courteous, but he showed himself so severe toward infractions of the rule that occasionally he was thought to be cruel. As for fasting, vigils, and charity, he had reached perfection.

When the time of his death was approaching, he had a dream, as he himself related to the blessed Bishop Avitus, in which he was transported to heaven into the presence of the Lord. There he saw the Cherubim and Seraphim who were shading the Divine majesty, and having opened a book, they signified to the Prophet Isaiah the words which he was to prophesy, while a host of angels surrounding the Throne of God made the heavens resound with their praises. And as he was contemplating this in ecstasy, he woke up. Examining this dream attentively, he recognized that God was announcing to him the end of his life. Then he said to the abbot whom he had established as superior of the monastery, "The place near the river, where I was intending to build an oratory, is very pleasant. I beg you, then, to carry out my desire, which is to consent to take my bones there."

When he was dead, he was buried in the oratory of his original cell. When the abbot wished to carry out the task which the Saint had commanded him, he found in that place, by God's leave, lime prepared long before and a foundation of the very size he had wanted to make. Then, when the work was done, he opened the tomb of Abbot Bracchio, whose body was found intact, as if he had died the night before. And so, two years after his death, he was taken to that place with great joy by the congregation of monks whom he had trained himself.

NOTES

St. Bracchio died on February 9, 576. St. Gregory knew him personally and heard from his own lips the above account of the miraculous ball of fire, as he states in *The Glory of the Confessors*, ch. 39.

Duke Sigivald is mentioned in St. Gregory's *History of the Franks* (Book III, chs. 6, 13 and 23). He was killed by King Theodoric.

The Manatense monastery existed as the Abbey of Menat until the French Revolution. It was 17 kilometers from Poinsat, the first residence of St. Bracchio.

St. Bracchio joined St. Aemilianus c. 534 A.D.

13

Saint Lupicinus of Lipidiaco

LAY RECLUSE OF THE AUVERGNE

Commemorated January 24 (†500)

THE athletes of Christ and those who triumph over the world, desirous
of losing this fleeting life, have wished to arrive at that life which abides
in perpetual joy, where is heard no sighing and which is terminated by
no end, whose light never goes out and whose serenity will be obscured
by no cloud of gloom. For this reason they always counted as nothing the
offenses and sorrows of the present life, knowing well that for the few
torments they suffered they will obtain great joys later. That is why
whoever aspires to take part in this combat should not be frightened by
any terror, should not be turned aside by any difficulty, should not be
discouraged by any sorrow in order to be worthy to be admitted to the
enjoyment of eternal happiness with God's elect. Such has been the path
of the holy man whose life is written and read here.

1. Lupicinus, a man of great sanctity and very strong in the works
of God, had originally been given over to seeking alms in the houses of the
devout and would give to those in similar circumstances what he was able
to acquire by this means. When he reached middle age he came to the
village of Berberens, which is now called Lipidiaco. There he found old
walls in which he shut himself up, and he withdrew from the sight of all
men, receiving through a small window a little bread and water, which

245

would sometimes last him three days, even though he was given very little. The water was brought in by a little channel, and as for his small window, it was shut by a rag. Both openings had been so concealed that it was not possible for anyone to see his blessed face.

Since he took delight in this place, day and night singing psalms in praise of God, he sought a means of afflicting his body more, for he remembered these words of the Apostle: "The sufferings of this present time are not worthy to be compared with the glory which shall be revealed in us" (Rom. 8:18). The whole day he carried on his neck, while he was chanting the praises of God in his cell, a huge stone which two men could scarcely move. At night, to mortify himself the more, he had fixed on the cane which he carried two thorns with the points turned out and which he would place under his chin in order to hinder his sleep.

Finally, toward the end of his life, his chest was caved in by the weight of the rock he carried, and he began to spit blood on the walls around him. But very often during the night, devout men would draw near his cell secretly, and there heard as if there were the voices of several persons who were singing psalms, and many of the infirm—and especially those tormented by fever of foul pustules—were healed simply by having been touched by his hand or by having received his blessing with the saving sign of the Cross.

2. When he was bent over with old age, he called his servant and said to him, "The time is past for hiding matters, and the time has come to tell them. So know that in three days I will be delivered from this world. Now call all the faithful, my brothers and my sons, to come visit us. I want to bid them farewell." On the third day his brethren came in crowds to his door; he opened it, and when he had greeted and embraced them all, he made his prayer to the Lord, saying, "I give Thee thanks, O Lord Jesus Christ, Who hast ordered my deliverance from all the stumbling-blocks of this world, and Who hast so vouchsafed to preserve me in this world from such things, that the author of all crimes has found nothing of his."

And turning toward the people, he said, "I beg you, beloved, to magnify the Lord with me, and let us exalt His name together (Ps. 33:3). For it is He Who has raised me up from the mire; Who has drawn me from the work of darkness and made me a participant of the joy of His friends; Who sent me His Angel to call me from this earthly dwelling and promised to lead me to eternal rest, in order that, having become a fellow of those whom He honors with His friendship, I will also be worthy to be admitted to His Kingdom."

O blessed man, who was worthy to be consoled in this body to the point of knowing those things which will be enjoyed in Heaven before leaving this world, and who could obtain here below the Divine power which David so often asked: "Make known to me, O Lord, my end, and the number of my days, so that I may know what is lacking to me" (Ps. 38:5). Finally, having lain upon the ground, he gave up to the Lord his soul which was sighing after Heaven. Then all fell prostrate and shed tears. They strove some to kiss his feet, some to remove some scrap from his clothing, others in rivalry to gather from the wall the blessed blood which he had spat, and each called himself unfortunate if he withdrew without being able to carry away from him some relics. The wall is still witness today of what we have just said, for it presents as many hollows as it merited receiving the spittle spat from the blessed one's mouth. It was the same with the channel through which the holy man drew the water necessary for his use: by kissing it with faith they drew health from it. I myself have seen many who, having dug out the spittings from that sanctified mouth, have been honored with receiving from it healing of various infirmities.

3. When the Saint was dead, as we have said, there was a certain respectable lady, who, after having had the body washed and reclothed in fitting garments, wished to convey it to the village of Trezelle; but the people of Lipidiaco were opposed to it, saying, "It is our land which nourished him—his body belongs to us." But the lady replied, "If you rely upon the needs of his life in order to oppose me, I also often sent him wheat and barley, which he ate himself or gave to others." The others replied, "He went out from among us, he drank the water from our river, and he mounted up to Heaven from the earth where we are. Is it right, then, that you who come from another country tear him from our hands? Now know that not one of us will allow it: he will be buried here." The lady answered: "You wish to determine his origin and his race? He came from foreign lands. You speak of the waters of your river? They contributed less to quenching his thirst than the waters of Heaven."

And, after they had bandied about such words, the inhabitants of Lipidiaco dug a grave and were intending to bury the Saint's body when the lady called for help, put the peasants to flight, and took up the holy body by force. She then had it conveyed in a coffin to the village of Trezelle, after having set out along the route troops of psalm-singers with crosses, tapers, and fragrant incense. The people, seeing this, repented and sent after the lady to say to her, "We have sinned in resisting you, and we sincerely recognize that the Lord's will is that it be so in this matter. Now we ask you not to be excluded from his funeral but to be admitted to the offices for him." She granted them to follow the procession, and thus both peoples were united and came together to the village of Trezelle, where, after the celebration of the Liturgy, they buried the blessed body with the greatest honor and joy.

In that village the most blessed one often manifested himself in miracles. But in Lipidiaco also he did not neglect to give even after his death many marks of his sanctity, as we have said above; for these two places were protected by the same Saint. And perhaps some unbelievers will try by their barking to refute what we have said. But let them know that I have seen the priest Deodatus, who is in his eighties, who related to me these things just as I have written them, declaring to me on oath that he had blended no falsehood with them.

NOTES

This Saint Lupicinus should not be confused with Saint Lupicinus of Condat (ch. 1). He died on Jan. 24, 500.

Lipidiaco is the present Dompierre-sur-Bebre, northeast of Clermont. Trezelle was a neighboring village.

14

Saint Martius the Abbot

BLESSED WARRIOR OF CHRIST

Commemorated April 13 (†525)

THE Divine goodness grants us a great benefit when it prepares for us a refuge for the remission of our sins if we forgive the negligence of others, if we are indulgent towards those who have offended us, if we reply to hatred with our blessing, our Lord Jesus Christ having said to us, "Love your enemies, do good to them that hate you, and pray for them which despitefully use you, and persecute you, that ye may be the children of your Father which is in Heaven" (Matt. 5:44-45). Behold the great treasure one amasses when he scorns anger, when he is reconciled with the one who has condemned him, when he forgives the one who has judged him. Contempt for anger makes you a son of God the Father, a co-inheritor with Christ, and establishes you as a dweller in the heavenly Kingdom.

Whence it is manifest that his sins are blotted out who grants in this world the grace of pardon to the one who has offended him. For such is the judgment our Lord has delivered on this matter: "If ye forgive men their trespasses, your Heavenly Father will also forgive you (Matt. 6:14). And, when He teaches His humble servants to pray to Him, He says, You shall speak thus to your Father: Forgive us our debts, as we forgive our debtors (Matt. 6:12).

This blessed abbot, Saint Martius, was a person celebrated for his holiness, instructed in Divine letters, and who kept in his heart the good of this judgment, of pardoning with a good heart him who offends you.

249

And not only did he pardon the fault, but he even accompanied the pardon with some present in order never to disgrace the person of the offender. But first let us say some words about his life before speaking of that grace whose benefit he received.

1.   Blessed Martius, abbot in the city of Clermont, was, it is said, originally from that territory. From his childhood he led a religious life and dedicated himself wholly to the works of God. Truly, he was sparing in his meals, generous in almsgiving, assiduous in vigils, very devout in his prayers. He used all his energy in subduing luxury by the bit of abstinence and the combat of frugality, for fear of giving the least hold on himself. Not without reason was he called Martius, he who, with the sword of the Holy Spirit cut off at their birth, in martial triumph, hostile thoughts which swarm in mortal souls. He was not deaf to these exhortations of the epistle which tells us, "Arm yourself with the armor of God and the sword of the Holy Spirit, so that you may be able to set at naught the flaming darts of the devil" (Eph. 6:11, 16, 17).

When he had come to the legal age of majority and shone in the city like a brilliant star, he thought that there was still something lacking to him. He went away some distance, took a pickaxe, and began to hack away at a rocky mountain in which he hollowed out cells and made himself little dwellings. This was in order that, held more tightly by the bond of sobriety, he might offer more easily to God Almighty the incense of his prayers and the whole burnt offerings of his praises on the altar of a pure heart, recalling these words spoken by the Lord in the Gospel: "Enter into your closet, and with the door closed pray to your Father, and your Father Who sees in secret will reward you" (Matt. 6:6). He knew that the Angels would not fail to console him with their visitations, if he withdrew himself from the sight of men. Thus he prepared for himself, in this rock which he had hollowed out of the mountain, the things necessary for a dwelling, making himself in the heart of these grottos—and out of the very rock—a bench and a couch or bed on which to rest his body, fatigued by laborious work. But all these objects were stationary, because they had been cut into the rock. When he wanted to sleep, he would put nothing underneath him except only the habit with which he was clothed, having only that for pad, mattress, and blanket. He possessed for his own only the worship of God, in which he remained constantly. The liberality of devout persons provided him his subsistence.

2. Finally the eternal Lord, Who does not cease to glorify His saints, began to make known to men His servant's worth, pointing out to them in what manner he rendered to the Divinity the worship due Him, when He vouchsafed the Saint the grace of healing illnesses. For he cast out demons from the bodies of the possessed in the name of Jesus Christ and halted the poison of malignant pustules by the sign of the Cross. He also healed tertian and quartan fevers by an infusion of blessed oil and granted to the people many other benefits by the will of Him Who dispenses all good things.

Attracted by the renown of such a great man, some people began to crowd about him, joyful over being able to be formed by his teaching. What more? He gathered men, formed monks, and made them perfect in the work of God. Indeed, his was great patience, and he armed himself with so much good in order to repulse the shafts hurled against him to harm him, that you would have thought him protected by a true cuirass of kindness.

The monks had a garden full of a large quantity of various vegetables and fruit trees, which was at once pleasing to behold and delightful for its fertility. In the shade of these trees, whose leaves murmered sweetly in the breath of the zephyr, the blessed old man was wont to sit. A bold man without fear of God, tormented by the desires of gluttony, forced the garden hedge and entered by stealth, something the Lord has condemned in the Gospel: "He who does not enter by the door is a thief and a robber" (John 10:1). Now this was during the night, and those things could not be done except during that time, because "everyone who does evil hates the light" (John 3:20). This man, then, after having picked vegetables, onions, garlic, and fruits, went to leave, laden with the burden of his culpable fraud, through the opening by which he had entered. But he could not find the opening anywhere, and overcome by the weight he was carrying and pricked by his conscience, he let forth deep sighs under the burden of this double affliction, leaning against the tree trunks from time to time. He ran round and round the whole garden, and not only did he not find the entrance, but he could not even see any longer the way he had opened under cover of darkness.

Then he was in a double fear: either of falling into the monks' hands or of being taken by the judge. In the midst of these burning thoughts, the night slipped away and the day, which he did not desire, drew nigh. At this time the abbot would use the night for singing Psalms, and he

learned, by a revelation from God, I think, what was happening. At day-
break he called the prior of the monastery and said to him, "Run quickly
to the garden; an escaped ox has gotten in, but he has done no damage.
Approach him, and having given him needful things, let him go, for thus
it is written, 'Thou shalt not muzzle a threshing ox' (I Cor. 9:9; Deut. 25:4)."

The prior did not understand what this meant, but he went to carry
out the order. The man, seeing him come, threw down the things he had
taken, took to flight, and then, plunging his head into the middle of the
thorns and brambles, in the manner of swine, tried to get out the same
way he had come in. The monk seized him and said to him, "Do not fear,
my son, because our elder sent me to lead you out from this place." Then,
gathering up all the man had thrown away, the fruits with the vegetables,
he put this load on the man's shoulders. Opening the door, he dismissed
him saying, "Go in peace, and hereafter do not repeat the base act you
have committed."

3. This priest, like a true lamp enlightening the world with a pure
light, frequently cast out infirmities by the efficacy of his virtues. A
certain Nivardus, for a long time racked with fever and constantly drinking
water in order to quench the fire of his illness, became dropsical to the
point where his belly and stomach swelled visibly like a bladder. In des-
peration from such an infirmity, he asked to be taken by cart to the Saint's
abode. He was raised from his bed, placed on a cart, and driven to the
cell of Saint Martius, humbly begging the priest of God to lay his hands
on him. The Saint prostrated himself in prayer before the Lord, turned
toward the sick man, and gently rubbing his limbs, gave him back his
health in the sight of all. Now, it is said that this swelling with which the
body of Nivardus was afflicted disappeared so completely under the Saint's
fingers that afterward no trace of this illness remained.

I learned these things from my father, for this Nivardus was bound
to him by a close friendship. He even affirmed having seen the Saint and
said that when he was still young, about eleven years old, he had some
attacks of tertian fever. Then his friends led him to the man of God, who
was already old and near the end of his days and who could scarcely see
any more. And when he had placed his hand on the boy, he asked, "Who
is this, or whose son is he?" They answered, "This boy is your servant
Florentius, son of the Senator George." And the Saint said, "May the Lord
bless you, my son, and may healing be granted to your weakness." When

the boy had kissed his hands and thanked him, he went away healed. Moreover, he affirmed that he no longer felt in his whole life any effect of that sickness.

4.   At length, at the age of ninety, covered with the sweat of a good combat, having come to the end of the course of his life and always keeping watch over his faith in God, the Saint went to receive that crown of righteousness which the Lord was to give him on the day of reckoning.   Then his body, bathed with great honor and clothed in becoming garments, was buried in the monastery oratory.   That his holy tomb has been made famous by the Divine virtues manifested there, there is no need of other witnesses than the crowd of the sick who go there and return home healed immediately.   And indeed, the sick who go there from various lands not only find solace, but also most often they feel the shivers of fever which agitate their limbs succeeded by perfect health, by the grace of our Lord Jesus Christ, Who, having of old called the dead from the tomb, now glorifies by illustrious miracles the tombs of the Saints.   To Him may there be glory unto the ages of ages.   Amen.

NOTES

Saint Martius reposed on April 13, 525. Up to the 18th century his tomb was kept in a chapel in the Abbey of St. Illidius (see ch. 2) in Clermont, but now it is lost.

15

Saint Senoch the Abbot

BLESSED HEALER OF TOURS

Commemorated October 24 (†576)

"VANITY of vanity," says the Preacher, "and all is vanity" (Eccl. 1:2). Is it then true that all which takes place in the world is vanity? Whence it happens that God's saints, whom no ardor of passions burn, no goad of concupiscence pricks, no mire of infamous luxury soils, and whom the tempter with his artifices does not even harm in imagination, so to speak, regarded themselves as being perfectly just, and following this, being puffed up with the pride of arrogant presumption, have often fallen, so that those whom the sword of the gravest crimes could not dispatch have been easily smothered by a light smoke of vanity. Thus it happened to him of whom we are going to speak, who, when he shone with many virtues, would certainly have fallen into the abyss of arrogance if he had not been held back by the solicitous exhortations of faithful brethren.

Blessed Senoch (died Oct. 24, 576), a Teiphale by nationality, was born in the Poitou village called Tigfauge, and, having turned toward the Lord, he became a cleric and founded a monastery. In the territory of Tours he found old walls on the ruins of which he built comfortable dwellings; he also found there an oratory where it is said that our illustrious St. Martin had prayed. He rebuilt it with great care, and having set up in it an altar in which was contrived a receptacle suitable for the relics of saints, he invited the bishop to come and bless it. The blessed bishop Euphronius went there, and after blessing that altar he bestowed on him the honor of the diaconate.

255

After the celebration of Liturgy, when they wished to enclose the reliquary in the prepared place, it was discovered that the reliquary was too large and could not be set in place. Then the deacon prostrated himself in prayer with the bishop, and shedding tears, he obtained what he asked. Astonishing thing! The place which had been too narrow became enlarged by the Divine power, and the reliquary shrank to such an extent that the latter fit easily, to the great wonder of those present.

Gathering together three monks in this place, he served the Lord diligently and in the beginning walked in the narrow path of life, taking very little food and drink. During the days of the Holy Great Lent (Quadragesima) he increased his abstinence still more, for then he would eat only barley bread and drink only water, taking care to consume but one pound of each every day. Finally, he endured the harshness of winter, content with using absolutely nothing to cover his feet, and wearing iron chains on his neck, feet, and hands. Then, withdrawing from the sight of his brethren in order to lead a strictly solitary life, he shut himself up in a cell, praying continually, spending his days and nights in vigils and prayers, without allowing himself any distraction. The faithful, in their devotion, frequently brought him money, but instead of burying it in hiding places, he would put it in the purses of the poor, for he often recalled this oracle from the mouth of the Lord: "Do not lay up for yourselves treasure upon earth, because where your treasure will be, there also will be your heart" (Matt. 6:19, 21). So he gave away what he received, thinking only of God, in order to provide for the various needs of the indigent. Whence it happened that during his lifetime he freed from the bond of slavery and the burden of their debts more than two hundred unfortunate people.

2. After we had arrived in the country of Tours, he came out of his cell to see us. After greeting and embracing us, he went back again. He was, as we have said, very abstinent, and healed the sick. But, just as holiness came from abstinence, so also vanity began to creep in from holiness. For when he left his cell, he went with arrogant pride to pay a visit to his parents in the Poitou village we named above. Having returned, all inflated with pride, he sought to please only himself. But when we had reprimanded him and he had listened to what we said to him about those vainglorious ones who were banished from the Kingdom of God, he purged himself completely of his vanity and so humbled himself that there did not remain in him the slightest root of pride, which he confessed, saying,

"Now I recognize the truth of the words proceeding from the Apostle's sacred mouth: 'Let him who glories glory in the Lord' (I Cor. 1:31)."

But since the Lord was working through him many miracles for the sick and he said that he wished to shut himself up in order that he appear to no human countenance, we gave him the counsel not to confine himself in such reclusion except during the days between the repose of Saint Martin and the solemnity of the Lord's Nativity, or likewise during the forty days before the Feast of Pascha—during which the authority of the Fathers obliges us to fast with greater abstinence—but for the rest of the year to place himself at the disposition of the sick. He listened to our opinion, voluntarily received our words, and obeyed them without variance.

3. At last, having said something of his way of life, we come now to the miracles which the Divine Power was pleased to accomplish through him for healing many infirmities. A certain blind man by the name of Popusitus came to him (at that time the blessed Senoch had already been ordained priest) and asked him for something to eat; but when his eyes were touched by the holy priest's hand with the sign of the Cross, he recovered his sight immediately. Another young man from Poitou, laboring under the same affliction and hearing of the confessor's works, begged him that he might receive the light he had lost. Without delay the Saint invoked the name of Christ and made the sign of the Cross over the blind man's eyes. Immediately there was a flow of blood and light entered, and after the passage of twenty years, the light of day illuminated the two extinguished stars in the unfortunate man's brow.

Two young men who were sick in all their members and who were bent round like balls were brought into the Saint's presence. When he had touched them with his hands, their limbs became straight, and in the space of an hour he delivered both of them: he doubled his beneficent work by a double miracle. A boy and a girl were also presented to him with their hands all drawn up. Now it was the Mid-Pentecost, and when they begged the servant of God to grant them the use of their hands, he, because of the great concourse of people who had flocked to the church, deferred doing what they asked, declaring himself unworthy that God should accomplish through him such marvels for the infirm; at last he yielded to everyone's entreaties and took the hands of the unfortunate ones in his own; when he touched them the fingers straightened out, and he sent both away healed. Likewise, a woman named Benaia came with her eyes shut and went away with those same eyes opened, after he had touched them with his healing hand.

Nor do I believe it ought to be hidden how it often happened that, by his words, the venom of serpents did no harm. In fact, two persons swollen up from having been bitten by a serpent came to cast themselves at his feet, begging him to drive out by his virtue the venom which the fang of an evil beast had diffused in their mortally stricken members. He made his prayer to the Lord, saying, "O Lord Jesus Christ, Who in the beginning created all the elements of the world and has ordained that the serpent, envious of man's excellence, abide under the curse (Gen. 3:14), drive out from these Thy servants the evil of his venom, in order that they triumph over the serpent and not he over them." While pronouncing these words, he touched all parts of their bodies, and forthwith the swelling was compressed and the venom deprived of all its harmful effect.

The day of the Lord's Resurrection had arrived, and a certain man, on his way to the church, saw a large herd of animals destroying his crop; he groaned, saying, "Woe to me, for the work of a whole year is going to perish without there remaining anything." And taking an axe, he cut off branches in order to stop up the opening in the hedgerow. But immediately his hand drew up and held tightly in spite of itself what it had freely taken hold of. Stricken with pain and dragging behind him the branch on which his hand had fastened, this man came in sorrow to find the holy confessor and told him all that had happened. Then the Saint, having rubbed the man's hand with oil sanctified by blessing, took away the branch and healed the hand.

Thereafter he healed many of snake-bite and the poison of malignant pustules by making over them the sign of the Cross. Some, tormented by the hatred of the deadly demon, as soon as he laid his hands on them, recovered the integrity of their intelligence previously troubled by these demons which he cast out. And to all those whom he healed by the hand of God, if they were poor, he would give with great joy food and clothing. And he had such care for the needy that he took the trouble of building them bridges to cross the rivers, lest someone have reason to mourn the shipwrecks which occur from the flooding of the waters.

4. When this holy man was renowned in the world by such marvels and was about forty years old, he was seized by a slight fever which kept him in bed for three years, which was announced to me when his end drew

near. I hastened to his bedside, but I could elicit no word from him, for he was very exhausted, and after about an hour he gave up the spirit. To his funeral flocked a multitude of those redeemed persons, of whom we spoke above, that is, of those whom he had delivered from slavery or from their debts, or whom he fed or clothed. They lamented, saying, "To whom are you leaving us, holy Father?" Later, when he was laid in the sepulchre, he often manifested himself by evident miracles. On the thirtieth day after his death, when Liturgy was being celebrated at his tomb, a sick man named Chaidulfus drew near to ask alms and recovered the use of his limbs as soon as he had kissed the pall which covered the sepulchre. Many other marvels were accomplished there, of which I have made known these to be held in memory.

ST. VENANTIUS THE ABBOT

16

Saint Venantius the Abbot

CONQUEROR OF DEMONIC POWERS
Commemorated October 13 (†c. 400)

THE Divine power makes a present at once unique and multiple to the churches and the peoples of the earth when it continually bestows on the world not only favorable intercessors for sinners, but even teachers of eternal life. Thus, what appears to be only a single gift is at the same time double when it is bestowed by the Divine Majesty, because those who wished to ask have abundantly received, following these words: "Ask and ye shall receive" (John 16:24), and the like. Thus, the human mind must seek carefully and incessantly what was the life of the saints in order that, challenged by this study and set on fire by this example, it always might tend toward what it knows to be pleasing to God and might be worthy to be delivered by Him or be hearkened to. See, then, what the saints sought from the Divine Majesty, asking Him continually to instill these virtues in their hearts, to accomplish them in their deeds, and to express them by their mouths, in order that, with their spirits purified in thought, word and deed, they might think in a holy way, speak with justice, and act with honesty.

Whence it happens that while they were subjecting themselves to what could be pleasing to the Divinity, they obtained to be discharged from the debt of sin, to be drawn out of the contagious mire of vices, and to be invited, by reason of their worth, to enter into the heavenly Kingdom. They in fact would hold before their eyes the examples of their predecessors and extol the Lord Almighty because of the virtues of those whom they were seeking — as we have

261

said — to take as models. And we also, in trying to say something in praise of the devout servant of God, the abbot Venantius, return to the Divinity His own gifts, which have certainly been fulfilled by His right hand, instead of our speaking of the things themselves which the saints have wrought; and we pray to Him to open the mouth of a dumb man in order to make known the works of this hierarch, for if we truly recognize ourselves to be slight in knowledge, we also know well in our conscience that we are sinners.

1.   Saint Venantius (d. Oct. 13, c. 400) was a native of the territory of Bourges, of free and Christian parents according to the dignity of this world. When he came to the age when his youth was in bloom, he was engaged by his parents in the bond of betrothal. And when, following the inclination of that age of life, he yielded with grace to love the girl, often bringing dainties to her and going so far as to offer her slippers, there came to him, by an inspiration of God, (the idea) to come to Tours. There was at that time a monastery near the basilica of Saint Martin where the abbot Silvinus, under an austere rule, led a flock consecrated to the service of God. The pious young man, coming to the abbot and seeing the miracles of blessed Martin, said within himself, "It seems to me better to serve Christ without defilement than to be involved by marital union in worldly contagion. I will leave my fiancee from the country of Bourges and will join myself by faith to the universal Church, in order that I not contradict by my deeds the feelings I have in my heart."

Turning these thoughts about in his mind, he came before the abbot, and casting himself at his feet, he manifested to him his intimate feelings while shedding tears. And the abbot, giving thanks to God for the faith of this young man and addressing to him a priestly admonition, tonsured him and admitted him to the ranks of the monastic flock. From that moment he showed himself so full of humility toward his brethren and of charity toward all, and he came to such a high degree of sanctity, that all were attached to him as to a near relative. As a result, when the abbot died, he was called to replace him by the choice of the brethren.

2.   One Sunday he was invited to celebrate Liturgy and said to his brethren, "My eyes are already covered with darkness, and I can no longer read from a book. Have me replaced by another priest." While the priest was officiating, he stood near him, and when the moment arrived when, according to Christian custom, the holy offering was to be blessed by the sign of the Cross, he saw as it were at a window in the apse a ladder positioned, by which a venerable old man was descending, honored with the clerical state, who with his outstretched hand was blessing the sacrifice offered on the altar. These things took place in the basilica of Saint Martin, but no one was worthy to see them except him, and we do

not know for what reason the others did not see them. However, he later told it to his brethren, and there is no doubt that the Lord made these things visible to His faithful servant, to whom He had vouchsafed to reveal the secrets of the heavenly mysteries.

The same Saint Venantius came back one Sunday, supported by his staff, from visiting the basilicas of the saints after praying there. He stopped motionless in the middle of the courtyard of the church of the blessed confessor, listening with his eyes fixed toward heaven for a long time; then, taking some steps, he began to groan and emit long sighs. Questioned by those with him to know what it was, or whether he had seen something Divine, he replied, "Woe to us, languid and slothful as we are. I see that in heaven the solemnity of the Liturgy is far along, while we slothful ones have not yet begun the celebration of this mystery. I tell you truly, I have heard the voices of the Angels in heaven proclaiming 'Holy!' in praise of the Lord." Then he ordered that Liturgy be celebrated immediately in the monastery.

Nor will I pass over how once, when he was again returning from the churches after praying there according to his custom, as we have said before, while in the basilica during Liturgy they were singing the words of the Lord's Prayer, at the moment when the cantors said, "Deliver us from evil," he heard a voice which came from a tomb and said the same: "Deliver us from evil." One can well believe that he did not hear this without being of perfect merit. It was also given to him, when he had come to the grave of the priest Passivus, to learn from him both the nature of his merits and the amount of his heavenly consolation.

3. And although these are great matters, I believe I ought to speak now of the grace the Lord bestowed on the sick through him, for it cannot be doubted, as we have said above, that the hand of God has acted through him to whom the Lord wished to reveal such things of which we have spoken.

A young boy named Paul, who suffered great pains in his thighs and calves, came to the Saint and, casting himself at his feet, began to beg him to obtain by his prayer, from God's mercy, relief from his troubles. Straightway the Saint made his prayer; then, having rubbed the sick boy's limbs with blessed oil, he had him lie down on his bed, and at the end of an hour he ordered him to get up. The child got up, and by the Saint's hands was returned well to his mother.

The slave of a certain Faretrus, whom his master hated, took refuge in the priest's oratory. The master was filled with arrogance, and taking advantage of the holy man's absence, he carried off his slave and killed him. But he was immediately seized with fever and died. Often the Saint by his prayers stopped quartan, tertian and other fevers. By the life-giving sign of the Cross, he fought the poison of malignant pustules, and invoking the name of the Trinity he delivered the possessed from the demon. Often he also had to contend with the demons, but he emerged victorious from his combats. One night, having risen from his bed to go say the office, he saw two large live rams before his door, as if they had awaited his arrival, and as soon as they saw him they rushed toward him in fury. By opposing them with the sign of the Cross, he saw them disappear and entered into his oratory without fear.

Another night, returning from the oratory, he found his cell full of demons and said to them, "Whence have you come?" "From Rome," they answered, "and we left there to come here." He said to them, "Withdraw, wretched ones, and do not draw near to a place where the name of God is invoked!" At these words the demons vanished like smoke.

4.   The man who had received the grace of working these great miracles and others like them, having fulfilled the course of the present life, departed this world to possess eternal life, and his sepulchre is often glorified by a large number of resplendent miracles. An evil demon had troubled the spirit of a servant of a monastery called Mascarpion, who was possessed by the demon for three years and would come to make demonic grimaces by the blessed man's tomb. He was, we believe, delivered from this demon by the Saint's prayers, and he lived many years in sound mind.

The wife of Julian, who was suffering from quartan fever, was delivered from all fire and every chill as soon as she had touched the blessed man's tomb. Baudimund's wife was in the same state, and she was healed immediately when she had prostrated herself and prayed near the Saint's bed. We have also heard many other things about him, but these which we have written we consider to suffice for the belief of right-believing Christians.

NOTES

St. Venantius's monastery appears in a 10th-century charter as "abbatiola S. Venantii." The possible remains of this monastery were discovered in Tours in 1941.

17

Saint Nicetus, Bishop of Trier

EQUAL IN GLORY TO THE APOSTLES

Commemorated December 5 (†566)

I F it is necessary to add faith to the things which are said, it is principally, I think, to those which are related to us of the works of the saints for the merit of the faith, because we have not seen all the things of which we have written, but some have been confirmed for us by certain recountings, some by the witness of approved authors, and we have seen others of them by the witness of our own eyes. But what is worse is that men whose perverted intelligence does not want to believe what is written and, moreover, does not want to submit to what is proved to them, disdain as fictions even those things they have seen. They do not even have that confidence which the Apostle Thomas bore in his heart when he said, "Unless I see I will not believe" (John 20:25). "Blessed are they who have not seen and have believed" (John 20:30); for as soon as Thomas saw he immediately believed.

But, as we have said, there are many who not only do not believe the things they have seen, but who mock them. Whence, intending to write something about the virtues, the courage, the greatness of soul, the holiness of Saint Nicetus, Bishop of Trier, I expect to be criticized by some, who will say to me, "You who are young, how can you know the deeds of the elders? How will what they did come to your knowledge? These things which you have written are not regarded otherwise than as fictions which come to you."

That is why it is necessary to make known the narrator from whom I have learned the things which I will tell, in order to confound those who wish to obscure the truth. So let them know that the matters reported below I have taken from blessed Aredius,* abbot in the city of Limoges, raised by the bishop Nicetus himself, and who received from him the clerical order. And I do not believe he could be mistaken, since at the time when he recounted these things, God through him was illuminating the eyes of the blind, causing the paralyics to walk, and returning reason to the possessed after casting out the demons which possessed them. Nor is it to be believed, either, that he had wished to wrap himself in clouds of falsehood whom God often protected so well against clouds of rain that he was not touched by a single one of the falling drops, while those with him were completely wet.

In short, if it is necessary to doubt such a witness, it is also necessary to distrust the benefits of God. The aforementioned priest was thus saying to me of the bishop in question, "It is true, beloved brother, that I knew many things about Saint Nicetus by the witness of good men; but I have seen more of them with my own eyes or I have learned them from himself, although I drew them out of him with difficulty. And even though he acknowledged in simplicity certain things which God had vouchsafed to accomplish through him, he was so far from being thereby puffed up by vainglory that he did not speak of them to me without regret and without tears in his eyes, saying to me, "I wish, beloved son, to manifest to you these things in order that, living in great innocence of heart, you meditate on similar things. For no one would know how to raise himself to the height of God's virtues unless he were 'innocent in hands and pure in heart,' as sings David in his song (Ps. 23:4)." Having thus spoken to me, he began his account.

1. The bishop Saint Nicetus (†Dec. 5, 566) was destined for the clergy from the moment of his birth. Indeed, as soon as he was born, his head was seen to be completely devoid of hair, as happens with the newborn, but all around was a ring of fine hair, such that you would call it a clerical crown. As a result of this, his parents raised him with the greatest care, instructed him in letters, and entrusted him to the abbot of a monastery.

He showed himself in this place so devoted to the Lord that when the abbot died he succeeded him. In the exercise of his functions he bore himself in such a way for the instruction and correction of the brethren that not only did he wish that they abstain from doing evil, but he permitted no one to sin in word, saying, "My beloved, we must avoid all joking and idle words, for, in the same way that we ought to present our bodies to God entirely pure, even so we ought never open our mouths except for God's praise, because there are three

---

* See the life of St. Aredius, Part V, ch. 25 below.

reefs whereon a man runs aground: when he thinks, when he speaks, or when he acts. You then, beloved, avoid frivolity, malice, and the worst deeds." He thus would give these and many other exhortations to his brethren in order to make them pure and fit for God.

He was also very respected and honored by King Theodoric, because he had often revealed to him his sins and crimes in order to make him better by such reprimands. And because of this, when the bishop of the city of Trier died, the king designated Nicetus for the episcopate. The people by their consent and the king by his decree were unanimous in this regard, and he was led by honored persons of the highest dignity near the king to be consecrated bishop. Now when these had arrived near the city at sunset and prepared to set up their tents to stay there, they hurried to set their horses free and release them into the wheat fields of the poor. Seeing this, blessed Nicetus was touched with compassion and said, "Quickly chase out your horses from the poor man's crop; otherwise I will cut you off from my communion." The men answered him indignantly, "What are you saying? You have not yet entered into the episcopal dignity, and already you are threatening excommunication?" He replied, "I tell you truly, the king tore me away from my monastery in order to impose this burden upon me; the will of God will surely be done and not that of the king, when he will intend evil, because of the resistance I will raise." Then, rushing forth, he chased the horses from the field, and he was conducted to the city in the midst of these men's admiration.

He did not honor the person of powerful men but feared only God, both in his heart and in his works. One day, sitting in the bishop's chair, he was listening to the series of readings; he felt I do not know what upon his neck. Having tried two or three times to remove it with his hand, he was not able to find anything capable of burdening him so strongly. Turning his head right and left, he smelled a sweet odor and understood that this burden was that of the episcopal dignity.

2. From the time he assumed the episcopate, he showed himself so terrible to all those who did not observe God's commandments, that he declared with a herald's voice the approach of death. About this I think I ought to say something to confirm priestly censure, whether for the instruction of the people or for the amendment of the lives of present kings.

At the death of King Theodoric, his son Theodebert entered into possession of the kingdom and did many unjust things, concerning which the bishop often reproved him strongly, whether the king himself was the perpetrator or whether he neglected to punish those who committed them. One Sunday, behold, the king came into the church with men whom the bishop had excommunicated. After the lessons prescribed by the ancient canon were read and the gifts offered upon the altar of God, the bishop said, "The solemnity of the Liturgy will not be completed here today, unless those deprived of communion go out of the church first." The king wished to resist, but a young boy from among the people was suddenly seized by a demon and began to cry out with all his might in the midst of the pains of the torment he was suffering, proclaiming the virtues of the Saint and the crimes of the king. He said that the bishop was chaste and the king adulterous; that the former was humble through fear of Christ and the latter proud through royal glory; that the one would be presented before God without stain and that the other would soon be destroyed by the author of his crime. And when the king, struck with fear, asked that the possessed boy be ejected from the church, the bishop said, "First let those who follow you, that is, the incestuous, homicidals, and adulterers, be expelled from the church, and God will order the other to be quiet."

Immediately the king gave the order for all those who had been condemned by the episcopal sentence to leave the church. When they had been expelled, the bishop commanded the demoniac to be put out of the church. But he had fastened himself to a column, and ten men could not tear him from it. Then the Saint of God, making the sign of the Cross under his vestment, for fear of bringing vainglory upon himself, commanded the demon to release him. Immediately he fell to the ground with those who were drawing him with all their strength; then, an instant later he got up healed. After the service he could not be found, and no one knew whence he came or where he had gone. Nevertheless, the majority thought he had been sent by God to make known the works of the king and those of the bishop. Then it happened that at the bishop's prayer the king became gentler, so that the pastor marked for heavenly rewards could with justice hear, as if it had been said of himself, this prophetic word: "He who brings forth what is precious from the vile shall be as my own mouth" (Jer. 15: 19).

The bishop preached every day to the people, uncovering the vices of each and continually praying for the forgiveness of those who confessed them. As a result, the venom of hatred often was kindled against him, because of the frankness with which he pointed out the actions of many. But he would go to offer himself to the persecutors and bare his neck to the sword raised to strike, and God did not allow him to suffer any harm. He had indeed desired to die for justice, if he had found for that a cruel enough enemy, and he would say, "I would willingly die for justice." He also excommunicated King Clothaire several times for unjust actions, and the latter threatened him with exile in vain; he was never afraid.

3. At one time, when he had been led into exile, he was repulsed by the other bishops, who were flatterers of the king; abandoned by all his own people, he said to a deacon who alone remained faithful to him, "Now what are you going to do? Why have you not followed your brethren, to go where you will, as the others have done?" He said, "As the Lord my God lives, I will not abandon you as long as I have breath in my body." "Since you speak thus, I want to reveal to you what it has pleased God to make known to me; tomorrow at this hour I will take back the honor of which I have been deprived, and I will be returned to my church, and those who have deserted me will come back to me in great confusion.

The deacon in astonishment waited for the result of these words which would soon be tested. The next day there arrived a messenger from King Sigiburt entrusted with letters announcing the death of King Clothaire. Sigibert wrote that he was going to take possession of his kingdom and that he wished to have the bishop's friendship. Upon learning this, Saint Nicetus returned to his church, re-entered into his authority—to the great confusion of those who had abandoned him—and received them all nevertheless with good will. Who would be able to say now how he had strength in preaching, vigor in discussion, constancy in strife, wisdom in instruction? He always had the same steadfastness in adversity as in prosperity, without fearing threats and without being deceived by endearments. For truly, as he who told me these things (Saint Aredius) was saying, there was little to which he did not have to be exposed, like the Apostle Paul (II Cor. 11:26)—in danger from rivers, in danger from thieves, in danger in the city, in danger among false brethren, and many others.

One day he was crossing the Moselle in a boat when he was pushed by the current against the pilings of a bridge. Hanging on only to one piling with his hands, he held the boat with his foot and thus could be saved by onlookers, although he nearly drowned. To him the snares of the tempter, as he thought, were not strangers. Moreover, the author of all crimes several times presented himself before his eyes as if to do him harm. One day when he was travelling, he got down from his horse to relieve himself and went into some dense brush. Behold, all at once he saw before him a frightful snake, of great length, of formidable girth, black in color, with eyes shining and large as those of a mad bull, and with a large mouth which it opened as if to swallow the man of God. But when he made the sign of the Cross, this apparition vanished like rising smoke, and there was no doubt that the prince of crime had shown himself to the Saint in this instance.

4. As we have said, he was very strong in fastings. For it was during the time when the others would take their meals that he, with his head covered by

his hood lest he be recognized in public, would often go through the basilicas of the saints followed by a single servant. God also gave him the gift of healing. While he went through the abodes of the saints clothed as we have just said, he came to the temple of the bishop Saint Maximin in the courtyard of which three demoniacs were lying, overcome with sleep after many convulsions. Seeing them fast asleep, he made before them the sign of the Cross, and immediately awakening with loud cries, they made an effort to vomit and were delivered.

The inguinary plague was raging among the people of Trier in the precincts of the city, and the priest of God was assiduously imploring the Lord's mercy for the sheep confided to him. All at once, at night, a loud noise was heard, like a violent clap of thunder upon the bridge, and such that one would have thought the city to have been split in two. And while all the people, full of fear, were sitting upon their beds in expectation of death, there was heard in the midst of the uproar a voice more distinct than the others, which said, "What ought we to do, countrymen? For at one of the city gates the bishop Eucharius is watching; at the other Maximin is standing; Nicetus is established in the middle.* So there is nothing for us to do than to leave this city to their protection." As soon as this voice had made itself heard, immediately the sickness stopped, and from that moment no one died. From this it is not to be doubted that that city was protected by the bishop's virtues.

One day, invited by the king, he said to retinue, "Let us look for a great many fish, so that when we go before the king we have wherewith to fulfill our obligation and furnish abundantly for our friends." They said to him, "Our trap, into which the fish have been accustomed to come, is completely empty, and our ponds themselves have been pulled away from their places by the river's impetuousness." Hearing this, the Saint entered his cell, called a servant, and said to him, "Go, tell the head cook to take fish from the river." He carried out the order but only made the man laugh. When he returned, the bishop said to him, "I see you took this order I gave you, and that they did not want to listen to it. Go and tell them to go." And after they had received the order harshly two or three times, they ended by going angrily to the fishery, and looking at it, they found it so full of fish that scarcely ten men could take out all that were there. Divine power often furnished Saint Nicetus what was useful for him.

5. I did not think I ought to pass over in silence what was shown to him by the Lord concerning the kings of the Franks. He saw in a dream a great tower

---

* The church built over the grave of St. Eucharius is outside the south gate of Trier, the church over the grave of St. Maximin is outside the north gate, and the cathedral where St. Nicetus served is in the middle. Both St. Eucharius and St. Maximin were bishops of Trier, the former in the 3rd century and the latter in the 4th century.

St. Nicetus' cathedral in Trier as it looks today. Built in 325 by order of St. Constantine, it was restored in the 6th century by St. Nicetus. Reconstruction and decoration of it continued until the 19th century.

whose height was such that it nearly touched the sky. It had a large number of windows through which angels were looking, while God stood on its top. One of the angels was holding a large book in his hand and saying, "This king will live so much time and that one so much," and he named them all, one after another, those who were living and then those yet to be born. He announced the good or bad nature of their reigns and the length of their lives. When he would call the name of each, the other angels would respond, "Amen." And thereafter it thus came to pass for each as the Saint announced in this revelation.

Once, when Nicetus returned from a journey by water to find the king, he fell asleep. Behold, the river, disturbed by wind, began to rise up in high waves, so much that one would have thought the boat on the point of sinking. Now the bishop, as we have just said, was sleeping I know not what sleep, when it seemed to the sleeper that someone was choking him. Awakened by those around him, he made the sign of the Cross over the water, and the storm ceased. Then, since he was emitting frequent sighs, they asked him what he had seen. He answered them, "I had intended to keep silence, but I will speak. It seemed to me that I was holding a net in order to pick up the whole world and that I had no other help than this boy Aredius." And it is with reason that the Lord wished to show him as a fisherman, for every day he took whole peoples for the Divine service.

A man came to him who had very long hair and beard and who, casting himself at the Saint's feet, said to him, "I am he, my Lord, who found myself in danger on the sea and was delivered by your help." But the Saint, having reproved him sternly for his wishing to give him glory for that, said to him, "Say how God saved you from that danger, for my power could not save anyone." The man answered, "Recently, after I had embarked on a vessel in order to go to Italy, a crowd of pagans entered the vessel with me, so that I found myself the only Christian in the middle of this host of peasants. But a storm arose, and I began to call upon the name of the Lord and to beg Him that your intercession could deliver me from death. The pagans, in their turn, called upon their gods: this one Jupiter, that one Mercury, another Minerva, yet another Venus. And when we were in danger of perishing, I said to them, 'Men, stop calling upon these gods, for they are not gods but demons. If you want to be drawn out of the danger we are in, call upon Saint Nicetus, in order that he obtain from God's mercy that we be saved.' With one voice they cried out in these words: 'God of Nicetus, save us!' And then the sea was calmed immediately, the wind fell, the sun reappeared, and our vessel directed itself where we wished. For myself, I made a vow not to have my hair cut before I had presented myself before you." Then this man, having had his hair cut by the bishop's order, went away to Auvergne, from where he said he came.

I would have been able to say yet more things I have taken from the abbot I have named, but I think the book ought to be ended.

6. When he knew that the time of his death was drawing near, he informed his brethren, saying, "I have seen the Apostle Paul with John the Baptist, who were inviting me to eternal rest and who were showing me a crown adorned with celestial pearls and saying to me, 'See the things you will enjoy in the Kingdom of God.' " He related these words to a small number of faithful persons; then, after a few days, finding himself afflicted with a slight fever, he gave up his soul to God and was buried in the basilica of Saint Maximin the bishop. His tomb is famous today for the Divine miracles which take place there.

NOTES

Not to be confused with St. Nicetius of Lyons, who was St. Gregory's uncle.

18

Saints Ursus and Leobatius

HOLY ABBOTS OF SENAPARIA

Commemorated July 28 (†c. 500)

WHEN the Lawgiver-prophet began to speak of the creation of the world and to show the Lord forming the expanse of the heavens by the majesty of His right hand, he added, "And God made two great lights and the stars and placed them in the firmament of heaven, so that they rule over the day and the night and shine in the firmament of heaven" (Gen. 1:16-17). Likewise, in the firmament of human understanding He placed — as the authority of the Fathers affirms — two great lights, that is, Christ and the Church, in order that they shine in the darkness of ignorance and illuminate our humble intelligence as the Evangelist John says of the Lord, because truly He is the light of the world, Who "enlightens every man who comes into the world" (John 1:9). He also placed in this firmament stars, that is, the patriarchs, prophets, and apostles, who instruct us with their doctrine and illuminate us with their miracles, as He has said in the Gospel: "You are the light of the world" (Matt. 5:14), and again, "Let your light so shine before men that they may see your good works and glorify your Father Who is in heaven" (Matt. 5:16). The Apostles, to whom these words were addressed, have rightly been taken for the whole Church, which does not have wrinkles and which remains without blemish, as the Apostle says: "That He might present the Church to Himself pure, having no blemish or wrinkle or anything similar." (Eph. 5:27).

Now, thanks to the doctrine of the Apostles there are up to our times men who, like unto stars in this world, not only were resplendent by the light of their merits, but also shone by the grandeur of their teachings; and who have lighted the whole universe by the rays of their preaching, going to teach in every place,

275

founding monasteries for Divine worship, instructing men to abstain from earthly cares and to despise the darkness of concupiscence in order to follow the true God, by Whom everything has been created. That is what the account will show, given by faithful brethren, about the abbots Ursus and Leobatius.

1. The abbot Ursus (d. about 500) was an inhabitant of the city of Cahors, and from the beginning of his life he was very devout and filled with love for God. Having left Cahors, he came into the territory of Biturious, where he founded three monasteries, at Tausiriacus, Onia, and Pontiniacus, and after he had left them under the government of priors commendable for their sanctity and wise management, he went on into the territory of Tours and came to a place to which someone had once given the name Senaparia.

He built an oratory and founded a monastery there. Committing it to the prior Leobatius with the charge of having the rule observed, he went to build yet another monastery, which is now called Loccis, situated on the river Indre, in the hollow of a mountain, above which was built a castle bearing the same name as the monastery. There, having established a congregation of monks, he made in his heart the resolution to go no more to another place, but to labor in this place with his own hand with the whole congregation and there to earn his livelihood in the sweat of his brow, enjoining among other things upon his brethren what the Apostle Paul said to his: "Labor with your hand, so that you may have wherewith to give to those in need" (Eph. 4:28), and also, "Let him who will not labor not eat" (II Thes. 3:10). The Lord also granted him the gift of healing, so that by a single breath from his mouth he cast out demons from the bodies of the possessed. The Lord also vouchsafed to work other miracles through him. He was abstinent in food and drink and ceaselessly enjoined upon his monks to keep their eyes and their thoughts from all excess.

2. While he was living in this way, when his brethren were grinding wheat necessary for their food, turning the millstone by hand, he had the thought of lessening their fatigue by putting a mill in the Indre River. Having had two rows of pilings placed in the river, with a large pile of stones for making sluices, he directed the water into a canal and thus used the current to make the mill wheel turn rapidly. By this means he lessened the monks' labor, so that a single brother sufficed for this task.

Now a Goth named Sichlaire, a favorite of King Alaric, desired to appropriate this works for himself and said to the abbot, "Give me this mill for my own property, and I will give you in return what you want." The abbot answered him, "Our poverty built it only with great pain. We cannot give it now, lest my brethren die of hunger." "If you wish," said Sichlaire, "to give it to me in good will, I will thank you; otherwise, I will take it by force, or else I will certainly make another for which I will turn aside the water by sluices which will no longer allow your wheel to turn." The abbot replied, "You will not do what God does not will, and you will not take it."

Then Sichlaire, boiling with anger, had another works similar to that one built below it. And when it happened that the water rising up under the mill-wheel accumulated to the point of preventing the wheel from turning as usual, the mill became inoperative. The watchman went to find the abbot at midnight, it is said, while he was keeping vigil in the oratory with the brethren. "Father," the watchman said, "rise and pray devoutly to the Lord, for the wheel of our mill is stopped by the inundation of the new canal Sichlaire has made." Upon hearing this, the abbot immediately sent a brother to each monastery which he had founded in order to say, "Prostrate yourselves in prayer until I inform you otherwise." He himself did not go out from the oratory, where he fervently addressed his prayer to the Lord, awaiting the coming of His mercy. Thus he did for two whole days and nights. The third day began to break when the monk who had charge of the mill reported that the wheel was turning as usual with great speed. Then the abbot went out of the oratory with the brethren, approached the bank, and looked for the mill which Sichlaire had built, but could not find it. Drawing nearer in order to look into the depth of the water, he could see no trace of it, and no one after that saw of it wood, or stone, or iron, or any other kind of trace, and it could only be conjectured that in the same place where he had built it, the earth had opened by Divine power to swallow it and make it disappear from the eyes of men. Then the abbot sent messengers to say to his brethren, "Rest now from your labors, for God has avenged our injury."

3. Endowed with these and similar virtues, he fulfilled the course of his life and passed to the Lord. Thereafter, at his tomb the possessed were healed and the blind recovered their sight. After his death, those whom he had placed at the head of the monasteries he had founded, were made abbots by the benevolence of the bishops. Leobatius became abbot in the monastery of Senaparia in the territory of Tours, where he lived in great sanctity and came to a ripe old age; he died and was buried there.

NOTES

In Senaparia, now called Sennevieres, there was built a Romanesque church dedicated to St. Leobatius.

St. Leobatius is also known as St Leubais.

ST. MONE-GUNDE

19

Saint Monegunde

A DEVOUT WOMAN, A WONDERWORKER

Commemorated July 2 (†530)

THE excellent gifts from on high which are bestowed on the human race cannot be comprehended by sense, nor expressed in words, nor represented in writing, since the Saviour of the world Himself, from the beginning of creation, willed to make Himself seen by the patriarchs, and to be announced by the Prophets, and at last did not disdain — the Almighty and Immortal Creator — to enclose Himself in the womb of the Ever-Virgin and Most Pure Mary, to clothe Himself in the garment of mortal flesh, to go to death for the reparation of man dead through sin, and to rise victorious. While we were seriously injured by the blows of our sins and all covered with wounds which we had received from brigands lying in wait for us, after He had mingled oil and wine, He led us to the inn of heavenly medicine, that is, to the dogma of the Holy Church. By an unfailing reward promised to those who keep His precepts, He exhorts us to live after the example of the saints. He gives us as models not only robust men, but even the weaker sex, fighting not feebly but with virile vigor. He gives a place in His heavenly Kingdom not only to men who fight as is proper, but even to women who take a hand in these combats by their wholesome toils: which He causes to be seen by us in our day in blessed Monegunde, who, having left her native land as did that prudent queen who came to hear the wisdom of Solomon, betook herself to the basilica of blessed Martin in order to wonder at the miracles which occur there every day and there to take in as at a priestly source what becomes worthy to be admitted into the groves of paradise.

1. The most blessed Monegunde (d. July 2, 530), from the city of Chartres, was married according to her parents' wish and had two daughters, from whom she gave herself over to deep joy and said, "God has made me fertile and given me two daughters." But the bitterness of this world soon dissapated this earthly joy, for both of her daughters were led by a slight fever to the final debt of nature. After this happening, this mother, desolate and lamenting over the loss of her children, ceased not to weep night and day, so that neither her husband, nor her friends, nor any of her neighbors could console her. Coming to herself at last, she said, "If I receive no consolation for the death of my daughters, I fear thereby to offend my Lord Jesus Christ. But now, leaving off these lamentations, I will sing with the blessed Job, consoling myself: 'The Lord gave, the Lord hath taken away; as it was pleasing to the Lord, thus hath He done; blessed be the name of the Lord' " (Job 1:21).

Saying this, she put off her mourning dress, had a cell made for herself where there was only a little window through which she could see the day, and there, scorning all things earthly and caring no longer for the company of her husband, occupied herself only with God to Whom she entrusted herself, praying for her own sins and for the sins of the people, having only one little girl in her service in order to get her necessary things. She would take barley flour and ashes mixed with water, kneading the mass with care, and make from it a dough from which she would shape loaves with her own hands, and baking them herself she would fortify herself after long fasts. The rest of the food from her house she would give to the poor.

One day it happened that the girl who served her (I believe she was seduced by the wiles of our enemy who always is in the habit of harming those who are good) withdrew from her, saying, "I cannot remain with this mistress who practices such abstinence, and I would rather go into the world where I will have food and drink in abundance." Five days had already elapsed since the departure of this girl, and her devout mistress received neither the usual flour nor water. Nevertheless, she remained still, always abiding firmly in Christ, in Whom one who is established cannot be shaken, whether by any whirlwind or by any stirring of waves. Also, she never believed that this life could be given by any perishable food, but rather by the Word of God, as it is written (Deut. 8:3, Matt. 4:4), remembering this proverb from Solomon's wisdom: "The Lord will not let the soul of the righteous die from hunger" (Prov. 10:3), and also, "The righteous man liveth by faith" (Rom. 1:17).

But since the human body cannot sustain itself without the use of earthly things, she asked by humble prayer that He who had given the people manna from Heaven to nourish them (Ex. 16) and water from the rock to refresh them

(Num. 20:11) would also will to give her the food necessary to sustain her poor body. Immediately, at her prayer, snow fell from the sky and covered the ground. Seeing this as the working of grace, and stretching out her hand through the window, she gathered snow upon the wall. Obtaining water by this means, she made bread as she was accustomed to do, until five days later the Lord provided her some other food.

Adjoining her cell, she had a little orchard where she had the custom to go to take a little recreation. Having gone there, she was walking about looking at the plants when a woman, who had placed wheat on the roof to dry because it was an elevated spot, and who was filled only with worldly thoughts, looked at the Saint indiscretely. Immediately this woman's eyes were darkened, and she became blind. Then, knowing her fault, she went to the Saint and told her what had happened. She hastened to prayer and said, "Woe to me, if for a little offense against my littleness the eyes of others are closed." And when she had completed her prayer, she laid her hand upon the woman, making the sign of the Cross, and immediately she recovered her sight.

A man of the same country, who had previously lost his hearing, came full of devotion to the cell of the Saint, whom the parents of this unfortunate one begged to be willing to lay her hands on him. But she said she was not worthy for Christ to work such things through her. Nevertheless, throwing herself upon the earth, as if she had wanted to kiss the Lord's footsteps, she humbly supplicated the Divine clemency for the sick man; and while she was still lying on the ground, the ears of the deaf man were opened and he joyously returned home freed from all sorrow.

2. Glorified among her relatives by such signs, in order not to fall into vainglory she left her husband, her family, and all her household and went full of faith to the basilica of Saint Martin the bishop. While on her way, she came to a village of the territory of Tours, named Evena, where there were the relics of blessed Merdardus of Soissons, for whom that very night they were keeping vigil. The Saint, after passing the night attentively in prayer, went at the appointed hour with the people for the celebration of Liturgy. While the priests were celebrating the service, a girl came in, swollen by the venom of a malignant pustule, who threw herself at Monegunde's feet, saying, "Help me, for a cruel death is trying to tear me from life." The Saint, who was prostrate in prayer as was her custom, prayed for this girl to God, the Creator of all things; then, getting up, she made the sign of the Cross. As a result, the lesion broke open in four parts, pus ran out, and an unfortunate death left the girl.

After this, the blessed Monegunde came to the basilica of Saint Martin and there, on her knees before the sepulchre, gave thanks to God for being able to behold the holy tomb with her own eyes. She settled herself in a little room where she spent all her days in prayer, fasting, and vigils. Nor did she leave this place unhonored with her miracles. The daughter of a certain widow came there with her hands all drawn up, and as soon as the Saint touched her with the sign of the Cross, after having prayed, the girl's fingers straightened and left the palms free.

While these things were taking place, her husband, who had heard of the Saint's reputation, gathered his friends and neighbors, went after her and took her back home, where he placed her in the same cell she had occupied before. But she did not cease to work at her usual labor and gave herself over to prayer and fasting, in order to obtain in the end the place wherein she desired to dwell. Again she took the desired path, imploring the aid of blessed Martin in order that he give her the means to arrive at his church, since he had caused her to conceive this desire. Thus she returned to the same cell she had lived in before and there dwelt without any difficulty and without being sought any more by her husband.

Thus gathering together a few nuns there, she persevered in faith and prayer, eating only barley bread and drinking only a very little wine on feast days, diluting it with much water. She did not have a soft bed of hay or fresh straw but only one of woven rushes, commonly called matting. She put this matting on a bench or laid it out on the ground: this was her usual seat, her bed, her pillow, her coverlet — in a word, all of her bedding — and she taught those whom she had called to her to do the same. Living there in the praises of God, she gave to the sick a multitude of healing remedies.

3. A certain woman brought to her her daughter who was full of ulcers and on account of them, as some say, she was secreting pus. The Saint prayed, took saliva from her mouth, anointed her running sores with it, and made this young girl well by the help of same virtue used by Him Who, with some dust and spittle, formed the eyes of one born blind (John 9). A boy living in that area had swallowed a harmful drink, following which, it is said, serpents developed in the interior of his body and caused him sharp pains by their bites, so that he could not get any rest, be it for a moment. He could no longer drink or eat, and if after a while he would take something, he would immediately vomit it. This unfortunate boy was brought to the blessed woman and begged her to heal him by her virtue. And when she protested that she was unworthy to work such a miracle, nevertheless, yielding to the prayers of his parents she touched his stomach several times, stroking him gently with her hand, and she felt the place where the venemous serpents' corruption had settled. Then she took a green vine leaf, coated it with saliva, made the sign of the blessed Cross over it, and then put it

against the boy's lower abdomen. The pain abated a little, and he slept on a bench, he whom continuous pain had previously deprived of sleep. After an hour he got up to empty his stomach, threw up the offspring of a corrupt race, and went away healed, giving thanks to the servant of God.

Another boy, drawn up by paralysis, was brought on the arms of others to her, whom he begged to heal him. Prostrate in prayer, she prayed for him to the Lord. Then, when she had finished her prayer, she got up, took the boy by the hand, set him on his feet, and sent him back healed. A blind woman who was brought to her begged her to lay her hand on her, but she replied, "What is this to you and to me, men of God? Does not Saint Martin abide here, he who every day shines by the working of so many miracles? Go to him and entreat him that he deign to visit you." But the woman persisted in her request, saying, "God always accomplishes remarkable works through those who fear His name. That is why I come to beg you, you who have received from God the gift of healing." Then the servant of God, deeply moved, laid her hands on those dead eyes; immediately the cataracts disappeared and she who had been blind could see far and wide the world revealed to her. Many of the possessed also came to her; as soon as she laid on her hands she put to flight the evil enemy and gave back health. And of all those whom she allowed to come to her, none waited long for healing.

4. But already the time was drawing nigh when God would call her to Himself, and her strength began to leave her. Seeing this, the nuns who were with her wept bitterly and said, "To whom are you leaving us, holy Mother? To whom are you entrusting us whom you have gathered here to keep God in mind?" She said to them while shedding a few tears, "If you preserve peace and holiness, God will protect you, and you will have the great bishop Saint Martin for your shepherd. As for me, I will not go away from you, for if you call upon me I will be in your hearts." But they implored her, saying, "Many of the sick will come to you, asking to receive your blessing, and what will we do when it comes to pass that you are no more? We will put them out in confusion, when we no longer see your face. So we beg you, for the time when this will be hidden from us, to agree at least to bless oil and salt which we can give to the sick who will seek a blessing." Then she blessed for them oil and salt which she gave back to them and which they kept with the greatest care.

And thus the most blessed one died in peace. She was buried in her cell and thereafter made herself known through numerous miracles, for the blessing of which we have just spoken gave health after her death to the sick who received its beneficial effects.

A deacon named Boson had a foot swollen as a result of a malignant pustule, so that he could no longer walk. He had himself carried to her tomb and there prayed. The nuns took some of that oil which the Saint had left and put it on his foot; immediately the pustule opened, the poison flowed out, and the man was healed. A blind man brought to her tomb prostrated himself in prayer, and right away becoming drowsy, he slept and saw the blessed one in a dream, who was saying to him, "I judge myself unworthy to be counted among the saints; nevertheless, you will recover the light of one eye here. Then run to the feet of the blessed Martin and fall down before him in compunction of soul. He will give you the use of the other eye." The man woke up and recovered sight in one eye. He went where the order he had just received impelled him. There, entreating with a new prayer the blessed confessor to show his virtue, he felt the night which enveloped his still blind eye dissipate, and he went away seeing completely.

A mute also came and fell down at this blessed tomb, and his heart was so contrite in faith that he dampened with a stream of tears the stones of the cell. When he got up, he left with his tongue loosened by Divine power. Another mute came after that, and falling down in prayer he begged in his heart — not being able to by voice — for the Saint's help. In his mouth were placed a little of the blessed oil and salt of which we have spoken, and immediately there came from between his lips blood mingled with pus, and he received the use of his voice.

A man who had a fever also approached this tomb, and he had scarcely touched the pall which covered it when the fever abated and he went away healed. A cripple named Mark, having been brought on arms to the tomb, prayed there for a long time. Aften nine hours he got up on his feet and went home. A boy named Leonidus, who had been gravely ill for four months, not being able to walk or even to eat, by reason of the violence of a persistent fever, was brought to the tomb near death. There he received his health and came away returned to life.

What shall I say about so many others who have been healed of fever by simply having kissed with faith the pall which covers the Saint's sepulchre? What shall I say of the possessed who, brought to her cell, had no sooner crossed the threshold than they recovered their right minds? The spectre did not delay in leaving their bodies when it felt the virtue of the Saint, by the action of our Lord Jesus Christ, Who freely gives eternal rewards to those who fear His name.

The cell of St. Monegunde, where she was buried, was near St. Martin's tomb. Her relics were later placed in St-Pierre-le-Puellier.

St. Monegunde's small monastery was mentioned in a charter of 1031, but there is no record of it after that.

St. Gregory of Tours' *Glory of the Confessors* (ch. 24) contains the follow-account about St. Monegunde:

"In the same city of Tours, Blessed Monegunde died on the 2nd of July in the year 570. She was from the territory of Carnotena. . . . She traveled as far as Tours in order to be free from talking. It is fitting that God often revealed miracles through her. For if anyone would come upon bad circumstances, one could call upon her in prayer, and immediately she would cast herself down in supplication to the Lord. Then, gathering the leaves of vegetables or fruit trees, according to one's liking, one would smear saliva and make the sign of the cross over the wound, and put a leaf on it. Immediately all poison would vanish in such a way that one would endure no more than illness and nothing worthy of death. Those who suffered from pain in the throat were quite often healed after having been given some holy water. The infirm now constantly flock to her sepulchre and are healed. . . ."

20

Saint Leobardus the Recluse

WHO LABORED AT MARMOUTIER NEAR TOURS

Commemorated January 18 (†6th century)

THE Church of faith is edified every time the deeds of the saints are recounted devoutly. And, although it experiences great joy to see those who from the beginning of their lives have lived a devout life arrive safely at the harbor of their perfection, the Church also rejoices, as God has ordained, in those who, abandoning the world, have had the strength, with the help of Divine mercy, to bring to completion a pious undertaking.

1. Blessed Leobardus, born in the territory of Auvergne, was not, it is true, of senatorial birth, although of a free state. He had God in his heart from the beginning of his life, and even if he did not come from a pious family, he was glorious at least by his own merits. When it was time, he was sent with the other children to school, where he learned by heart portions of the Psalms, and without knowing that one day he would be a cleric, he was already preparing himself for the Lord's service. When he had come to a marriageable age, his parents, following the custom of the world, wanted to persuade him to give the earnest of betrothal to a young girl in order to marry her. When he refused to do this, his father said, "Beloved son, why do you resist my fatherly will and refuse to marry in order to raise up for our lineage offspring who will be of benefit in the future? For we give ourselves up to vain labors if there will be no one to enjoy them. Why fill our house with wealth if no one of our blood will have use of it? Why purchase for money so many slaves for our domains if all this must come under the control of a stranger? The Divine Scriptures witness that children

287

ought to obey their parents' voice (Eph. 6:1); be aware that if you show your-self disobedient toward your parents, you will not be able to avoid heavenly chastisements!''

Speaking thus, although he had another son, his father easily persuaded him at his young age to do what the young man did not wish. So Leobardus gave the ring to his fiancee, then gave to her the kiss, gave her the slipper (see ch. 16:1 above), and celebrated the feast day of the betrothed. While this was taking place, his father and mother fell asleep in the sleep of death and left the world, having gone through the course of life.

After Leobardus and his brother had fulfilled the time of their mourning, the former went to the other's house laden with gifts which he wanted to give him on the occasion of his nuptials, but he found him so drunk with wine that he could not recognize Leobardus and did not want to receive him in his house. Leobardus withdrew, sighing and shedding tears. Coming to a shed full of hay, he let his horse eat, tied it nearby, and lay down on the hay to sleep. In the mid-dle of the night he woke up, got up from his bed, and raising his hands to heaven gave thanks to Almighty God that he had been born, that he was alive, and that God nourished him with His gifts, and he continued in that way for a long time. While he was uttering long sighs and copious tears were rolling down his cheeks, Almighty God, "who predestined those whom He foreknew to be conformed to the image of His Son" (Rom. 8:29), touched his heart, inspiring him to leave the world in order to submit himself to the Divine service.

2. Then, becoming as it were the priest and custodian of his own soul, he began to preach to himself, saying, "What are you doing, my soul? Why do you remain in hesitation? Vain is this world, vain are its lusts, vain is the glory of the earth, and all that is in it is only vanity. It would be better to abandon it and follow the Lord than to give any approval to worldly deeds." Speaking thus, the next morning he mounted his horse in order to return to his house, and while he was following his route joyously, he began to consider in his mind what he would do or where he would go. He said, "I will go to the tomb of blessed Mar-tin, from which comes a beneficent power for the sick, and I believe that his prayer will open to me the way to go to God, since his prayer to the Lord has brought back the dead from Tartarus."

Continuing on his way, praying always, he entered the basilica of Saint Martin, near which he stayed some days. Then he crossed the river and devoutly betook himself to a cell situated near Marmoutier, from which a certain Alaric had just withdrawn. He began there to make parchment with his own hands and prepared it for writing. There he strove to understand the Holy Scriptures and to remember the Psalms of David, which in the course of time had escaped his memory; and instructed in this way by the reading of the Divine Scriptures, he recognized the truth of what the Lord had previously placed in his heart. And let no one consider fictitious what I am recounting: I call God to witness that I know it from the mouth of blessed Leobardus himself.

After a short interval of time, he showed himself so perfectly humble that he was honored by all. Having taken a pick, he excavated the stone of the cell where he was in order to enlarge it. In all this he gave himself over with delight to fasting, prayer, psalmody, and reading, and never ceased to celebrate the Divine worship and prayer; from time to time he would write in order to divert himself from bad thoughts.

3. Meanwhile, not failing to show himself always to be the enemy and envious of the servants of God, the tempter, on the occasion of a dispute which a humble monk of the Lord had with his neighbors, placed in his mind the thought of going out of his cell in order to go to another. Since we were in that area, having come there in order to pray as we were wont to do, he manifested to us the corruption of poison which was ravaging his heart. Sighing with sharp grief, I began to exhort this man, assuring him that this was a snare of the devil. And after leaving him, I sent him books of the 'Life of the Fathers' and the 'Institutions of the Monks,'* in order that he learn what recluses ought to be and with what prudence monks ought to behave. When he had re-read them, not only did he drive out of his mind the bad thought which he had had, but even more it so developed his knowledge that he astonished us with his facility in speaking of these matters. He expressed himself in a very gentle manner, his exhortations were full of charm, he was full of love for people, he had his eyes open for kings, and he prayed continually for all ecclesiastics who feared God.

He was not like some who take pleasure in wearing long hair and beard, for at fixed intervals he would cut his hair and beard. He abode twenty-two years occupied in this way in his cell and obtained such a great grace from God that from his saliva alone he took away all effect from the poison of malignant pustules. He extinguished the fire of fever with wine which he had sanctified by the sign of the Cross, quelling with righteousness febrile heat in others — he who had smothered in himself the ardor of criminal passions.

One day there came to him a blind man who was weeping with humility over his misfortune and begging the Saint to touch with his hand his eyes deprived of light. For a long time he refused; finally, overcome by the man's tears

---

* The former by Rufinus and the latter by St. John Cassian. St. Romanus (of the Jura) received these two books from Abbot Sabinus at the beginning of his monastic life (see the *Life of the Jura Fathers*, ch. 1).

and touched with compassion, he prayed to the Lord for three days, and on the fourth, placing his hands on the man's eyes, he said, "Almighty Lord, Only-Begotten Son of the Father, Who reigneth with Him and the Holy Spirit unto the ages, Who gave light to one born blind (John 9) with the saliva from Thy blessed mouth, give sight to this Thy servant, in order that he know that Thou art the Almighty Lord." Saying this, he traced the sign of the Cross on the blind man's eyes, and immediately the darkness dissipated and sight was restored to him. The abbot Eustachius, who was present, can attest to the truth of this miracle.

4. At last, broken by the continual labor of having to hew the rock, which he did not cease to hollow out below the mountain, worn out by the austerity of his fasts, although strengthened by his incessant prayer, he began to feel little by little the vigor leaving his body. One day when he was extremely tired, he had us called to him. We went to him, and after he had wept over the necessity of his demise, he begged us, the sinful one, to give him Communion. Having received it and having drunk the wine, he said, "My time is fulfilled: God ordains that I be delivered from the bonds of this body, but several days must yet pass. I will be called by Him before the holy day of Pascha." O blessed man, who served the Creator of all things to the point of knowing, by Divine revelation, the moment of death! It was in the tenth month of the year when he spoke thus, and in the twelfth he again fell gravely ill.

One Sunday he called his servant and said to him, "Prepare me some food to eat, for I feel very weak." And when the servant replied, "It is ready, my lord," he said to him, "Go and see if the office is already over and whether the people have gone out from Liturgy." He had said that, not because he wanted to take food, but in order that no one be witness to his death. The servant came back after having gone out, and entering the cell, he found the man of God, his body rigid, and his eyes closed, who had given up his ghost — which evidently demonstrates that the Angels took him, since the holy warrior did not wish that a man be present at his demise. At this sight, he who served him raised his voice in lamentation. When the other brethren had flocked in, his body was washed and he was clothed fittingly and he was placed in the tomb which he had cut out himself in his cell. That he had been admitted into the company of the righteous is something not to be doubted, I think, by any of the faithful.

End of the Book of the Life of the Fathers.

V

Additional Lives
of the Fathers

by St. Gregory of Tours

PREFATORY NOTE

In addition to the twenty chapters of the *Life of the Fathers*, the writings of St. Gregory contain several other substantial Lives of 6th-century saints of Gaul. These are presented here as a supplement to the complete text of the *Life of the Fathers*.

The first of these Lives is of a saint personally known to St. Gregory: St. Salvius, Bishop of Albi. His Life, contained in the *History of the Franks* (Book VII, 1 and V, 50), affords one of the classic examples in Christian literature of a saint who beheld Heaven itself and returned to tell of it; it may well be placed beside such Eastern Lives as that of St. Andrew the Fool for Christ of Constantinople.

21

Saint Salvius

SEER OF HEAVENLY MYSTERIES

Commemorated September 10 (†584)

T HE FEELING OF REVERENCE which I have for him compels me to say something about St. Salvius. He often used to tell how, during his years as a layman, while he was occupying himself with worldly affairs he never permitted himself to be ensnared by the carnal desires which so frequently fill the minds of young people. When the Holy Spirit finally found a place in his heart, he gave up the struggle of worldly existence and entered a monastery. As one now consecrated to Almighty God, he understood that it was better to serve the Lord in poverty and to humble oneself before Him, rather than to strive after the wealth of this transient world. He spent many years in his monastery and observed the rule instituted by the Fathers.

When the time came for the abbot of this monastery to die, Salvius took over the charge of feeding the flock, for he had by then reached the fullness of his physical and intellectual powers. Once he had been given this appointment, it was his duty to be more with the brethren, in order to maintain discipline; but instead he became even more withdrawn, and chose for himself a cell which was still more remote. Once he was elected abbot, he lived just as ascetically as before, devoting all his time to reading and prayer. He was persuaded that it was more fitting for him to remain secluded among his

295

monks, than to appear in public and be addressed as abbot. Being thus persuaded, he bade farewell to the monks. He became a recluse, and in the solitude
of his cell he subjected himself to even greater abstinence than before. At the
same time he took good care to observe the law of Christian charity, offering up
prayers for all who came to visit the monastery, and giving them the bread of
offering with abundant grace. Again and again those who came with grave
afflictions went away healed.

One day when Salvius lay in bed, gasping for breath and weakened by a
high fever, his cell was suddenly filled with a bright light and the walls seemed
to shake. He stretched out his hands to heaven, and as he gave thanks he
breathed forth his spirit. The monks, together with his own mother carried his
dead body out of the cell with lamentation; then they washed it, vested
it and placed it upon a bier. They passed the long night in weeping and singing
psalms.

When morning came and all was ready for the funeral, the corpse
began to move on the bier. Salvius' cheeks became flushed, he stirred himself
as if awakened from a deep sleep, opened his eyes, raised his hands and spoke:
"Oh merciful Lord, why hast Thou done this to me? Why hast Thou decreed
that I should return to this dark place where we dwell on earth? I would have
been much happier in Thy compassion on high, rather than having to begin
once again my profitless life here below." Those around him were in perplexity.
When they asked him the meaning of the miracle which had occurred, he gave
no reply. He rose from the bier, feeling no ill effects from the illness which he
had suffered, and for three days he remained without food or drink.

On the third day he called the monks, together with his mother. "My
most dear friends," he said, "hear what I am about to say. You must understand that all you see in this world is entirely without value. *All is vanity*,
exactly as the prophet Solomon proclaimed. Blessed is he who behaves in such
a way in this earthly existence that he is rewarded by beholding God in His
glory in heaven."

As he said this, he wondered whether he should say more or stop
with this. He was silent for a while, but the monks begged him to tell them
what he had seen. "When my cell shook four days ago," he continued, "and
you saw me lying dead, I was raised up by two angels and carried to the highest
peak of heaven, until I seemed to have beneath my feet not only this miserable
earth, but also the sun and moon, the clouds and stars. Then I was conducted
through a gate that shone more brightly than the light of the sun and
entered a building where the whole floor shone with gold and silver. The light
was impossible to describe. The place was filled with a multitude of people,

neither male nor female, stretching so far in all directions that one could not see where it ended. The angels made a way for me through the crowd of people in front of me, and we came to the place towards which our gaze had been directed even when we had been far away. Over this place there hung a cloud more brilliant than any light, and yet no sun or moon or star could be seen; indeed, the cloud shone more brightly than any of these with its own brilliance. A voice came out of the cloud, as the voice of many waters. Sinner that I am, I was greeted with great respect by a number of beings, some dressed in priestly vestments and others in ordinary dress; my guides told me that these were the martyrs and other holy men whom we honor here on earth and to whom we pray with great devotion. As I stood here there was wafted over me a fragrance of such sweetness that, nourished by it, I have felt no need of food or drink until this very moment."

"Then I heard a voice which said: 'Let this man go back into the world, for our churches have need of him.' I heard the voice, but I could not see who was speaking. Then I prostrated myself on the ground and wept. 'Alas, alas, O Lord!' I said. 'Why hast Thou shown me these things only to take them away from me again? Thou dost cast me out today from before Thy face and send me back again to a worldly life without substance, since I am powerless to return on high. I entreat Thee, O Lord: turn not Thy mercy away from me. Let me remain here, I beseech Thee, lest, falling once more to earth, I perish. The voice which had spoken to me said: 'Go in peace. I will watch over you until I bring you back once more to this place.' Then my guides left me and I turned back through the gate by which I had entered, weeping as I went."

As he said this, those who were with him were amazed. The holy man of God wept. Then he said: "Woe to me that I have dared to reveal such a mystery! The fragrance which I smelled in that holy place, and by which I have been nourished for three days without food or drink, has already left me. My tongue is covered with sores and has become so swollen that it fills my whole mouth. It is evident that it has not been pleasing in the eyes of my Lord God that these mysteries should be revealed. Thou knowest well, O Lord, that I did this in the simplicity of my heart, and not in a spirit of vainglory. Have mercy on me, I beseech Thee, and do not forsake me, according to Thy promise." When he had said this, Salvius became silent; then he began to eat and drink.

As I write these words, I fear that my account may seem quite incredible to some of my readers; and I am mindful of what the historian Sallust wrote: "When we record the virtue or glory of famous men, the reader will readily accept whatever he considers that he might have done himself; anything which exceeds these bounds of possibility he will regard as untrue." I call Almighty God to witness that everything that I have related here I have heard from the lips of Salvius himself.

Many years later Saint Salvius was forced to leave his cell in order to be elected and consecrated bishop against his will. According to my reckoning, he had held this position for ten years when the plague broke out in Albi and most of the people died of it. Only a few of the citizens remained alive, but Saint Salvius, as a good shepherd, refused to leave his city. He stayed there, exhorting those still among the living to pray without ceasing, not to grow faint in their vigils, and to concentrate their minds and bodies on doing only what was good. "Always act in such a way," he would say, "that if God should decide to call you from this world, you may enter not into His judgment, but into His peace."

After a certain council which Salvius and I attended together, I was about to depart for home when I realized that I could not leave without bidding farewell to Salvius and embracing him. I found him and told him that I was about to leave. We went a little way outside the house and stood there conversing. "Look at the roof of that building," he said; "do you see what I see?" I answered, "I see only the new tiling which the King has had put there not too long ago." "Can you see nothing else?" he asked. "No," I replied, "I can see nothing." I began to think that he was mocking me. "Tell me if you can see something else," I said. He sighed deeply and said: " I see the naked sword of the wrath of God hanging over that house." He was not wrong in his prophecy. Twenty days later the two sons of King Chilperic died.

When the time came that God revealed to Salvius the nearness of his own death, he prepared his own coffin, washed himself carefully, and put on his shroud. He died in blessed contemplation, with his thoughts turned towards heaven. He was an extremely holy man. He had no desire at all for possessions and refused to accept money; if anyone forced him to accept it, he would immediately give it to the poor.

While he was bishop, the patrician Mummolus carried into captivity many of the inhabitants of Albi, but Salvius followed him and persuaded him to free them all. The Lord gave him such influence over these people that the captors accepted a reduction in the ransom which they had asked and even gave presents to Salvius. In this way he liberated the people of his own diocese and restored them to their former condition.

I have heard many other edifying stories about him. He died in the ninth year of the reign of King Childebert (584 A.D.).

22

Saint Bricius

CLAIRVOYANT BISHOP OF TOURS

Commemorated November 13 (†444)

Following the repose of Saint Martin, bishop of the city of Tours, that most exalted and truly incomparable man, about whose miracles large volumes have been written in our own country, Bricius succeeded him as bishop. As a young man this Bricius would often set snares for Saint Martin, who then was still living in the flesh, because the Saint very often used to rebuke him for spending too much of his time on trivial things. One day, when a sick man came to Saint Martin to be healed, he met Bricius, who was still a deacon, in the square. In his rough way the man said, "I am hanging around here waiting for the holy man, but I don't know where he is or what he's doing." Bricius answered, "If you are looking for that deranged fellow, just look in that direction. In his typical half-witted way, he is staring at the sky." Going over to Saint Martin, the poor man was given what he desired. Then the Saint turned to his deacon Bricius and said, "So I seem to you to be half-witted, do I?" So confused was Bricius when he heard this that he denied that he had said any such thing, but Saint Martin continued, "I was listening to your words, even though you were some distance away. Amen I say to you, for God has just granted to me that you will take over the honor of this bishopric after my death; but you must know this, that during the period of the episcopate you will suffer much persecution." Hearing this, Bricius laughed and replied, "Was it not true what I claimed, that much of what you say is sheer lunacy?" Even after he had been ordained to the priesthood, Bricius continued to cause pain to the Saint by his sarcastic remarks. However, when he was elected as bishop, with the complete approval of the citizens of Tours, he spent his time in prayer.

Despite the fact that Bricius was arrogant and vain, he was considered to be pure in body. In the thirty-third year after his ordination, a lamentable charge was made against him. A woman to whom his servants used to give his clothes to wash, and who had herself given up wearing lay garments for religious reasons, became pregnant and gave birth to a child. The entire population of Tours rose in anger at this news. They placed the whole guilt on their bishop and as one man wanted to stone him to death. "Your piety as a holy man has all this time been merely a cover for your immoral acts," they cried. "God no longer allows us to defile ourselves by kissing your unworthy hands." Bricius adamantly denied the charge. "Bring the child to me," he demanded. The baby was brought in, still only thirty days old. Bricius said to the infant, "In the name of Jesus Christ, Son of God the Almighty, if I am really your father, I order you to say so, with all these people listening." "You are not my father," the baby answered. When the people begged Bricius to inquire who the father was, he replied, "That is not for me to do. I was only concerned insofar as the matter affected me. If you have any more interest in what has occurred, then ask the question yourselves." Then they rose in rebellion against him and dragged him away, crying, "You will no longer rule over us with the false name of pastor." To vindicate himself to the people, he put burning coals in his cassock, pressed them against his body and went in procession with the entire crowd to the tomb of Saint Martin. When he arrived at the tomb, he dropped the coals on the ground, but his cassock had no signs of burning on it. Then he continued with what he was saying: "Just as you witness that my clothing is completely unmarked by these burning coals, so is my body undefiled by intercourse with woman." Still they would not believe him, and they expelled him from their city, so that the saying of Saint Martin might be fulfilled: "Know this, that during the period of the episcopate you will suffer much persecution."

Having expelled Bricius, the people of Tours chose Justinian as their bishop. Bricius made his way to the Pope of the city of Rome. Weeping and lamenting over his fate, he said to the Pope, "I deserve to suffer all this reviling, for I have sinned against the holy man of God, calling him a madman and a lunatic on several occasions. When I beheld the miracles which he preformed I did not believe them." When Bricius had left, the people of Tours said to their new bishop, "Go after him and pay heed to your own situation, for if you do not follow him you will deserve to be despised by us all." At this, Justinian left Tours and came to the city of Vercelli in Italy. There he died on his journey, being struck by the judgement of God. When the people of Tours learned of the death of Justinian they persisted in their wrong-doing and appointed Armentius in his place.

As soon as Bishop Bricius arrived in Rome, he related to the Pope all that he had suffered. He took up residence in the papal see and often celebrated Liturgy there, but he continued to repent over his cruel treatment of the holy man of God. When seven years had elapsed he left Rome and with the Pope's permission set out once more for Tours. He came to a village called Mont-Louis, about six miles from the town, and took up residence there. Armentius became ill with a fever and died in the middle of the night. This was revealed to Bishop Bricius in a vision, and he said to his servants, "Get up quickly and let us hasten to the funeral of our brother, the bishop of Tours." As they arrived at one of the gates of the city and were preparing to pass through it, the deceased man was being brought out through another gate. After the funeral Bricius returned to his own cathedral and there lived happily for seven years. He reposed in the forty-seventh year of his episcopate. Saint Eustochius, a man of remarkable sanctity, succeeded him.

NOTE

The above account is from *The History of the Franks,* Book II, 1.

Saint Hospicius

23

Saint hospicius

HOLY RECLUSE OF NICE

Commemorated May 21

N EAR the town of Nice there dwelt a recluse named Hospicius. He was a great ascetic who had iron chains wound around his body, next to the skin, and he wore a hair-shirt over them. He ate nothing except dry bread and a few dates. In the period of Lent he lived on the roots of Egyptian herbs, which merchants brought home for him. Hermits are very fond of these. First he would drink the water in which they were boiled, and then he would eat the herbs themselves. The Lord deigned to perform remarkable miracles through Hospicius. At one time the Holy Spirit revealed to him the coming of the Longobards into Gaul. His prophecy was as follows: "The Longobards will invade Gaul and will destroy seven cities, because the wickedness of those cities has grown great in the eyes of the Lord. No one in them knows God, no one seeks Him, no one does good in order to alleviate God's wrath. The entire populace is without faith, given over to perjury, prone to stealing, quick to commit murder; and no justice is seen to prosper among them. They do not give their tithes, they do not feed the poor, they do not clothe the naked; no hospitality is offered to strangers there, and they are not given enough to eat. Thus, disaster is on its way to these people. I therefore tell you: Gather all your property together inside your walls, for otherwise the Longobards will take it. Fortify yourselves in the strongest places you can find."

All the people were astonished at what Hospicius said. They bade farewell to him and hurried home in great agitation. Then he spoke to his monks, saying, "Leave this place immediately and take all your possessions with you.

303

The people about whom I have told you are approaching already." "We cannot abandon you, holy father," they answered. "Do not fear for me," he said. "They will do me harm, it is true, but they will not kill me." The monks dispersed and the Longobards arrived. They destroyed everything that they could lay their hands on, and eventually came to the place where the holy man of God lived as a recluse. He showed himself to them through a window in his tower. Marching round and round the tower, they could find no entrance through which they could get to him. Two of them climbed up and ripped a hole in the roof. Seeing Hospicius wrapped in chains and wearing a hair-shirt, they exclaimed, "This is a criminal! He must have murdered someone. That is why he has chains tied around him." After an interpreter had been summoned, they asked Hospicius what he had done to deserve such punishment. He confessed that he had committed murder and that he was guilty of every crime in the calendar. One of the Longobards drew his sword and prepared to cut off the recluse's head. As he dealt the blow, his right hand was paralyzed in mid-air and he was unable to move it back to his side. He dropped his sword and let it fall to the ground. Seeing this, his companions gave a great shout, begging the holy man to tell them what they should do next. Hospicius made the sign of the Cross over the soldier's arm and it became whole again. The man was converted on the spot; his head was tonsured and he became one of Hospicius' most devoted monks. Two of the Longobard leaders, who had listened to what he said, returned home to their country safe and sound. The others, who had only derision for his warnings, died miserably in Provence. Many of them were possessed by demons and kept crying, "Holy man, most blessed man, why do you torture and burn us in this way?" He laid his hand upon them and healed them.

Some time after this there was an inhabitant of Angers who came down with a very high temperature and lost the power of speech and hearing. Although he recovered from his fever, he remained deaf and dumb. A deacon was about to depart for Rome from this region, to bring back relics of the blessed Apostles and other saints who guard over that city. When the sick man's parents heard of this, they asked the deacon to be so kind as to take their son along on the trip, for if he could only visit the tombs of the blessed Apostles he would immediately be healed. The two departed together and at length came to the place where Saint Hospicius lived. The deacon greeted him and gave him the kiss of peace. He explained the reasons for their trip and said that he was on his way to Rome. He asked the holy man to give him an introduction to any local sailors whom he might know. Right before they left, Hospicius felt miraculous power rising in him through the Spirit of our Lord. He said to the deacon, "Please show me this afflicted person who is travelling with you." The deacon hurried away to his lodging and found the invalid, who was once more suffering from a high temperature. The man made signs that there was a great ringing in his ears. Seizing his arm, the deacon rushed him off to the Saint. Hospicius laid his hand on the man's hair and pulled his head in through the window. He took some oil, consecrated it, held the man's tongue tightly in his left hand and poured the oil down his throat and over the top of his head. "In the name of our Lord Jesus Christ," he said, "may your ears be unsealed and your mouth opened, through that miraculous power which once cast out the evil spirit from the man who was deaf and dumb." As he said this, he asked the man what his name was. "I am called so-and-so," he replied, pronouncing words clearly. When the deacon saw what had happened, he said, "I thank you with all my heart, Jesus Christ, for having vouchsafed to reveal such a miracle by the hand of your servant. I was on my way to Peter, I was going to Paul and Lawrence, and all the others who have glorified Rome with their blood. I have found them all here, in this very place have I discovered them." Saying this, he wept and was filled with awe. The man of God took no vain credit for himself. "Be quiet, dear brother," he said. "It is not I who do this, but He Who created the world out of nothing, Who has made man for our salvation, He Who grants sight to the blind, hearing to the deaf, speech to the dumb, Who restores the skin which they have lost to the leprous, and finds a soothing remedy for all those who are sick." The deacon bade farewell to Hospicius and went on his way rejoicing with his companions.

After they had departed, a man named Dominicus — and this time I give you the real name — who had been blind from birth, came to put this miraculous power to the test. He stayed in the nearby monastery for two or three months, and spent all his time in prayer and fasting. Then Hospicius called for him. "Do you wish to gain your sight?" he asked. Dominicus replied, "It has always been my wish to learn about things which are unknown to me. I do not know what light is. One thing I am sure of, and that is that everyone who sees it praises it highly. As for myself, from the day I was born until now I have never had the power of sight." Hospicius consecrated some oil and, making the sign of the Cross over the man's eyes with it, he said, "May your eyes open, in the name of Jesus Christ our Redeemer." Immediately the man's eyes opened, and he stood lost in admiration as he looked upon the wonderful works of God, which he was seeing for the first time in this world.

Later there was brought to Hospicius a woman who, as she herself admitted, was possessed by three devils. He laid his hand on her and blessed her, marking the sign of the Cross on her brow with consecrated oil. The demons were cast out and the woman went away healed. By his blessing he healed another girl who was oppressed by an unclean spirit.

As the day of his death drew near, Hospicius summoned the abbot of the monastery to him. "Bring a crow-bar," he said, "break through the wall, and send messengers to the bishop of the city of Nice, in order that he may come and bury me. Three days from now I will depart from this world and go to my designated rest, which the Lord has promised to me." As Hospicius said this, the abbot of the monastery sent his men to the bishop of Nice to give him the news. Meanwhile, a man named Crescens came to the window. When he saw the chains around Hospicius' body, which was alive with worms, he asked, "My lord, how can you bear such terrible sufferings?" Hospicius answered, "He in Whose name I endure these sufferings offers me consolation. I tell you, I am being released from these chains and I am going to my rest." On the third day he removed the chains which were tied around him and knelt in prayer. After he had prayed and wept for a long time, he lay down on a bench, stretched out his feet, raised his hands to Heaven, gave thanks to God and so gave up his spirit. All the worms which had eaten into his saintly limbs disappeared immediately. Bishop Austadius arrived and committted the Saint's body to the grave. I heard all this from the mouth of the deaf and dumb man who, as I have told you, was healed by Hospicius. This man told me many other stories about the miracles performed by Hospicius, but I have chosen not to set them down, because I have heard that his life has been written by several others.

NOTES

The above account is from *The History of the Franks,* Book VI, 6.

The name of St. Hospicius has been preserved in a promontory near Nice called "Pointe de Saint-Hospice."

24

Saint Eparchius

MIRACLE-WORKING RECLUSE OF ANGOULEME

Commemorated July 1 (†581)

S AINT Eparchius, the recluse of Angouleme, was a man of great sanctity, and God wrought many miracles through him. Originally he was an inhabitant of Perigueux, but, after his conversion and ordination to the priesthood, he went to Angouleme and there built himself a cell. He gathered a few monks around him and spent his time in continual prayer. Whenever gold or silver was offered to him, he would spend it in supplying the needs of the poor or in freeing people from prison. Bread was never baked in his cell as long as he lived, for, as need arose, it was supplied by those who came there to worship. Eparchius arranged for the freeing of a great number of prisoners by using the alms and offerings of the faithful. By making the sign of the Cross over malignant pustules he would destroy the poison in them; by prayer he would drive out evil spirits from bodies which were possessed and many times he persuaded judges to pardon the accused, more by his power of gentle reason than by violent pleading. He begged so endearingly that when he asked for leniency they could not refuse him anything.

Once a man was being led away to be hanged for theft. He was a habitual criminal, thought by the locals to be guilty of many other crimes, as well as robberies and murders. Hearing all this, Eparchius sent one of his monks to beg the Count concerned to grant him the man's life, however guilty he may be. The crowd began to demonstrate: if this man were freed, they cried, it would be the end of law and order in the district and the Count would lose all authority.

Therefore, it was impossible to free him. He was tortured on the rack, beaten with sticks and cudgels, and sentenced to be hanged. The monk returned and sadly reported this to Eparchius. "Go back," he said. "Don't approach too near, but stay there. In His loving kindness, the Lord will grant me this fellow-creature whom man has refused to surrender. When you see him fall, pick him up and bring him back to me in the monastery." The monk did as he was told. Eparchius knelt in prayer and spoke to God for a long time, weeping as he did so. Consequently the gibbet collapsed, the chains were broken and the hanged man fell to the ground. The monk lifted him up and brought him back safe and sound to the abbot. Eparchius gave thanks to God. Then he had the Count summoned. "My dear son," he said, "you have always listened with sympathy to what I have had to say. Why were you so adamant today, when you refused to pardon the man whose life I asked you to save?" The Count replied, "I am always ready to listen to you, saintly priest, but today the crowd made a demonstration and I could not do what you asked, for I had a riot on my hands." "You did not listen, "Eparchius answered, "but God deigned to listen. He restored to life the man whom you handed over for execution. You see him there, where he stands unharmed." As Eparchius said this, the condemned man flung himself at the feet of the Count, who was quite dumbstruck when he saw still alive one whom he had seen enduring execution. This story was told to me by the Count himself.

Eparchius did many other things which I do not have space to relate to you. Having been a recluse for forty-four years he fell ill of a fever and died. They carried him out of his cell and buried him. A great crowd of people whom he had freed from the sentence of the law, as I have said, walked in his funeral procession.

NOTE

This account is from *The History of the Franks,* Book VI, 8.

25

Saint Aredius

HOLY ABBOT OF LIMOGES

Commemorated November 17 (†591)

Here begin the miracles and the repose of Abbot Aredius, who in this year (591) finished his life here below and went to Heaven at the command of our Lord. He came originally from Limoges, a man of free birth, descended from very important people in that area. He was sent to King Theudebert and joined the group of noble youths attached to the royal household. At that time Nicetus, a man of great holiness, was bishop of the town of Trier.* He was regarded by his flock to be a remarkably eloquent preacher, and he was famous far and wide for his good works and his miracles. Nicetus noticed the young man in the king's palace. Perceiving some Divine quality in his face, he ordered Aredius to follow him. Aredius left the king's palace and joined Nicetus. Together they went to the bishop's cell and spoke of those matters which are the concern of God. The young Aredius asked the saintly bishop to correct him in his errors, to be his teacher and to give him instruction in the Holy Scriptures. He was full of flaming zeal for his studies. Having passed some time with Bishop Nicetus he had his head tonsured. One day when the clergy were chanting psalms in the cathedral, a dove flew down from the ceiling, fluttered gently around Aredius and then alighted on his head. In my opinion, this was a clear sign that he was filled with the grace of the Holy Spirit. Embarrassed by what had happened, he tried to drive the dove away. It flew around for a while and then settled down again,

---

* See chapter 17 above.

first on his head and then on his shoulder. Not only did this happen in the cathedral, but when Aredius went off to the bishop's cell the dove went with him.
Day after day this was repeated, to the great surprise of Nicetus.

Both Aredius' father and brother died, and this man of God, filled, as I
have said, with the Holy Spirit, returned home to console his mother Pelagia,
who had no one to look after her, save her one remaining son. By now he was
devoting all his time to fasting and prayer, and he asked his mother to continue
being responsible for all the household duties, to be in charge of the servants, the
tilling of the fields and the culture of the vines, in order that nothing should
come between him and his praying. There was but one commitment for which
he wanted to remain responsible, and that was that he should have control of the
building of churches. What more is there that I can say? He built churches to the
glory of God's saints, collected relics for them and tonsured his own family re-
tainers as monks. He founded a monastery* in which was followed the Rule of
Cassian, Basil and the other abbots who had set rules for the monastic life. His
saintly mother provided food and clothing for all the monks. She did not allow
this heavy burden to interrupt her prayers to God. No matter what she was doing, she continued to pray and her words ascended like fragrant incense, finding
favor in the sight of God. Meanwhile, the sick began to flock from everywhere to
the saintly Aredius. He restored them to health by making the sign of the Cross
on each of them with his hand. If I attempted to write all their names down one
by one, I should never be able to list them all or to provide a complete record.
One thing I know, that no sick man ever came to him without going away
healed. Here are a few details of the more significant miracles which he per
formed:

One day he was on a pilgrimage with his mother to the church of Saint
Julian the Martyr. That evening they reached a place which was dry and barren,
for no water ran there. His mother said to him, "Son, we have no water. We
cannot possibly spend the night here." Aredius prostrated himself in prayer and
continued to supplicate our Lord for a very long time. Then, standing up, he
stuck the stick which he was holding in his hand in the ground. He twisted it in
a circle two or three times and then with a joyful smile pulled it out. So much
water gushed out that not only was there plenty for their own present needs but
they were also able to water their animals.

Not very long ago, when Aredius was on a trip, great rain clouds began to
appear. As soon as he saw this, he bowed his head a little over the horse which
he was riding and raised his hand to God. No sooner had he completed his prayer

---

* The monastery of Saint Yrieix in the Limousin.

than the cloud split into two parts: all around them the rain poured down in torrents, but not a single drop fell on them.

A citizen of Tours named Wistrimund, commonly known as Tatto, was suffering terribly from a toothache. His entire jaw was swollen. He went off to find this saintly man. Aredius placed his hand on the infected place, and immediately the pain stopped and never tormented the man again. This story was told to me by Wistrimund himself. As for the miracles which our Lord performed through the power of Saint Julian the Martyr and the blessed Saint Martin, I have recorded most of them in my *Book of Miracles* just as he himself related them to me.

When with Christ's help Aredius had done these miracles and many similar ones, he came to Tours right after the feast of Saint Martin. He remained with me for a while, and then he told me that he was not long for this world and that his death was surely near. He bade farewell and then went on his way, thanking God that he had been vouchsafed before his death to kiss the tomb of the holy bishop. He returned to his cell, made his will and set all his affairs in order, appointing as his heirs the two bishops, Saint Martin and Saint Hilary. Then he fell ill of dysentery and began to ail. On the sixth day of his illness, a woman who had long been possessed by an unclean spirit of which the Saint had not been able to heal her, and whose hands were bound behind her back, began to cry, "Run, citizens! Leap for joy, you people! Go out to meet the saints and martyrs who are gathering together for the passing of Saint Aredius! Here is Julian of Brioude, and here is Privatus of Mende. Martin has come from Tours and Martial has come from Aredius's own city. Here come Saturninus of Toulouse, Dennis of Paris and all the others now in Heaven to whom you are accustomed to pray as God's saints and martyrs." She began to shout all this just as night was descending. Her master had her tied up, but he was unable to hold her. Breaking her bonds, she rushed off to the monastery, shouting as she went. Only a short time later did the saintly man breathe his last, and there was considerable evidence that he was taken up by angels.

At the time of his funeral, just as the grave was closing over him, Aredius cleansed this woman from the curse of the demon who infested her, together with another woman possessed by a yet more evil spirit. It is my belief that it was by God's will that he was unable to heal them while in the body, so that his funeral might be glorified by the miracle. When the ceremony was finished, a third woman who was dumb and suffered from a gaping rictus, came to his tomb and kissed it, and thereby received the gift of speech.

NOTES

The above account is from *The History of the Franks*, Book X, 29.

St. Gregory includes the following passage about St. Aredius in his book *The Miracles of St. Julian* (ch. 40):

"When Aredius the priest from Limoges, a very devout man of whom I made mention in the second book of the miracles of blessed Martin, came to me, I carefully examined his life and began to inquire about the miracles which the most blessed Julian had performed in Limoges. This priest Aredius had built in honor of the blessed martyr a sacred church which he enriched by the relics of Saint Julian. Because he was a very humble man, he hesitated for some time and at last spoke these words after being especially urged: 'When I approached the church of blessed Julian for the first time I bore away a little bit of wax from his tomb. From there I came to the fountain into which the blood of the blessed martyr was poured, and after washing my face I filled a small vessel with water for the blessing. I call Almighty God to witness, for before I reached home it was changed into balsam in color, consistency and fragrance. When the priest came to dedicate the temple I told him all these things, and he was unwilling to enclose anything else in the sacred altar in the place of the relics except the little vessel whose water had been changed to balsam, for he said, "These are true relics which the Martyr has glorified by heavenly powers." ' "

Further information about St. Aredius is found in St. Gregory's *Miracles of the Blessed Bishop Martin*, Books II, 39; III, 24; and IV, 6; and *The Glory of the Confessors*, chapters 9 and 102. A Life of St. Aredius *(Vita Sancti Aredii Abbatis)* is included in the apocryphal works of St. Gregory (H. L. Bordier, *Les Livres des Miracles*, Paris, 1864, vol. 4, pp. 160-208).

St. Aredius is known in France as St. Yrieix. His saintly mother Pelagia reposed in 572.

26

Saint Vulfolaic

THE STYLITE OF TRIER

Commemorated November 17

ONCE while travelling I came to the town of Carignan, where I was warmly welcomed by the deacon Vulfolaic, who took me to his monastery. This is located about eight miles from the town, atop a hill. Vulfolaic had built a large church on the hillside and made it well-known for its relics of Saint Martin and other saints. While I was there I asked him to tell me of the gladsome event of his conversion and how he, a Longobard by birth, had happened to enter the service of the Church. At first he was unwilling to relate his story, for he was very sincere in his desire to avoid worldly glory. I adjured him with great oaths, beseeching him not to hold back anything of what I was asking him, and promising not to reveal what he told me to a living soul. For a long time he resisted, but in the end he relented to my supplications and entreaties.

"When I was a small boy," he said, "I came to hear the name of Saint Martin. I did not even know whether he was a martyr or just a famous ecclesiastic, what good he had done in this world, or which place had the honor of receiving his holy body for burial. Nevertheless, I used to have vigils in his name, and whenever I had any money I would give it as alms. When I grew a little older I made a great effort to learn to write. At first I taught myself merely to copy out the letters, and then I discovered what they meant when they were put in the right order. I became a disciple of Abbot Aredius, and with his encouragement I visited the church of Saint Martin. When the time came for us to leave, he collected a little dust from the sacred tomb as a holy relic. He put it in a small box

313

and hung it around my neck. When we arrived at his monastery near Limoges, he put this box away in his oratory. The dust increased in quantity until it not only filled the box but forced its way through the joints wherever it could find an opening. Inspired by this miracle, my heart was filled with joy, and as a result all my hope for the future was placed in the Saint's miraculous power. I then moved to the neighborhood of Trier, and on the hillside where you are now standing I built with my own hands the dwelling that you see in front of you. Here I found a statue of Diana, which the credulous local people worshipped as a god. I myself raised up a pillar, on which I remained standing with bare feet, no matter how much it hurt me. When winter came in its season, it so chilled me with its icy frost that the bitter cold caused my toenails to fall off, not once but many times, and the rain turned to ice and hung from my beard like the wax which melts from candles. This district is well-known for its harsh winters.''

I was very interested to know what food and drink he took, and how he managed to destroy the idols on the hillside. "All I had to eat and drink was a little bread and green vegetables, along with some water," he told me. "Crowds began to flock to me from the households in the region, and I kept telling them that Diana was powerless, that her statues were useless, and that the rituals they performed were vain and empty. I made it clear to them that the incantations which they chanted when they were intoxicated and during their debaucheries were quite unworthy of them. Rather, they should make a worthy offering of worship to Almighty God, Who had made Heaven and earth. I prayed night and day that the Lord would deign to cast down the statue and free these people from their false idolatry. In His mercy, God moved their simple minds, and thus they began to listen to what I had to say, to forsake their images and to follow the Lord. Then I summoned an assembly of some of their number and with their assistance I was able to destroy it myself. Already I had overthrown the smaller idols, which were easier to deal with. A great crowd gathered at Diana's statue: they tied ropes around it and began to pull, but all their efforts were futile. I hurried to the church and lay prostrate and weeping on the ground, praying to God for help, that with His Divine power He would destroy what human strength was unable to overturn. Having finished praying, I came out once more, went up to the workmen and took hold of the rope. The idol crashed to the ground at the very first heave we gave. I had it broken to pieces with iron hammers and then made into dust.

"Having gone home for some food, I found that my whole body from the top of my head to the soles of my feet was covered with malignant pustules, so much so that it was not possible to find the space of a single finger-tip which was free from them. Going to the church by myself, I stripped myself naked by

the holy altar. It was there that I kept a bottle full of oil which I had brought
home with me from Saint Martin's church. With my own hands I anointed my
entire body with this oil, and then I went to sleep. It was almost midnight when
I awoke. As I rose to my feet to say the appointed prayers, I discovered that my
body was completely healed, just as if I had never had any sores at all. Then I
understood that these ulcers had been caused by the malice which the devil
bore for me. He is so full of spite that he does all he can to hurt those who seek
God.

"Certain bishops came to me whose plain duty it was to encourage me
to press on wisely with the task which I had begun. Instead they said to me,
'It is not right, what you are attempting to do! Such an obscure person as you
can never be compared with Simeon the Stylite of Antioch! The climate of this
region renders it impossible for you to continue tormenting yourself in this way.
Come down from your pillar and live with the brothers whom you have gathered
around you.' Now, it is considered a sin not to obey bishops, so, of course, I
descended and went off with those brethren and began to take my meals with
them. One day a certain bishop persuaded me to go to a household some distance away. Then he sent workmen with sedges, hammers and axes, and they
smashed to pieces the pillar on which I used to stand. Returning the next morning, I found it absolutely destroyed. I wept bitterly, but I have never dared to
again set up the pillar which they smashed, for that would be to disobey the
commands of the bishops. Consequently, I have been content to live among the
brethren, and here I have stayed to this day."

When I requested that Vulfolaic tell me about the miracles which Saint
Martin had performed there, he related to me the following stories:

"A certain Frank, who was descended from a very noble family among
his own people, had a son who was deaf and dumb. The boy was brought by his
parents to this church, and I ordered that he sleep on a bed in the building itself,
beside my deacon and one of my priests. He spent all day in prayer, and at night,
as I have said, he slept in the church. God had pity on him and Saint Martin appeared to me in a vision, saying, 'You can now move your ward out of the
building, for he is healed.' The following morning, as I was reflecting on the
vision I had seen, the boy came up to me and spoke. His first words were to give
thanks to God for what had occurred. Then he turned to me and said, 'I am
thanking Almighty God for having given my speech and hearing to me.' Then he
returned home, for he was completely healed.

"A certain man, who was often charged with thefts and other offences,
made a habit of clearing himself by swearing false oaths. He was accused by
certain people of having committed a robbery. 'I will go to Saint Martin's

church,' he said, 'and prove my innocence by the oaths I will swear there.' As he went in through the door, his axe slipped from his hand and he himself fell on the floor, having a severe spasm in his heart. At this, the miserable wretch confessed his crime in the very speech in which he had planned to swear his innocence.

"Another man was charged with having burnt down his neighbor's house. 'I will go to Saint Martin's church,' he said, 'and swear that I am innocent, and thus return home acquitted of this charge.' There was no doubt that he had actually burnt down this house. As he made to come in to take the oath, I went to meet him and said, 'Your neighbors claim that, whatever you say, you cannot be exonerated from this crime. Now, God is everywhere, and His power is just as great outside the church as it is inside. If you have some false conviction that God and His saints will not punish you for perjury, look at His holy sanctuary which stands in front of you. You can swear your oath if you insist, but you will not be permitted to step over the threshold of this church.' He raised his hands to Heaven, crying, 'By Almighty God and the miraculous power of His priest Saint Martin, I deny that I was responsible for this fire.' As soon as he had sworn this oath, he turned to go, but he appeared to be himself on fire! Falling to the ground, he began to cry that he was being burnt up by the saintly Bishop. He kept shouting in his agony, 'As God is my witness, I saw a flame descend from Heaven! It is surrounding me and is burning me up with its harsh smoke!' Saying this, he died. This was a warning to many people not to dare to perjure themselves in this place."

The deacon related many other miracles to me, but I cannot repeat all of them here.

NOTES

The above account is from *The History of the Franks,* Book VIII, 15-16.

St. Vulfolaic is known in France as St. Walfroy. His ascetic exploit on the pillar was like that of the great stylites of Eastern Christendom, St. Simeon (†460) and St. Daniel (†493).

EPILOGUE

The Life of Fr. Seraphim

The American Translator of *Vita Patrum*

by Fr. Damascene

Fr. Seraphim lecturing for the "New Valaam Theological Academy."

father Seraphim the Philosopher

TEACHER OF ANCIENT PIETY

Reposed August 20 (†1982)

IN HIS LOVE FOR MANKIND, God has placed in every person an innate longing for His Divine Truth. In order for the fullness of Truth to be revealed, however, one must first renounce the opinions of this world and inwardly die to it. This renunciation occurs through suffering, in which man's spirit is torn, like the curtain of the temple, away from his fallen, carnal self and is led to seek enlightenment from above. It is then that our gracious Lord, if He finds a loving heart that may serve as a sure receptacle of His Truth, imparts a higher understanding to the devout seeker.

Few in our days have sought the Truth with such singleness of purpose as did the righteous Fr. Seraphim. He was a philosopher according to the original meaning of the word: a "lover of wisdom." Just as Solomon once found favor in God's sight by desiring wisdom above all else, so did Fr. Seraphim become chosen to be God's servant through his earnest, painful longing to acquire the Truth at all costs. Having at last discovered it, he became free of the bonds of earth and ripe for eternity, as say the Scriptures: "You shall know the Truth, and the Truth shall make you free" (John 8:32).

1. Fr. Seraphim was born outside the saving enclosure of the Church, in order that, through his spiritual quest, conversion and subsequent missionary work, he might lead other searching souls into the Body of Christ. His quest for Truth became apparent at an early age. His mother, noticing how much her son was studying for school, once said to him, "You will be a smart man someday."

319

"I don't want to be smart," the boy replied, "I want to be wise." The older he grew, the more intense became his inquiry into the nature of his existence. His studies led him through the literature and traditional philosophies of many different cultures, and especially to the wisdom of the ancient Orient, for the acquisition of which he spent many years studying the languages of ancient China. But his hungry soul remained unfed, and he existed on the edge of despair, isolated and alone. For hours he would walk along deserted beaches at night, thinking that, without the Truth he sought, life was devoid of meaning, wondering if perhaps the oblivion of death was preferable to having such a burning yet unfulfilled desire. Little did he know then that his silent longings had not gone unnoticed, for God, in His limitless mercy, was soon to open to him another world.

God's providence worked through one of Fr. Seraphim's friends, who once recommended that he visit an Orthodox Christian Church. Heeding this advice, he walked into an Orthodox cathedral and witnessed a solemn and beautiful service, handed down from the times of the early Christians. Feeling as though he had stepped into the ranks of angels in Heaven, he joyfully said within himself, "I've come home." His philosophic quest thus brought him at last into the presence of Christ, Whose true image he had not been able to find until he had made personal contact with the ancient Christian experience of the Orthodox Church. In this way he discovered that the Truth he had been seeking resided not in a single philosophy, but rather in the Divine Person of our Lord Jesus Christ, Who has said, "I am the Way, and the Truth, and the Life" (John 14:6).

Not many years later, when he received Holy Communion for the first time, Fr. Seraphim felt a Divine taste in his mouth which lasted for several weeks. Being humble before God, he thought that all newly-baptized Christians had the same experience; and it was only later that he learned that he had indeed received a special gift of grace.

2. This rare man, Fr. Seraphim, not satisfied merely with being externally a member of the Church, begged God that He would bring him into the very heart of the Truth, wherein all the saints and righteous ones have found the means for their salvation. His newfound "pearl of great price" — the true Gospel of Christ — was so precious to him that he wanted to dedicate his entire life to serving it. He wanted to do something with what he had received, not just bury his talent in the ground.

While this yearning still burned within Fr. Seraphim, he fell ill with a serious ailment, which grew worse and worse until he feared that he would die from it. How great was his anguish when he thought that he would be taken away so soon, before he had even begun to serve God! In such a state, he went one day to a small store that sold, among other things, icon cards. He looked entreatingly at one of the icons. an image of the Mother of God, and spontaneously said within himself, from the depths of his troubled soul, "Most Holy Mother of God, please hear me! Before I die, let me do something to serve your Son!" The Holy Virgin did not withhold Her mercy from the needy supplicant; and thus it happened that shortly after this incident, Fr. Seraphim, already recovering from his illness, heard a knock at his door. When he opened it, he found a young seminarian, a man with ideals similar to his own, wanting to serve Christ but not yet knowing exactly how to do it. They later decided to open an Orthodox Christian bookstore, so that other seekers like themselves could be provided with soul-profiting reading. In this way was granted Fr. Seraphim's wish to work for God His other need, that of entering into the fullness of the Church, was fulfilled at about the same time through a righteous man who arrived in the city in which Fr. Seraphim was living, San Francisco. This man was Blessed Archbishop John Maximovitch, a wonderworker sent by God to Fr. Seraphim as a living vessel of Divine Truth, which Truth he did not hesitate to impart through his holy example and words of instruction. Fr. Seraphim deeply loved his spiritual teacher, and Archbishop John in turn did all he could to help his disciple.

With the blessing and encouragement of Archbishop John, Fr. Seraphim and his seminarian friend became co-laborers in a missionary brotherhood dedicated to St. Herman of Alaska. In addition to working at the bookstore, they began to publish a periodical, "The Orthodox Word," for the mission of true Christianity. And here is where God, wanting to make use of His willing servant, provided Fr. Seraphim with the opportunity to exercise all his talents — his penetrating mind and his writing ability — for the spreading of the Gospel. Fr. Seraphim devoted all his energy to his God-pleasing literary work so that, at the time of final reckoning, he would be found not empty handed, but with his talents increased a hundredfold.

3. Ever since his conversion, Fr. Seraphim did much reading of the Holy Fathers of the Church, and he was especially drawn to the ancient desert-dwellers and ascetics. In these desert-dwellers, he found living illustrations of Christ's otherworldly teaching: transfigured beings who disdained all attachment to things temporal and who sought only that which lies beyond this corruptible earth. So much was he inspired by their example that he longed to have a small taste of the life of silence and prayer, unhindered by the tumult of the world. For this reason, he and his partner decided to move their publishing work to the mountains. Soon they found some land suitable for their needs: a forested area high on the top of a ridge, miles away from the noise of cities. After they had

lived there for a few years, they were tonsured monks, and thus their brotherhood became a monastic one. Their literary work continued, and expanded to
include the printing of books.

Having been delivered from death and granted more years of life through
the intercessions of the Mother of God, Fr. Seraphim cherished the time he was
able to spend in his forest hermitage. His heart so overflowed with thanksgiving
that he would be seen blessing and kissing the trees. Because he valued every
moment of life as a gift from God, he was filled with a sense of urgency and
repeatedly warned: "It is later than you think. Hasten, therefore, to do the
work of God."

Through daily Divine services, constant exposure to spiritual literature,
and separation from the world, Fr. Seraphim's experience of spiritual life deep-
ened. He lived for another world, guarding himself against idle talk and soberly
viewing ordinary events in the context of heavenly reality. His loving heart,
warmed and softened by his early years of suffering and his profound conversion, combined with his brilliant mind, his noble, truth-loving character and his
depth of spiritual experience, to make him a Christian teacher unparalleled in
our days. Having steeped himself in the writings of the Holy Fathers, having
come to them as a loving son and learned from them Divine wisdom, having
lived like them and acquired their way of thinking and feeling, he became as one
of them. He successfully transmitted the spirit of the Holy Fathers in his writings, thereby feeding the souls of thousands of readers and enabling them to
attain oneness of soul with the Christians of past centuries.

4. When Fr. Seraphim was made a priest, his responsibilities increased
even more. He was called upon to pastor a parish flock in a nearby town. For a
man who longed for desert solitude, this was certainly a burden, and yet he bore
it without a grudging word. "Whatever God sends us," he would say, "we must
accept and do our best with. Each day brings a new struggle, a new chance to
increase our prayer and new ways in which to serve God."

He was a loving pastor not only to those in the town parish, but also to
the many brothers who came to the monastery. Late at night, he would be seen
kneeling before the altar of the monastery church, praying fervently with tears
for those souls which had been placed under his direction.

All of his pastoral work, as well as his literary work, he did solely for the
glory of God and for the salvation of his neighbor. He shunned all ephemeral,
earthly rewards which might be gained in this life, even those rewards which may
be amassed through the institutional, purely human side of church life. And yet
his holy life did not go unrewarded by God. Once, in the altar of the town
parish, during the reading of the canons at Sunday Matins, one of the acolytes

*Fr. Seraphim when he served with Bishop Nektary
for the last time: Alameda, California, 1981.*

saw Fr. Seraphim surrounded by Divine, uncreated Light. From this it is known
that during his life here on earth, Fr. Seraphim received a foretaste of the
heavenly bliss prepared for him by Our Lord Jesus Christ.

Fr. Seraphim's early mentor Archbishop John, although he had reposed
many years before, did not cease to take care of his spiritual son. Once a certain
Brother Gregory, having been entrusted by Fr. Seraphim with a large sum of
money, went to buy food for the monastery. When the time came to make pay-
ment, he suddenly realized he did not have the money. Telephoning Fr. Seraphim in a state of great agitation, he was told to return to the church in which
Fr. Seraphim was serving. As he approached the church, he was met by Fr. Seraphim. "You have it right there," said Fr. Seraphim, pointing to the brother's
chest. "Archbishop John told me. You didn't think of praying to him, did you?"
The brother felt his chest and with simultaneous joy and shame he found the
money in the pocket which he thought he had certainly searched. Fr. Seraphim
then comforted him, explaining that after he had finished speaking on the
telephone, he had gone to church and there, praying before a portrait of Archbishop John, had asked him to help find the money. Archbishop John mystically
informed Fr. Seraphim that Brother Gregory had the money in his pocket.
"Thus," concluded this brother as he finished relating the tale, "a sure trial and
temptation was transformed into a revelation of the mystery of holiness and
grace."

5.   Fr. Seraphim was only forty-eight years old when Our Lord was
pleased to take him into His kingdom. As it is written in the Wisdom of Solomon: "He, being made perfect in a short time, fulfilled a long time: for his soul
pleased the Lord: therefore hasted He to take him away from among the
wicked" (Wis. 4:13). When the course of his blessed life was drawing to an end,
he was suddenly afflicted with acute pains in his stomach. Being of such a
humble disposition, he never complained or tried to draw attention to his sickness, but only retired to his cell to pray. Soon, however, his brethren realized
that his ailment was a serious one, and took him to a hospital for treatment.
After the doctors had operated on him, they said that the disease would probably be fatal. The news spread, and people travelled from distant places to be at
Fr. Seraphim's bedside during his last hours. Day and night they stood near him,
consoling him by singing the sacred hymns of the Church. How great was the
lamentation, how fervent were the prayers of the faithful! So many people were
about to be deprived of their beloved spiritual father and teacher. And yet there
was joy mixed with the sorrow, for all were aware that, from among those assembled in that hospital room, one person was soon to step over the threshold
of death and stand before the throne of Almighty God. It was as if the ceiling of

the room had opened up, as if everyone was in the presence of the blessed world beyond death.

Here, during his last, painful days in the hospital, Fr. Seraphim finished the holy task he had begun when he first took on the yoke of Christ: he eradicated the vestiges of his selfish, human will so that he could belong wholly to God, with Whom he would spend eternity. Again it is written in Holy Wisdom: "And having been a little chastised, they shall be greatly rewarded: for God proved them, and found them worthy for Himself. As gold in the furnace hath He tried them, and received them as a burnt offering" (Wis. 3:4-5). In truth was the spiritual gold of Fr. Seraphim's soul purified by suffering, for he was tied to the hospital bed as one crucified, his arms and legs shaking from the intense pain that ran through his body. He could not speak because of the air tubes which the doctors had placed in his mouth. All he could do was pray, gazing imploringly into heaven. As his co-laborer in the wilderness said, "Fr. Seraphim suffered as he did in order to receive the glory of Martyrs."

A young catechumen was standing at his bedside when a priest came in the room to give Fr. Seraphim Holy Communion. Before administering the sacred Body and Blood of Christ, the priest read the Gospel and then, holding the book over Fr Seraphim's reclining body, began to bless him with it. Suddenly Fr. Seraphim, exerting every last bit of strength in his dying, convulsing frame, raised himself up to kiss that sublime and holy Book that had given him Life. There was not a face in the room that was not covered with tears. The catechumen standing there said later that this incident was so inspiring that it erased all thoughts of hesitation concerning his baptism.

6. Finally, when the soul of the blessed one was sufficiently purified, it departed unto the Lord. Fr. Seraphim's body was brought to his monastery to be buried on his beloved mountain, and, for the three days following his repose, was kept in the monastery church. There, as Fr. Seraphim lay in his simple wooden coffin, his face became radiant and smiled with such a serene smile that all were moved by the sight.

During the funeral, the church was filled to overflowing with faithful pilgrims. All came up to his coffin to kiss the blessed hands which wrote so many soul-profiting books, articles and church services. When the coffin was about to be taken from the church and buried nearby, one of the pilgrims, a woman named Helen, was vouchsafed to see Fr. Seraphim shining with celestial light above the coffin, facing the altar and swinging a censer.

Forty days after Fr. Seraphim's repose, a bishop named Nektary came to the monastery and led the singing of a Glorification hymn: "We glorify thee, our holy Father Seraphim, instructor of monks and converser with angels." During

his sermon, he called Fr. Seraphim "a righteous man, possibly a saint." The veri-
ty of this appraisal is attested to by the numerous miracles which Fr. Seraphim
has performed since his death. Here we will include a few of these, described by
the priest Alexey Young on November 11, 1983:

"About two months after the repose of Fr. Seraphim it came to my attention that a cousin (non-Orthodox) of one of my spiritual children (Barbara
M.) was in the hospital with a serious ailment. She asked to see me and asked
that I pray for her. She was suffering from a constriction of vessels in the leg,
causing shortage of circulation. The immediate crisis was a gangrenous big toe.
I saw this toe myself: it was green and rotting — a terrible sight. The doctors
were preparing to amputate the toe within a week or so, and said that it was likely she would lose the whole foot and possibly the limb from the knee down. I
annointed her toe and leg with oil from Fr. Seraphim's grave and asked his intercession on her behalf. Within a short period of time the gangrene had completely
disappeared. The doctors decided it was not necessary to amputate the toe or
anything else and announced that they were 'amazed' at what had happened.
Today, more than a year later, she has had no re-occurrence of her affliction, to
the continuing surprise of the doctors, who have no explanation for it. I'm convinced that this healing was worked through Fr. Seraphim. (By the way, I myself
spoke to the doctor on more than one occasion, and so am able to personally
verify the medical details as well as the initial prognosis.

"And now I have a second miracle to report: Two weeks ago today my
brother-in-law, Stefan (whom I baptized last July and then married to my sister,
Anna), was in a serious auto accident here in town. He broke both legs (com-
pound fractures in the left leg) and also shattered the left ankle and the left big
toe. He was immediately taken into surgery, where the doctors worked for 4½
hours to clean out the wounds (the bones had broken through the flesh in more
than one place); road dirt had been ground into the flesh and bones and the
danger of life-threatening infection was very great. I saw the photos of his left
leg and foot just before they took him into surgery and it was an appalling sight:
the left foot was just hanging; the ligaments and tendons had all been torn away,
and the bones completely crushed.

"During that first operation we prayed in the waiting room. Remembering that Bishop Nektary had sung a Glorification to Fr. Seraphim, I served a
Molieben to Fr. Seraphim on behalf of Stefan. Starting the next day, and every
day thereafter, he was anointed with oil from Fr. Seraphim's grave. Through the
bandages we were even able to reach one of the mangled toes of the left foot.

"After the surgery the doctor told us there was a good chance that he
would lose the foot. Also, there was a possibility that if infection set in it could

become 'life-threatening.' But we had great confidence in the prayers of our Righteous One before the throne of God, and we waited, patiently.

"Six days later the surgeons operated again. This was a critical time, for based upon what they saw when they removed the bandages, they would have a good idea about whether or not the foot could be saved. Afterwards the surgeon himself said that it was a 'miracle'! Not only was everything mending well, but there was no sign of infection — in itself a miracle.

"Of course Stefan now has three months in a wheel chair, and then he will have to learn to walk all over again. There are still many difficulties, and possibly more operations, in the near future. But I believe that in this, as in so many other things, Fr. Seraphim again heard our prayers, and turned on our behalf to God's throne in order to give us help. Truly, God rests in His saints!

"Of both of the above miracles I am personally a witness. In addition, photographs exist of the second case which would quickly convince anyone — lay person or physician — that something of a truly extraordinary nature took place."

Several other miraculous visitations did our Lord Jesus Christ work through His servant, Fr. Seraphim. To God, Who raised up such a man for our inspiration and enlightenment, may there be glory unto the ages of ages. Amen.

BIBLIOGRAPHY

THE WORKS OF ST. GREGORY OF TOURS

1. *The History of the Franks (Historiae Francorum).* English translations by O. M. Dalton (Oxford, 1927, two volumes) and Lewis Thorpe (Penguin Books, 1974).
2. *The Glory of the Blessed Martyrs (In Gloria Martyrum Beatorum).*
3. *The Passion and Miracles of St. Julian the Martyr (De Passione et virtutibus Sancti Juliani martyris).* Unpublished English translation by Betty Marie Jorgensen, submitted as a Master's thesis at the University of Washington, 1931.
4. *The Miracles of Blessed Martin the Bishop (De Virtutibus beati Martini episcopi).* English translation of Book I in *Gregory of Tours: Selections from the Minor Works,* translated by William C. McDermott (Philadelphia, University of Pennsylvania Press, 1949).
5. *The Life of the Fathers (Vita Patrum).*
6. *The Glory of the Confessors (In Gloria Confessorum).*
7. *The Miracles of Blessed Andrew the Apostle (De Miraculis beati Andreae apostoli).* Attributed to St. Gregory, but not included in his own list of his works.
8. *The Passion of the Seven Sainted Martyrs Sleeping at Ephesus (Passio sanctorum Martyrum Septem Dormientium apud Ephesum).* English translation in *Gregory of Tours: Selections from the Minor Works,* translated by William C. McDermott (Philadelphia, 1949).
9. *On the Offices of the Church (de Cursibus etiam eççliasticus unum librum condidi).* This book, which was mentioned by St. Gregory in *The History of the Franks,* has been lost. Some scholars claim it has been found under the title *The Course of the Stars (De Cursu Stellarum ratio),* but their claims are doubtful since the discovered work does not have St. Gregory's name attached to it and is not in the spirit of his other works.
10. *Commentary on the Psalms (In Psalterii tractatum commmentarius).* This work is lost except for the introduction, chapter-headings and two fragments.
11. A book on the Masses of St. Sidonius Appolinaris, which is lost.
12. *The Life of St. Aredius the Abbot (Vita Sancti Aridii Abbatis).* Included in the apocryphal works of St. Gregory; original Latin version in *Les Livres Des Miracles* (H. L. Bordier, Paris, 1864, Vol. IV).

BOOKS OF RELATED INTEREST

Albertson, Clinton, tr., *Anglo-Saxon Saints and Heroes*, Fordham University Press, 1967.

Alliez, Abbe, *Histoire du Monastere de Lerins*, Vol. I, Paris, 1861.

Bede, Venerable, *A History of the English Church and People*, Penguin Books, 1955. Written 150 years after St. Gregory's *History of the Franks*.

Benoit, Paul, *Histoire de l'Abbaye et de la Terre de Saint-Claude*, Montreuil-sur-Mer, 1890, two volumes.

Bordier, Henry, *Les Livres des Miracles (de Saint Gregoire)*, Paris, 1864, Vol. IV. Includes the Latin text of the Life of St. Gregory of Tours by Abbot Odo. A French translation was published in the same author's translation of *The History of the Franks*, Paris, 1859.

Cassian, St. John, *Conferences*, translated by Colm Luibheid, Paulist Press, 1985. This edition contains only 9 of St. John Cassian's 24 Conferences, but it is the only readily available English translation.

Congar, Yves, O. P., *After Nine Hundred Years*, Fordham University Press, 1959.

Dalton, O. M., *The Letters of Sidonius*, Oxford, 1915. St. Sidonius Appolinaris, a 5th-century bishop of Clermont, mentioned the monasteries of the Jura in his letters (Book IV, 25).

Dill, Sir Samuel, *Roman Society in Gaul in the Merovingian Age*, London, 1926.

Hoare, F. R., ed., *The Western Fathers*, New York, Harper Torchbooks, 1965. Includes the Lives of St. Martin of Tours (by Sulpicius Severus), St. Honoratus of Arles, St. Germanus of Auxerre, St. Ambrose of Milan, and Blessed Augustine of Hippo.

Malnory, A., *Sainte Cesaire, Eveque d'Arles*, Paris, 1894.

Martine, Francois, *Vie des Peres du Jura*, Paris, 1968. Includes the *Life of the Jura Fathers* (Sts. Romanus and Lupicinus) in Latin and French.

McDermott, William C., *Monks, Bishops and Pagans*, Philadelphia, University of Pennsylvania Press, 1949. Includes all the material from the same author's *Gregory of Tours: Selections from the Minor Works*. One of the selections, "The Seven Wonders of the World," has been taken from the anonymous work *The Course of the Stars*, and was probably not written by St. Gregory.

Talbot, C. H., tr., *The Anglo-Saxon Missionaries in Germany*, New York, Sheed & Ward, 1954.

Theodoret, Blessed, *The History of the Lovers of God*. English translation under the title *History of the Monks of Syria*, Kalamazoo, Michigan, Cistercian Publications, 1985. This collection of Lives of Syrian Fathers is an exact parallel to St. Gregory's *Life of the Fathers*.

Webb, J. F., tr., *Lives of the Saints* (of England), Penguin Books, 1970.

INDEX

ACKNOWLEDGEMENTS

We would like to thank the following people for helping to make the publication of Vita Patrum *possible:*

Mrs. Helen Kontzevitch
Daniel Olson
Paul Bartlett
Agafia Prince
R-monk Damascene C.
R-monk Gerasim E.
Hieromonk Nazary S.
Monk Sergius S.
R-monk Steven K.
R-monk John M.
R-monk Lazarus S.
Thomas Reske
Lector Gleb Collymore
Thomas Anderson
John Ragland
Rev. & Mrs. Vladimir
  Anderson
Mrs. Valentina Harvey
Mary Mansur
Katherine Mansur
R-monk Juvenaly N.
†Archbishop John M.
Nun Brigid M.
R-nun Maria S.
R-nun Paisia R.
R-nun Sophia L.
R-nun Nina B.
Catherine Borovsky
Christina Shane
R. M. Gregory
Reader David Carpenter
Reader David O'Neil
Br. Michael McGee
Paul Baba
George Black
Christopher Haddad
R-monk Peter H.

†Archimandrite Spiridon E.
George Anderson
Mr. & Mrs. Michael
  Anderson
Rev. and Mrs. Alexey
  Young
Thomas Delp
James Reed
Mr. & Mrs. A. Makushynski
Monk Mamas
Hieromonk Ioannikios
Mr. & Mrs. Andrew Bond
Jean Besse
Nicholas Mabin
Nicholas Blazik
Daniel Gorham
Serge Zavarin
Ephraim Zeebel
Rev. Basil Rhodes
Barbara Murray
Christopher Amerling
Basil De Tourney
Boris Dmitriev
Nun Victoria
R-monk Laurence C.
Maria Illyin
Maria Pafnoutieff
Solomonia Minkin
Michael Farnsworth
John d'Ancy
Constantine Roussyan
Excostudian Steven
Rev. Vladimir Mordvinkin
Macarius Shaeffer
Mr. & Mrs. Harvey Schmit
Mrs. Frank Rose
Mrs. Nina Podmo

Matushka Macrina Volkoff
Mr. & Mrs. George Jenkins
Rev. Abbot Thomas Davis
Maria Kraft
Alexander Pernitz
R-nun Nadezhda Russell
Michael Riggin
Br. Richard Betts
George Williams
Nicholas Mareno
Nina Seco
Daniel Mattson
Symeon Hill
Paul Bassett
Martinian Prince
Br. Athanasius H.
Sr. Barbara R.
Br. Thomas D.
Br. Christopher B.
Br. Mark Richard Y.
Br. Leonid R.
Br. Michael McHugh
Br. Stephen Rodier
Br. James Barfield
Mr. & Mrs. David DeMars
Naomi Henthorne
Mr. & Mrs. Nectarios
  Rozadilla
Paula Kaiser
Br. John N.
Sr. Katherine McCaffrey
Sr. Marie Rodier
Mr. & Mrs. Edward
  Opheim
Mr. & Mrs. Chris Opheim
Gregory Wolfer
Mr. & Mrs. Matthew Dick